S0-AFN-879

Ancillaries Available with
Practical English Handbook, Eleventh Edition

For Instructors

- **Instructor's Annotated Edition.** The copy you are holding is the student edition of the text with answers to exercises overlaid in a third color.
- *The Writing Teacher's Companion* by Rai Peterson. This acclaimed book gives sound, practical advice on all aspects of teaching composition, from devising assignments to evaluating papers to managing the classroom.
- **Computerized Diagnostic Tests** (Windows, ISBN 0-618-03957-0; and Macintosh, ISBN 0-618-05426-X). Students are tested in five major areas of English grammar—sentence errors, sentence struture, punctuation, mechanics, and diction.

For Students

- *Practical English Workbook,* Seventh Edition, by Floyd C. Watkins, William B. Dillingham, John T. Hiers, Matthew G. Hearn, and Byron K. Brown. Collection of supplemental sentence and paragraph exercises that follows the organization of the handbook. Each unit opens with a brief grammar review. Accompanying *Instuctor's Resource Manual* contains answers to exercises.
- **E-library of Exercises.** The E-library of Exercises is an online interactive study program designed to complement any Houghton Mifflin writing text. Self-tests in 30 areas are available. There are over 650 exercises in total. Scores are available to students as soon as they finish a test. Available on the Houghton Mifflin English Web site (*http://www.hmco.com,* select English).
- **Web Research Guide.** This site offers students tips, not only on searching and using the Internet to find information, but also on developing practical skills for making sense of the information they find (evaluating information). Includes tutorials designed to help students practice finding and evaluating information by content, source, and relevance to their assignments. Available on the Houghton Mifflin English web site (*http://www.hmco.com,* select English).
- *Writing Arguments* by Joseph F. Trimmer. This booklet contains some additional material on arguments beyond that included in *Practical English Handbook.* It also includes exercises and a sample paper.

Offered at Special Prices

- *Practical English Handbook* and *The American Heritage College Dictionary,* Third Edition.
- *Practical English Handbook* and *Compact American Dictionary.*
- *Practical English Handbook* and *Writing Online: A Student's Guide to the Internet and the World Wide Web,* Third Edition, by Nick Carbone.
- Composition readers. Houghton Mifflin offers discounts ranging from 10 to 50% on packages containing *Practical English Handbook* and a composition reader.

As part of Houghton Mifflin's ongoing commitment to the
environment, this text has been printed on recycled paper.

Houghton Mifflin Company ▪ Boston   New York

Instructor's Annotated Edition

Practical English Handbook

ELEVENTH EDITION

Floyd C. Watkins
Late of Emory University

William B. Dillingham
Emeritus, Emory University

John Hiers
Valdosta State University

with the assistance of
Byron Brown
Valdosta State University

Senior sponsoring editor: Dean Johnson
Senior project editor: Rosemary Winfield
Senior production/design coordinator: Sarah Ambrose
Senior cover design coordinator: Tony Saizon
Senior manufacturing coordinator: Sally Culler
Senior marketing manager: Nancy Lyman

Cover designer: Sarah Melhado Bishins
Cover art: © Photonica, Hiroya Kaji

Authors of works quoted in the text are identified with the quotations. Grateful aknowledgment is made to the following publishers and authors for permission to reprint from their works:

Diane Ackerman, "The Real George Washington," from *Parade* magazine, February 21, 1988. Reprinted by permission of The Writers Shop. All rights reserved.

Ethan Bronner, "College Applicants of '99 Are Facing Stiffest Competition," from *The New York Times,* June 1999, Saturday, Late Edition. Copyright © 1999 by The New York Times. Used by permission.

John Leo, "Finally, the People Vote on a Taboo," from *U.S. News and World Report,* March 4, 1996. Copyright © 1996 by U.S. News and World Report. Used by permission.

Denise Levertov, "In Mind," from *Poems 1960–1967.* Copyright © 1966 by Denise Levertov. Reprinted by permission of New Directions Publishing Corp. and Laurence Pollinger, Ltd.

Alice Walker, "The Flowers," from *In Love & Trouble: Stories of Black Women.* Copyright © 1973 by Alice Walker. Reprinted by permission of Harcourt, Inc.

Douglas L. Wilson, "What Jefferson and Lincoln Read," *The Atlantic Monthly,* January 1991. Copyright © 1991 by Douglas L. Wilson. Used by permission.

Copyright © 2001 by Houghton Mifflin Company. All rights reserved.

No part of this work may be reproduced or transmitted in any form or by any means, electronic or mechanical, including photocopying and recording, or by any information storage or retrieval system without the prior written permission of Houghton Mifflin Company unless such copying is expressly permitted by federal copyright law. Address inquiries to College Permissions, Houghton Mifflin Company, 222 Berkeley Street, Boston MA 02116-3764.

Printed in the U.S.A. Library of Congress Catalog Card Number: 00-133883

ISBN: Student edition 0-618-04301-2; IAE 0-618-04300-4

123456789-KPT-04 03 02 01 00

Contents

Punctuation   203

Preface

With each new edition of the *Practial English Handbook,* its authors have aimed at retaining the simplicity, directness, and usefulness of the original version while addressing the changing needs of students as they learn and of instructors as they teach. The Eleventh Edition reflects rather dramatic structural changes without sacrificing the venerated practicality of previous editions; it reflects comprehensive reviews of all chapters for contemporary pedagogy, illustration, and technology but always with a sharp eye on the successful elements of other editions. This edition, like all others before it, offers numerous improvements, a partial list of which follows. We have

- rearranged major chapters to first introduce logical thinking and the essay as a whole;
- revised the chapter on writing papers, with new guidelines, illustrations, and exercises;
- refurbished the chapter on Writing About Literature, with a new introduction and a new section on Writing About a Story;
- reworked the chapter on research, with a broader view of online sources and more comprehensive discussions and illustrations of Web-based research;
- added a new model research paper, which is more accessible in content, length, and style;

- updated and refocused lists of general reference aids and periodical indexes;
- expanded the treatment of computer-assisted writing;
- revised the glossaries for ease of use and clarity of definition;
- added new exercises and revised many others, as requested by our users;
- streamlined, clarified, and freshened other explanations, illustrations, and exercises as necessary.

As ever, we owe much to the close reading, cogent criticism, and energetic help of many colleagues, who, like the authors, bring years of experience in the composition classroom and in Writing Centers. You and the authors of this text continue to be linked by common experiences and goals. Many of you have told us openly and honestly what you expect of a good handbook; others have frankly and constructively criticized; all of you have offered invaluable suggestions. One cannot imagine how a handbook could evolve through eleven editions without your help. Most of you cannot be listed by name in a brief preface, but we certainly owe a continuing debt to all of you. Especially enriching this edition are the insights and revisions of Professor Byron Brown of Valdosta State University and Professor Matthew Hearn of Lipscomb University. We also express our gratitude to the following for their assistance: Katherine Bruner Tave, Southwestern Oregon Community College; Deborah M. Sinnreich-Levi, Stevens Institute of Technology (NJ); Michael Roos, Raymond Walters College (OH); Roselyn J. Schmitt, College of St. Benedict (MN); George Jochnowitz, City University of New York—College of Staten Island; Gerald Concannon, Massachusetss Maritime Academy; Kay Hoyle Nelson, Aurora University (IL); Lillian Cook, Panola College (TX); Jay Long, Baptist Bible College (PA); Anna Battigelli, State University of New York—Plattsburgh; Susan C. Gunn, Kent State University (OH); Kathy Martin, Lewis-Clark State College (ID); Jennifer Trevisol.

Floyd C. Watkins
William B. Dillingham
John T. Hiers

A Memo to Writers

For ten editions this book began with grammar or basic errors and proceeded to increasingly more complex kinds of writing and papers. Now this Eleventh Edition starts with thinking clearly and precisely and proceeds to aspects of the writing process that are necessary for accurate, interesting, and graceful writing.

Start by going to your own experience and knowledge. Know as much as you can about what you want to say. Then turn to any part of the book that helps you with devices, ways, and means. Let the table of contents, the index, your instructor, and your curiosity guide you to what you need to know. What help do you need with accuracy in thinking, grammar, spelling, sentence structure, correcting errors, diction, paragraphing, or researching for a deeper and broader view? You may confront any problem at any stage. That is part of the difficulty and the fascination with writing.

Accurate
Thinking
and Writing

1 Accuracy and Logic   *acc*

As an observer and a reader, you gather information of many kinds: facts, stories, opinions, and examples. Remember, take notes; keep records. You need to discriminate between abstraction and data, truth and error, accuracy and falsehood. The same principles govern reading (gathering information) and writing (disseminating knowledge).

Going from factual knowledge to a conclusion or to a generalization about the facts is the **inductive method** of reasoning. It is used especially in scientific thinking. A writer or a reader following the pattern of inductive reasoning asks whether the facts are true, whether exceptions have been noted, whether conclusions are accurately drawn from the data, and whether the conclusions are precise or exaggerated.

The **deductive method** of thinking applies generalizations and principles to new facts, situations, and circumstances. One confronts deductive reasoning by asking whether the principle is more than mere personal opinion, whether it is impartial, whether it is applied relevantly, and whether exceptions have been noted.

Induction and **deduction** are different processes; some find one more attractive than the other, but nobody lives by one alone. Both are necessary for meaningful and intelligent writing. All searchers and thinkers discover new facts, and all make new applications.

A speaker or a writer, a listener or a reader, needs to distinguish among rumor, fact, opinion, and belief. Be careful not to purvey errors or falsehoods. Express doubts or uncertainties when you do not know the truth.

Listen and watch for errors in reasoning called **logical fallacies.** Try to confront them with reason, correct information, and good manners rather than with strong emotions.

These are difficult commandments, but they are crucial for understanding, integrity, and peace. Every good person, scholar, and worthy citizen strives to obey them.

1a Use only reliable sources.

If your sources are shaky, or if authorities you consult seem questionable, do not base opinions and arguments on them. Beware of outdated information, published or unpublished gossip, and the proclamations of amateurs, novices, and nonspecialists.

Of course, even good authorities sometimes make mistakes, and a person who is not an expert in a field may nevertheless know what he or she is talking about. The point is to believe the truth but not be gullible.

QUESTIONABLE AUTHORITY
> My banker advises borrowers to use only the highest grade of gasoline.

AUTHORITY
> The manufacturer's manual says that any unleaded gasoline may be used in this car.

QUESTIONABLE AUTHORITY
> My coach recommends that all of his players be vaccinated to prevent what is called the common cold.

AUTHORITY
> My physician says that vaccinations to prevent the common cold do not yet exist.

QUESTIONABLE AUTHORITY
> The runner-up in last year's beauty contest is studying to be an actress. She says that Shakespeare is too difficult to be taught in high school.

1b Check the authenticity of facts.

Consider the methods used to obtain materials stated as facts. (Facts can be demonstrated.) Distinguish carefully between facts and judgments based on them.

Be aware that in your writing, a few errors or even one error will cast doubt on the veracity of your work.

ERROR IN FACT

Hot water will freeze faster than cold water when placed in a freezer.

SCIENTIFIC FACT

Contrary to old folktales, cold water freezes faster than hot water.

MISINFORMATION PRESENTED AS FACT

A tree struck by lightning will not be hit again.

THE FACT

Lightning may strike twice in the same place.

IGNORANT OPINION

Nobody lives on a farm anymore.

THE FACT

In America 1 percent of the people live on farms.

1c Do not assert sweeping generalizations. State possible exceptions.

SWEEPING GENERALIZATION

All college graduates know grammar and write well. You cannot write well unless you have graduated from college.

THE FACTS

Some college graduates do not write good sentences. Some great writers, notably Ernest Hemingway and William Faulkner, never graduated from college.

SWEEPING GENERALIZATION

No woman can be the mother of three children and make a living for her family.

THE TRUTH

> A mother of three children can make a living for her family, even though doing so is difficult.

CAUTION: You cannot justify sweeping generalizations by adding a phrase such as "in my opinion." Overstatement to make a point may irritate, arouse doubt, or cause disbelief. Moderation (or even understatement) convinces where brashness and arrogance alienate. Generalizations about nationalities and race are often pernicious.

1d Do not exaggerate.

Exaggerations misrepresent. They may begin with truth but then greatly expand or falsely decorate it, often to the point of absurdity. They may overstate so much that they lose the point instead of making it. Do not succumb to the glories of exaggerations that you hear in daily living, especially in fields like advertising and politics.

Some words are absolutes, which should be used only with caution and care: *always, never, anybody, everybody, nobody, only, just.*

Exaggerate for humor and effect only when your audience is aware of your method and purpose. Show the actual truth by admitting that you are exaggerating.

EXAGGERATIONS

> All the news on television stations at 6 P.M. is sad and violent.
>
> Medicine is getting close to the point of eliminating all contagious diseases.
>
> Together, government and education can solve all the major problems in life.

1e Avoid reasoning in a circle (also called *begging the question*).

A writer may begin with a point and then use as proof the same point stated in slightly changed phraseology or a new vocabulary.

Such reasoning gets exactly nowhere; it frustrates more than it convinces.

EXAMPLES OF CIRCULAR REASONING

Universal education is necessary because everyone ought to have an education.

Some people enjoy disputes because they get much pleasure out of contention and arguments.

1f   Avoid false comparisons.

Good comparisons are convincing arguments. A fresh analogy can clarify and persuade.

False comparisons between two things that have surface similarities instead of real likenesses are to be carefully avoided.

FALSE COMPARISONS

Western states should elect cattle farmers and rodeo riders as mayors and governors. Managing a city or a state is just like herding cattle.

Anyone who is a good typist can become an accomplished pianist because typing and playing a piano both require that the fingers strike a keyboard with dexterity.

Analogies

Analogies are figurative comparisons that explain one thing in terms of another. They are most effective when you show a resemblance between two things with so many differences that they are not ordinarily compared. The following paragraph, for example, draws an analogy between human beings and lobsters.

We are not unlike a particularly hardy crustacean. The lobster grows by developing and shedding a series of hard, protective shells. Each time it expands from within, the confining shell must be sloughed off. It is left exposed and vulnerable until, in time, a new covering grows to replace the old. With each passage from one stage of human growth to the next, we, too, must shed a protective structure.

ADAPTED FROM GAIL SHEEHY, *PASSAGES*

1g   Stick to the point.

An argument should be pointed. Wordiness, irrelevance, and excessive detail may shift your focus to other issues and lead your readers off the track. The logical fallacies discussed next stray from the point and throw up a smoke screen.

Red herring

The term ***red herring*** comes from an old practice of causing confusion by moving a dead fish across the path of hounds following a scent. Do not shift the subject from one topic to another so that the first may be forgotten or ignored.

> Radio and television devote too much time to the weather when violence and crime are the major problems.

Argumentum ad hominem

The Latin term ***argumentum ad hominem*** (meaning an argument made "to the man") refers to attacking a person instead of confronting the real issue.

> The governor, a woman of much wealth, cannot understand the needs of the poor.

1h   Appeal to principles, reason, and common sense, not to emotions, ignorance, and prejudices.

Arousing the self-centered emotions of listeners or readers to create hostility toward others is a wrong, even shameful, method of argument. Do not use unflattering terms to describe people. The following fallacies are false and unfair.

Name-calling

Do not call names or attach labels in order to make a point, even when they may represent a modicum of truth. Profane, obscene, or bigoted terms will not convince reasonable listeners or readers.

The following words and many others like them may be extreme, false, and rude: *do-gooder, demagogue, Klansman, communist, Nazi, sexist, racist, pervert.*

Even milder terms or modifiers such as *plutocrat, politician, ignorant, alien, foreign, liberal, conservative, democrat,* or *republican* are often inappropriate.

Flattery

Flattery is excessive and insincere praise used to win a person's favor by complimenting. A candidate who tells voters that they support him because of their high moral character is flattering them.

Snob appeal or mass appeal

Appeals to people's desires to be like the elite or the discriminating or to follow the crowd and do what everybody else does are false persuasion not based upon reason.

1i   Draw accurate conclusions about cause and effect.

Exact causes of events and conditions are often difficult to determine. Similarly, attributing effects to a certain cause or causes can be partly or entirely wrong.

Past hoc, ergo propter hoc

The Latin phrase ***post hoc, ergo propter hoc*** means "after this, therefore because of this." One thing is not the cause of another merely because it precedes the other.

CAUSE
> There were heavy rains all summer.

DOUBTFUL EFFECT ASSERTED
> It is no wonder that grasshoppers destroyed the crops.

EFFECT
> The baby cries continuously.

DOUBTFUL CAUSE ASSERTED
> The mother should never have taken so many vitamins during her pregnancy.

Non sequitur

The Latin term ***non sequitur*** (which means "it does not follow") refers to drawing a conclusion that cannot be made from the information that has just been stated.

> Exercise strenuously and enjoy a healthy heart and lungs.
> A child who enjoys classical music will become a good musician.

1j Avoid the *either . . . or* fallacy (also called a false dilemma).

When more than two possibilities exist, do not limit the choices to two. One does not have to sink or swim if the water is shallow enough to be waded or if a boat is available.

■ Exercise 1

It is more important to understand and explain a fallacy than it is to identify its name. Indeed, a statement may be fallacious in several ways. Study the following examples, and discuss them in class or in any appropriate company on any appropriate occasion.

Collect additional examples of either fallacious or original and remarkably correct reasoning.

EXAMPLES

What are the kinds of logical problems in the following statement?

More doctors smoke Buffalo cigars than any other brand.

Why choose doctors instead of some other kind of professional?
How many doctors are referred to in this assertion?
More doctors than who else?
More than other doctors who do not smoke Buffalo cigars?

Grammatically and logically the placement of the word *more* raises questions. A precise statement might be the following—if it were known to be true:

Doctors smoke Buffalo cigars more than they smoke other brands of cigars.

What is the truth and logic of the following statement?

Pets are people, too.

They are unlike people in so many ways (mentally, biologically, educationally, politically) that it is difficult to see any basis for the statement. There may be no way in which pets are people. What is the person who wrote the sentence trying to say? That pets have many feelings and abilities somewhat similar to those people have?

That pets as well as people may be friends? That pets should be treated with the kindness usually given to people?

Study the following assertions and be prepared to name the fallacies in each, to comment on them in class, or to write brief comments.

1. All metropolitan evening newspapers are losing money or going out of business.
2. All metropolitan evening newspapers are going out of business. Urbanites do not read anymore.
3. A citizen in the modern world must become highly educated or earn a low income for a lifetime.
4. No metal ever exists in a liquid state at ordinary temperatures.
5. The woman who sells herbal teas at her fruit stand says that nature provides plants to cure all physical illnesses.
6. After Billye Washington started fishing in Wash Creek, the fish died. Her fishing license should be revoked.
7. Because all employees should be required to own stock in the firm, any applicant who does not own stock should not be employed.
8. Do not select Professor Breenbough as one of the great teachers of the year. He is a disgraceful reprobate.
9. Repairing automobiles is just like solving problems in algebra.
10. The teacher brought a glass of tobacco juice and some earthworms to class. When she put the worms in the glass, they died. One student said it had proved that if you smoke cigars, you never will be wormy.

Papers

---

2 Writing and Revising

Writing is work. It can also be fun. From the dawn of literacy, writing has meant release and fulfillment, even a try for the permanent. Writers have been guides, controllers, and motivators. Learn to write well for yourself, for your instructor, for your friends, and even, in the larger scheme of things, for the world.

Many student writers handicap themselves by waiting until they feel inspired to compose a finished paper in a single draft—something that is very difficult to do at the college level and often causes writer's block. Strong writers, however, understand that good papers usually evolve through a number of stages: preliminary thinking and idea-jotting (brainstorming), scribbling free-flowing thoughts and informal sentences (freewriting), composing those thoughts to create a form readable by others (drafting), overhauling the draft to improve the content and style (revising), and proofreading to correct punctuation, mechanics, spelling, and appearance (editing).

2a Find a worthy subject.

You know what you are well informed about. You can learn more. You probably have an instinctive feel for what you can say and write, for what will interest friends (notes, letters) and public readers (letters of opinion, papers, essays).

Choose good subjects. Subjects can come from your reading, from your experience, from what you already know, and from what you can learn.

It is easy to assume that beginning writers have nothing or too little to say. Think deep and wide. Your knowledge may surprise you by its extent. Urbanization, people's moving from large geographical realms to more concentrated and even crowded areas in metropolises, has changed the nature of experience.

If you cannot write from personal experience about a deer track in the orchard or about buttermilk cooled in a fresh spring of water or in a well, for example, write about your observation of refrigerated foods in the home, in transport, or in commercial storage. Good subjects are where you find them. If you yourself have not witnessed a Highland fling or another sort of folk dance, you may have observed a musical performance in a nightclub or in a choir loft.

As a student of writing, you will be given particular assignments that will require you to write in specific ways. Accumulate a reservoir of potential subjects so that you will have topics from which to choose and something ready to adapt to whatever you are assigned. Just a title or a note can begin an essay. Good writers know that from one perspective, it is impossible to create anything that is not taken in some way from their own experience.

Exercises in this chapter

Every subject listed next suggests a topic for writing that you can make your own. Every hint or suggestion will be a guide for you to use in adapting the subjects to what your instructor requires. Construct the subjects by using the suggested techniques, and make them into interesting and important writings.

Primary subjects—drawn from your own experience

When you witness a place, a thing, or an occurrence, be sure that you observe it meticulously, accurately, and significantly. Write about the outline of hills or mountains as viewed from a deep valley, the far horizon in flat and treeless country, action seen from a small spot in a stadium at a sports spectacular, or a tidal wave or a flood observed from a boat. Write about the excitement of watching activity in an anthill or a bird's nest.

Small or large, the subject should be one that you have chosen with knowledge and joy. The following suggestions merely name topics, not titles. You must provide verbs, the action; nouns, the names; and adverbs and adjectives, the descriptions. In other words, pin down the particularity, the identity, of a subject. Make it yours. Give it the mark of your character, your mind.

PERFORMANCES (OR THE AUDIENCE AT A PERFORMANCE)

A carnival, spectator sports (high school level to professional), water sports, a ballet, a musical production

THE NATURAL WORLD

A vegetable or flower garden, a stream, a field or a farm, a backyard, a busy square of earth, a hill or part of a mountain

ANIMALS

Dogs, cats, cats and dogs, wild animals, cows (a leader, a loner), ducks, a cow noticing a swimming duck for the first time, a fox, a guinea pig

THE WORLD OVERHEAD

Planes, a small plane towing an advertisement, blimps, clouds, storms, kites, balloons, a ceiling

SINGLE INDIVIDUALS IN A CROWDED WORLD

A tramp, a newsboy, a pedestrian, a loiterer on campus, a driver in a traffic jam, a swimmer or a nonswimmer on a beach

GROUPS OF PEOPLE

A clan, a small class in school, a large class, a discussion group, a gang, a circle of friends, a team

TALKERS AND NONTALKERS

Intellectuals, musicians, clowns, whisperers, booming voices. In a shower room, at a coffee house, at a garden party, in a tearoom

ALMOST UNBELIEVABLE EXPERIENCES

Strange encounters, mechanical accidents or marvels, unusual natural phenomena (storms, floods, rocks, forests, streams, beaches)

VEHICLES AND ROUTES TRAVELED

Canoes, ships, automobiles, bicycles, interstates, rivers, the ocean, trails, dirt roads, traffic jams, automobile accidents

ARTS

Sculpture, paintings, folk art, gospel singing, concerts, symphonies, film, poetry, fiction, ceramics

GAMES AND SPORTS

Hide and seek, kick the can, soccer, ice hockey on a pond, football

GENERATIONS AND PEOPLE OF DIFFERENT AGES

Babies, infants, teens, youth, the middle-aged, the elderly

Long lists of subjects may not attract or spark your talent. Be ready to find your own subject. Every person, even a beginning writer, knows topics of interest, even of ecstasy, anxiety, frustration, or fulfillment.

Indeed, many good ideas for papers have been lost or forgotten because writers failed to record them when they emerged. You cannot depend on a sharp memory to retain fleeting ideas. One solution to this problem is to keep a journal. Many of the greatest writers maintain journals in which they record their thoughts for later development. Of course, journal entries need not be extensive. However, they should be long enough to help you recall a promising idea.

Secondary subjects—drawn from reading or listening

For nearly all your life, you have watched television and movies, read newspapers and books, and listened to conversations and radio. Continue to watch, read, and hear. Even more important, *think* about what you learn. Give an account of your source and then write what *you* think and what your readers may not have thought. Also, try to be aware of what your readers may agree with or even what opinions they may share with you.

Let subjects percolate in your mind until you are given specific assignments. Then decide how you will adapt a topic to fit the patterns previously suggested.

2b Develop your ideas and plan your paper carefully and systematically.

Drawing a sharp distinction between finding a subject (see previous section) and planning to write about it (see the following section) will save time and prevent confusion.

Whether you discover your own topic or your instructor assigns one, put your ideas on paper or on your computer screen. The techniques discussed next will help you to develop a subject.

One of the most important elements for producing finished papers is having enough time. Generally, the earlier you begin the process of writing a paper, the better it will be—provided, of course, that you use your time effectively. Allow sufficient time for working through the essential stages of the writing process described next.

Brainstorming

Even after you have chosen a subject, ideas will come to the mind in sudden and unpredictable flurries. Get into the habit of **brainstorming**—letting your thoughts drift wherever they will. Sometimes ideas seem not to come at all. At other times, they may rush in at the strangest moments—during sleepless hours when it may take you a few seconds to grab a piece of paper or turn on the computer. Brainstorm by taking notes quickly; save ideas. Later, treasure the good ones and freely discard the bad ones.

Listing

Brainstorming should produce a list of some kind. Make a note on anything that may be helpful. At this point do not be concerned with order or comparative importance (major and minor points). List now, and think more about the points later. Probably you will list many more points than you can use. Suppose you are contemplating writing a paper on spontaneous acts of kindness in crucial moments and situations. The following thoughts might occur to you:

> Instant courage
> Saving a life
> Danger to victim and rescuer
> 911
> Fire departments and police
> No time to wait
> No time to think
> Knowing CPR
> Not wishing to get involved—or appearing too eager to do so
> Rescuers having no time to think of self
> Reactions of observers
> Taking chances to rescue a single or a last survivor
> Times when helping the victim is impossible or foolish
> Those unwilling to help
> Automobile accidents and plane crashes
> After the accident and the rescue have ended
> Some victims may not wish to be rescued
> First reactions to an accident
> Second thoughts

Freewriting

In a way, all of the words that name the thinking processes involved in planning to write are similar. **Freewriting** is a step beyond listing because (1) loosely, you turn the parts of the list into rough sentences, and (2) you write on one point for only as long as the immediate inspiration continues.

The best writing is not always planned. A writer may write down one spontaneous sentence, and then the next part may continue to unfold almost miraculously. Jot down any ideas that seem to pop into your head. Nothing has to be systematic. Just hope that you can find and impose a system later. Even great writers have reported that a character or an idea may take charge, even to the point of seeming to dictate what a writer should write. If you have a subject, and nothing further seems to come to you, wait. Forcing the mind beyond a moment of glory may lead nowhere or may cause dullness. Inspiration will come, seemingly almost on its own terms, when you are least looking for it.

Save the product of your freewriting if it is worthy. If not, erase it from your computer easily without worry or throw away the paper.

Clustering or grouping—planning the parts

The list of the parts of a topic, the sentences from your freewriting, after a time will fall into groups or clusters. Look for associations and relations and try to draw them as physical relationships. Put them into groups without regard for order or importance at first. (See example on page 21.)

Just as graphs and maps may be useful alternatives to words, this technique for generating and developing ideas can reveal connections among ideas and can stimulate new thoughts.

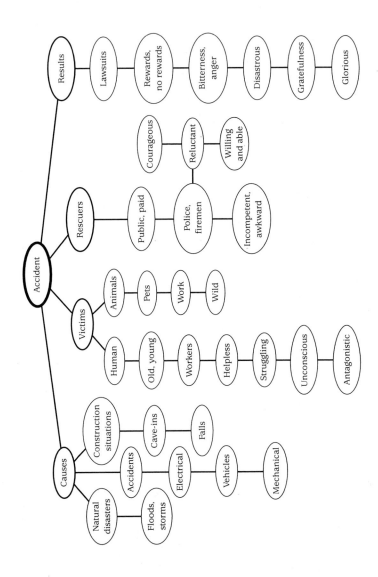

2c Organize systematically in your thinking or on paper.

William Faulkner sketched the plans for the seven days depicted in his novel *A Fable* on the plaster walls of his study in his home. In this famous rough literary outline, he used **grouping** and **clustering** to organize and remember. Parts of papers usually can be visualized mentally. Most also require reminder notes.

Scratch outline

The simplest kind of outline, the **scratch outline,** consists of a list of points placed in order but without subdivisions. The following topics for a scratch outline on want ads in a Sunday paper might suffice.

```
WANT ADS
ads—major part of paper
buyers and readers
long categories
as entertainment
real estate
personals and personal interest
employment
number and kinds of jobs
conclusion—imagination and invention
```

Topic outline

The **topic outline** is a formal, detailed structure that helps to organize materials. Prepare one to serve as a guide for what you will write. However, do not become a slave to the processes of outlining.

Observe the following conventions:

1. Number the main topics with Roman numerals, the first subheadings with capital letters, and the next with Arabic numbers. For further subheadings use lowercase letters *a, b, c,* then (1), (2), (3). The following is an example of the letters and numbers of an outline:

```
 I.  .............................................................................................................
     A.  ......................................................................................................
          1.  .................................................................................................
               a.  ...........................................................................................
                    (1)  ....................................................................................
                    (2)  ....................................................................................
               b.  ...........................................................................................
          2.  .................................................................................................
     B.  ......................................................................................................
 II.  ............................................................................................................
```

2. Use parallel grammatical structures.
3. Write topics, not sentences.
4. Do not place periods after the topics.
5. Make your outline cover the subject fully.
6. Arrange topics and subheadings logically and meaningfully.
7. Each succeeding level of an outline should represent a new level on a smaller scope.
8. Each subheading should have two or more parts.

INCORRECT OUTLINING

Want Ads in a Sunday Paper

I. Part of a Sunday Paper
    A. Uses of Want Ads
◄─────────── B. [another subheading needed]
II. Reading ads

EXAMPLE OF A TOPIC OUTLINE

Want Ads in a Sunday Paper

I. Part of Sunday Paper
    A. Uses of Want Ads
        1. Buyers
        2. Sellers
        3. Readers
    B. Length of Section
        1. Automotive
        2. Others
    C. Other Parts of Paper

   II. Reading Ads
      A. Entertainment—"Date Maker"
      B. Human Interest
         1. Rentals
         2. Expensive Real Estate
         3. Inexpensive Real Estate
         4. Personals and Personal Interest Sections
  III. Occupations
      A. Help Wanted
      B. Part-Time Help
      C. Hard Jobs
  IV. Conclusion—Imagination in Want Ads

Sentence outline

A **sentence outline** requires more planning than a scratch or a topic outline. The sentences will correspond closely with your major topic headings. If you compose the sentences before you write the paper instead of trying to select them afterward, they will be an aid instead of a burden.

EXAMPLE OF A SENTENCE OUTLINE

Want Ads in a Sunday Paper

   I. Want ads are a major part of the Sunday paper.
      A. The want ads serve many purposes for people.
         1. Buyers submit want ads for personal, economic, political, and vocational reasons.
         2. Readers read want ads for the same reasons as buyers.
      B. The length of want ads almost equals the length of a daily newspaper.
         1. The automotive section of the want ads is significantly larger than any other section of ads, comprising about five ounces in weight.
         2. The remaining 706 sections of want ads together weigh about seven ounces.
      C. Some categories may take more space in the paper than editorials, news, and events.
  II. Subscribers may read the want ads for enjoyment as well as profit.
      A. Want ads, including the "Date Maker" sections, can provide opportunities for entertainment for readers.

B. Other ads serve as human-interest ads, using enticing language to catch the reader's interest.
  1. Rental ads can offer property or hint at a relationship.
  2. Ads for expensive real estate can offer wealth, luxury, and elegance.
  3. Ads for inexpensive real estate also can offer wealth, luxury, and elegance through the right choice of words.
  4. The "Personals" and "Personal Interest" sections seem private and mysterious, since only a few readers may understand the meaning of an ad.
III. Want ads offering positions available in many occupations are also popular.
  A. Help wanted ads are popular, with advertisements for many different positions available.
  B. Part-time help wanted ads are also popular, providing opportunities for people seeking only part-time employment.
  C. Hard labor advertisements are rare, or carefully worded, since few people wish to have a strenuous labor job.
IV. To appeal to readers, want ads require invention and imagination from the writers.

2d Adapt your writing to reach a broad, general audience.

Try not to offend your reader—your audience. Concentrate on a general readership, educated adults who do not have highly specialized vocabularies—especially highly technical language—and who are interested in a wide variety of general subjects. Be fair and be sensitive to audiences whose feelings about your subject may differ from your own.

Your instructor, of course, is your first reader, although possibly not your only one. You would be ill advised to write about a subject if your views would bore or displease your reader—that is, writing about lowbrow music for a strict classicist or about a sedentary lifestyle for an athlete. You should resist the temptation to write solely for any single person. As they annotate the drafts of your papers, most professors regard themselves as readers with broad interests. Of course, you do not need to reject or compromise your

own interests or deeply held principles. Just try not to employ unpleasant tactics to force your readers to accept your perspectives.
With a good subject and a broad viewpoint, what you say should interest almost anyone.

Here are some questions that are helpful to keep in mind as you
consider possible audiences: (1) How much information does your
audience already have on your subject? (2) What is the average level
of your audience's education? (3) Is your audience likely to have
strong opinions about your topic? (4) What is your audience's line
of work or level of study? (5) Does your audience consist of a specific age group or socioeconomic class? Ignoring such important
considerations invites possible rejection of your work.

2e   Adopt a tone or an attitude appropriate for your readers and suitable to your subject.

For papers in a college course, you should generally adopt a serious
tone or attitude. Write in a style more appropriate for addressing a
professional rather than a child or a college friend at a party. (See
Section **41** on diction or level of language.) Considering your audience may help you to select the right tone. In a course, you are writing primarily for a teacher, someone who may be overly serious or,
on the other hand, quite whimsical.

One factor is your subject, which should be a controlling element. Usually write about food or appetite with a touch of humor
and about taxes or death with a somber mood of high seriousness.
Avoid being inappropriately frivolous about a serious subject or
with a serious audience and vice versa. Also, do not shift back and
forth from one attitude to another.

Trouble occurs when a writer is uncertain about what tone to
use. Avoid suddenly switching from one tone to another as the
writer of the following passage does:

> Art critics have the power to make or break young painters. Their
> opinions are especially influential among collectors and wealthy in-
> vestors. With praise from a few well-known critics, an artist can rise

shift in tone
almost overnight from struggling anonymity to distinction. Conversely, all it takes is strong negative criticism to doom a painter early in a career. Do these writers wield their enormous power responsibly? No! They care only for themselves. They are shameless frauds who invent nonsense about art and pass it off as the truth. They are arrogant and effete impostors who deserve to be severely scolded.

At the beginning of this passage, the tone is coolly objective. Then an ugly, ill-mannered outburst disrupts the mood.

2f Choose the tenses of verbs and the person and number of pronouns that will most effectively report what you know.

The third person singular and the past tense are customarily used for narratives. Essays use third person singular for an idea or an object (*it*) or for a person (*he, she*) and use the third person (*they*) for plurals, especially for conditions and groups and sometimes for the general and unknown. Ordinarily these persons and tenses are used without conscious contrivance, but the choice often can be planned and employed for special effect as, for example, when *it* refers to a woman or a child or when *he* or *she* is used to personify an animal or even a thing. The present tense used about a person long dead may convey all sorts of spiritual meanings.

The first person (*I, we*) usually is the choice for autobiographies, narratives, memoirs, and accounts of what the writer (sometimes with others) has done. *I* and *we* should speak and write boldly, frankly, and tactfully but never boastfully, immodestly, or deceptively. Readers may like you personally if you have a good grasp of your relative importance, but that *I,* sometimes called the "perpendicular pronoun," can annoy and cause antagonism when used too often and too arrogantly.

The second person is tricky. *Thee* and *thou* have special and even private meanings in modern English. *You* can be singular or plural. Stylistically, second-person usage is difficult to manage. It may sound like the person being addressed in cookbook instructions. It can be obtrusive (like the *I*) or imperative. When used with the present tense, *you* may seem immediate, personal, or even threatening.

Choose your words carefully. Using the first or second person or the present tense when the assignment does not permit it or when it is not a wise choice for the content or the tone can be disastrous.

2g State a precise thesis.

Know exactly what you wish to do in a paper. Pin down the central idea or purpose in a clear and precise **thesis statement** from which all details and examples will follow.

Some papers need more exactly defined theses than others. For narrative and descriptive subjects, establish a purpose and direction carefully. For argumentative, explanatory, and interpretive papers, go further by promising or stating main point(s).

Many thesis statements are ineffective, even bad. Some examples follow.

TOO VAGUE, FLABBY, UNINFORMATIVE

It is the purpose of this paper to provide a description of the want ads in a section of the Sunday paper.

TOO BROAD, CLAIMS TOO MUCH, PERHAPS EVEN UNTRUE

Want ads are the most profound and perceptive reflections of the human experience to be found in a Sunday paper.

The following is a more precise version.

DESCRIPTIVE, EXPLANATORY, A POINT TO BE PROVED

Want ads, a major part of a Sunday paper, are more substantial and entertaining than they are exact and dependable.

2h The paper's length should be appropriate to the subject and the assignment.

Select a subject that you can develop well in the length required. Do not choose a topic too large to be covered adequately or pad the paper just to achieve the required length.

Assignments of lengths are seldom artificial or arbitrary. Restricting a paper to a specified maximum page length is a prerogative of the instructor. The teacher may not be reasonably able to read long papers. In terms of the total work requirements for a course, it may not be wise to write a paper longer than that assigned.

Restricting a paper's length also involves mental discipline. Papers longer than the assignment are often wordy and uncontrolled. Writing them may be like spending too much money for an item or talking too much on a special occasion.

Papers that are too short for an assignment, on the other hand, may lack planning, content, or substance. It is much easier to reduce a paper's length than to expand it.

2i Write a first draft of your paper.

Sometimes the first version of a paper will be good, perhaps in several ways nearly good enough to be the last draft. Most papers, however, require much revision. Write as well as you possibly can the very first time and then be prepared to revise over and over.

Suppose that the assignment is to write a descriptive paper (not more than three and one half double-spaced computer or typewriter pages) about one of the sections of a large urban newspaper: the news, editorials, sports, society, travel, arts, business, classified or "want" ads, and so forth.

Imagine that you have selected the want ads as your topic. You have been reading them and using them for years; perhaps you have even placed one or two of your own. Put the topic aside for a time while you work, play, and perhaps even sleep. Writing a first draft will still involve planning, collecting your thoughts, selecting a strategy, and carefully reading many want ads.

Ideas will come when you least expect them, when you are not even struggling for them. No one can tell you exactly when to write. Possibly you will start two or more times and then run dry, have no inspiration, no thoughts. When you do get a good start, write as fast as you like for as long as you remain interested.

The following is a sample first draft of a paper on want ads.

Sample rough draft

"Want Ads in a Sunday Paper"

Want ads, a major part of a Sundy paper, are more informative than they are exact and dependable. A paper has to be big if it is to serve as many purposes as people expect it to do. Nearly everything it prints can be divided into to parts. Information given to readers by the paper itself and advertisements paid for with the intent of persuading reasders to make decisions that may benefit buyers of the ads.

The primary purpose of a paper, most readers agree, is to convey news ansd opinions about local and world events. Other purposes may be to inform readers about social occasions, sports, financial affairs, and the arts. Without want ads, the rest looks "pretty puny" and weighs only one and one fourth pounds or roughly twenty ounces approximately two sevenths of the entire Sundy issue. These parts also contains many advertisements, some full pages devoted only to selling something. Papers do not physically provide so much news and information as they offer materials about buying and selling, renting and using.

Buyers sponsor paid-for advertising, which should be intended to server the legal, professional, and busness world. Perhaps the least significant parts of a paper are the slick inserted pages of advertisements. With the comics and a brief magazine, they are overwhelming. They weigh over two poubds, about thirty-seven ounces in all, more than all the unsponsored information.

The want ad sections of the paper are extraordinarily long. Buyers place ads for many reasons—personl, economic, politics, and vocational. Also, through advertisements a newspaper wishes to serve the business, legal, and professional worlds. People read them for the same reasons and many others. Except for income from other advertisements, that's where the money's at.

In themselves want ads are bout as long as all of a daily paper. Some classifications (or categories) take up more pages than some other important sections such as editorils social news and events, and sindicated featurs. The number of ads for automobiles and trucks alone, for example, stretch the imagination and extends to thirty-eight pages. Not considering ten pages that are attached to other sections (Perspective and Personal Technology), in one Sunday paper they make up about five ounces of newspaper. That is a lot of cars and trucks. Who on earth will buy so many? The rest of the classifieds—seven ounces on the scales—have 706 categories. Even the manager in charge and his computer may not know the totals of the columns and the ads all together.

Want ads may be read for enjoyment as well as for profit. One old story tells about an amazed farmer who would read and call out to his wife: "Eliza, here is an ad by a man who wants to swap a peacock for a hog. Who on earth does he think would take him up." Classifieds may also seek or offer romance. One entire page called "DATE MAKER" has headings called "Women Seeking Men," "Men Seeking

Women," and so forth. One ad, for example, seems to promise many things.

DESTINY AWAITS!

Divorced, professional female, extremely attractive, outgoing, full-figured. Enjoys travel, dining, romance, pampering my man. In search of professional male, 35-50, attractive, financially secure.

Some want ads are much more personl than others. Writers uses enticeing language whether the subject is men and women or almost anything else. An entry in the section "Rentals to Share" may offer property or hint at a relationship.

ELMWOOD male seeks female to share large house, pool, gym, large bedrooms, private baths, fireplaces. References, $425/month + ¹/₂ utilities.

The ads for real estate offer wealth, luxury, elegance. One "home with acreage" in the paper, a horse farm or "an equestrian estate," has $3^1/_2$ baths and "bonus" (an extra room), a marble fireplace and a three-car garage. Nothing is plain and simple. A want ad can make a cabin sound like a palace. One mobile home offers a "VERY Deluxe Fireplace, den, two baths, all appliances, and air conditioning."

In the sections of "Personals" and "Personal Interests" the ads often seem private and mysterious. No one but the persons directly involved could understand some of them. Indeed, it has been rumored that agents of violence and foreign powers might convey messages in codes in a want ad like the following: "Peter, give the ball to Leroy whether he wants it or not." Religious love known only to the buyer of the ad may be the point of a brief message like "THANK YOU, ST. JUDE."

Vocation or occupation may define character. Nearly two hundred kinds of jobs are listed under full-time or part-time help wanted advertisements. The number of ads or columns in one category (or field) show the kinds of jobs or employment available. Jobs to be filled are as plentifull as automobiles for sale. Twenty-four columns advertise for help wanted in positions for accountants alone. In contrast, the paper lists "Activist" as a job field, but no one advertises a wish to employ an activist. (Possibly an example of an activist is one who distributes pamphlets for causes, such as the preservation of wildlife.)

The extent to which the world is mechanized or the ability of advertisers to call hard labor by other names may be indicated by the small number of advertisements for labourers. Few of the positions offered seem to require strenuous labour. To be employed as a janitor in a large muncipal airport, the applicant must "provide a ten-year history." Only five ads mention hard labour, and most of these sound as if they are placed by employment agencies. Labourers must be called by other names, or little labour is needed, or those who wish to hire labourers do not advertise.

Invention and imagination are required in advertisements that will appeal. Beauty, wonder, adventure, and money seem to be available just for asking and applying. Want ads serve many real needs in the world, but readers with caution and wisdom need to beware.

2j Revising your draft

You have completed your rough draft, and in the heat of inspiration, you think to yourself, "It is mighty good." You decide to turn it in as soon as you can and wait for the glory of a good grade. Tired from your labors, you take a short nap. When you wake, some of the enthusiasm has gone. You remember how a friend turned in a paper with very little revision of the first draft. It bounced back so quickly that she was astonished. It did not have even the usual large marks in editorial blue pencil. The instructor simply counted the pages and returned the paper with a failing grade or the option to write it once more and reduce its length.

So you review your paper briefly. To your surprise, it is much longer than you had thought it was—about a full page longer. The word counter for your computer, which you had not checked before, tells you it is several hundred words too long. You had thought that the assignment limits did not apply to anyone as creative or as well informed about the subject as you. So you took liberties.

Now you will have to undertake **global revisions.** Quickly you see that you can cut the wordiness and some of the overgeneralized ideas. At the beginning of the paper, you got carried away and speculated about the definition, description, and general character of newspapers. Leaving out the generalities will reduce the length significantly. You have heard that many papers improve when the first page is filed in a wastebasket. That proves to be almost entirely true of your beginning. You spent a lot of time weighing the various parts of the Sunday paper. The number of pages, columns, and ads describes lengths and proportions as well as the weights do, so you can leave out the pounds and ounces. One paragraph about a large estate can go, and you can omit the part about the activist, who may not be well defined anyway.

One of the fortunate aspects of writing is that you do not have to make mechanical and stylistic revisions in what you omit. You can begin without bothering to overwork your computer and make another copy. You can delete the big parts on your computer or on paper. You can then make the lesser, or **local,** changes in the same draft that contains the global deletions. You can run your spell-checker and also check questionable words in a dictionary. This kind of editing is indicated by color in the following version. The numbers refer to sections in this handbook that address the errors. Global deletions are marked out in black. If the paper gets too messy for even you to follow, use one draft for the large deletions and a second for the other revisions.

Global revisions and mechanical and stylistic revisions

Want Ads in a Sunday Paper 31d

Sunday 35

Want ads, a major part of a Sundy paper, are

more informative than they are exact and depend-

able. A paper has to be big if it is to serve as

many purposes as people expect it to do. Nearly

everything it prints can be divided into to parts.

Information given to readers by the paper itself

and advertisements paid for with the intent of

persuading reasders to make decisions that may

benefit buyers of the ads.

The primary purpose of a paper, most readers

agree, is to convey news ansd opinions about local

and world events. Other purposes may be to inform

readers about social occasions, sports, financial

delete

affairs, and the arts. Without want ads, the rest
looks "pretty puny" and weighs only one and one
fourth pounds or roughly twenty ounces approximately two sevenths of the entire Sundy issue.
These parts also contains many advertisements, some
full pages devoted only to selling something.
Papers do not physically provide so much news and
information as they offer materials about buying
and selling, renting and using.

delete

Buyers sponsor paid-for advertising, which
should be intended to server the legal, professional, and business world. Perhaps the least
significant parts of a paper are the slick inserted
pages of advertisements. With the comics and a
brief magazine, they are overwhelming. They weigh
over two poubds, about thirty-seven ounces in all,
more than all the unsponsored information.

The want ad sections of the paper are extraordi-

19
narily long. Buyers place ads for many reasons—

35   ~~personal~~   **political**
personl, economic, <u>politics</u>, and vocational. Also,

delete through advertisements a newspaper wishes to serve
the business, legal, and professional worlds.

People read them for the same reasons and many
others. Except for income from other advertisements,
              is
that's where the money~~'s at~~.   *41d*

                    about
    In themselves want ads are <u>bout</u> as long as
all of a daily paper. Some classifications
(or categories) take up more pages than some
                        editorials
other important sections such as <u>editorils</u> social *35*
            syndicated   **features**
news and events, and <u>sindicated</u> <u>featurs</u>. The *24b*
number of ads for automobiles and trucks alone,
           stretches
for example, <u>stretch</u> the imagination and extends
to thirty-eight pages. Not considering ten pages
that are attached to other sections (Perspective   **delete**
and Personal Technology), in one Sunday paper they
make up about five ounces of newspaper. That is a
lot of cars and trucks. Who on earth will buy so
many? The rest of the classifieds—~~seven ounces on
the scales~~—have 706 categories. Even the manager
in charge and his computer may not know the totals
of the columns and the ads all together.

    Want ads may be read for enjoyment as well as
for profit. One old story tells about an amazed
farmer who would read and call out to his wife:

"Eliza, here is an ad by a man who wants to swap a

peacock for a hog. Who on earth does he think would

32e   **up?**

take him ~~up~~." Classifieds may also seek or offer

romance. One entire page called "DATE MAKER" has

headings called "Women Seeking Men," "Men Seeking

Women," and so forth. One ad, for example, seems to

promise many things.

   DESTINY AWAITS!

   Divorced, professional female, extremely attractive, outgoing, full-figured. Enjoys travel, dining, romance, pampering my man. In search of professional male, 35-50, attractive, financially secure.

35
35   **personal**
11   Some want ads are much more ~~personl~~ than others.
            use   enticing
   Writers ~~uses~~ ~~enticeing~~ language whether the subject

is men and women or almost anything else. An entry

in the section "Rentals to Share" may ~~offer~~

property or hint at a relationship.

   ELMWOOD male seeks female to share large house, pool, gym,
   large bedrooms, private baths, fireplaces. References,
   $425/month + $^1/_2$ utilities.

                                        promise
42b   The ads for real estate ~~offer~~ wealth, luxury,

   elegance. One "home with acreage" in the paper, a

delete   horse farm or "an equestrian estate," has $3^1/_2$ baths

   and "bonus" (an extra room), a marble fireplace

   and a three-car garage. Nothing is plain and

simple. A want ad can make a cabin sound like a palace. One mobile home offers a "VERY Deluxe Fireplace, den, two baths, all appliances, and air conditioning."

In the sections of "Personals" and "Personal Interests" the ads often seem private and mysterious. No one but the persons directly involved could understand some of them. Indeed, it has been rumored that agents of violence and foreign powers might convey messages in codes in a want ad like the following: "Peter, give the ball to Leroy whether he wants it or not." Religious love known only to the buyer of the ad may be the point of a brief message like "THANK YOU, ST. JUDE."

Vocation or occupation may define character. Nearly two hundred kinds of jobs are listed under full-time or part-time help wanted advertisements. The number of ads or columns in one category (or

     shows   *11*

field) <u>show</u> the kinds of jobs or employment

             plentiful   *35*

available. Jobs to be filled are as <u>plentifull</u> as automobiles for sale. Twenty-four columns advertise for help wanted in positions for accountants alone.

delete
In contrast, the paper lists "Activist" as a job field, but no one advertises a wish to employ an activist. (Possibly an example of an activist is one who distributes pamphlets for causes, such as the preservation of wildlife.)

The extent to which the world is mechanized or the ability of advertisers to call hard labor by

35
          laborers
other names may be indicated by the small number of

35
advertisements for labourers. Few of the positions

        labor   *42b*

35
offered seem to require strenuous labour. To be

         municipal
employed as a janitor in a large muncipal airport,

the applicant must "provide a ten-year history."

35
         labor
Only five ads mention hard labour, and most of

these sound as if they are placed by employment

35
        Laborers
agencies. Labourers must be called by other names,

35
        labor
or little labour is needed, or those who wish to

35
        laborers
hire labourers do not advertise.

Invention and imagination are required in advertisements that will appeal. Beauty, wonder, adventure, and money seem to be available just for asking and applying. Want ads serve many real needs

in the world, but readers with caution and wisdom
    of false claims and to proceed with   *20b*
need to beware. caution and wisdom.

Before submitting a paper, read it over two or three times, at least once aloud. Listen for annoying repetitions. The following checklist should be helpful as you write and revise.

Checklist

Title

  Should accurately suggest the paper's contents
  Should attract interest without being excessively novel or clever
  Should not be too long

NOTE: Do not underline the title or put quotation marks around it.

Introduction

  Should be independent of the title. No pronoun or noun should depend
    on the title for its meaning.
  Should create interest
  Should establish the tone of the paper as serious, humorous, ironic, or
    otherwise
  Should include a thesis statement that declares the subject and purpose
    without use of worn word patterns such as "It is the purpose of this
    paper to. . . ."

Body

  Should develop the thesis statement
  Should be arranged in a logical sequence
  Should include topic sentences that clearly indicate the direction of the
    paper's development and the relevance of the paragraphs to the the-
    sis statement
  Should explain technical terms
  Should not contain choppy paragraphs

Should devote adequate space to main ideas and subordinate minor ideas
Should use appropriate concrete details and omit insignificant details

Transitions

Linking words, repeated terms and phrases, and repeated grammatical
structures (see Section 3f) should make clear connections between
sentences and paragraphs.

Conclusion

Should usually contain a final statement of the main idea, an overview
of what the paper has shown
Should usually be written in a separate paragraph
Should not merely restate or rephrase the introduction

Proofreading

Always read a manuscript through at least once just for proofreading. When proofreading, slow down your reading speed, and try to focus on individual letters. If possible, leave one day between completing the last draft and producing the final, finished copy. Examine your work carefully for wordiness, repetition, bad diction, vagueness, faulty punctuation, choppy sentences, and lack of transitions. Use your dictionary or your spell-checker to correct spelling, hyphenation, and word compounding.

2k   Model Papers

Final draft of model paper

```
Want Ads in a Sunday Paper and in the Online World

    Want ads, a major part of a Sunday paper and now

also of the online world, are more informative
```

than they are exact and dependable. Buyers place ads for many reasons—personal, economic, political, and vocational. People read them for the same reasons and many others. Except for income from sales of the paper and other advertisements, they are where the money comes from.

In themselves the Sunday want ads are about as long as all of a daily paper. Some classifications (or categories) take up more pages than some other important sections such as editorials, social news and events, and syndicated features. The number of ads for automobiles and trucks alone, for example, stretches the imagination and extends to thirty-eight pages. That is a lot of cars and trucks. Who on earth will buy so many? The rest of the classifieds (three sections of the paper) have 706 categories. Even the manager in charge and his computer may not know the totals of the columns and the total number of ads.

Want ads may be read for enjoyment as well as for profit. One old story tells about an amazed farmer who would read and call out to his wife: "Eliza, here is an ad by a man who wants to swap a peacock for a hog. Who on earth does he think would take him up?" Classifieds may also seek or offer romance. One entire page called "DATE MAKER" has categories like "Women Seeking Men," "Men Seeking Women," and so forth. One ad, for example, seems to promise many things:

> DESTINY AWAITS!
>
> Divorced, professional female, extremely attractive, outgoing, full-figured. Enjoys travel, dining, romance, pampering my man. In search of professional male, 35-50, attractive, financially secure.

Some want ads are much more personal than others. Writers use enticing language whether the subject is men and women or almost anything else. An entry in the section "Rentals to Share" may offer property or hint at a relationship as well:

> ELMWOOD Male seeks female to share large house, pool, gym, large bedrooms, private baths, fireplaces. References. $425/month + $1/2$ utilities.

The ads for real estate often promise wealth, luxury, and elegance. Nothing is plain and simple. A want ad can make a cabin sound like a palace. One mobile home offers a "VERY Deluxe Fireplace, den, two baths, all appliances, and air conditioning."

In the sections of "Personals" and "Personal Interests," the ads often seem private and mysterious. No one but the persons directly involved could know and understand some of them. Indeed, it has been rumored that agents of violence and foreign powers might convey messages in codes in an advertisement like the following: "Peter, give the ball to Leroy whether he wants it or not." Religious love may be the point of another message: "THANK YOU, ST. JUDE."

Vocation or occupation may define character. Nearly two hundred kinds of jobs are listed under "Full-Time Help Wanted" or "Part-Time Help Wanted." The number of ads or columns in a category (or field) may show kinds of jobs or employment available. Jobs to be filled are as plentiful as the number of automobiles for sale. Twenty-four columns advertise for help wanted in positions for accountants alone.

The extent to which the world is mechanized or the ability of advertisers to call hard jobs by other names may be indicated by the small number of advertisements for laborers. Few of the positions offered seem to require physical work. To be employed as a janitor in a large muncipal airport, the applicant must "provide a ten-year history." Only five ads mention hard labor, and most of these sound as if they were placed by employment agencies. Laborers must be called by other names, or little labor is needed, or those who wish to hire laborers do not advertise.

Invention and imagination are required in advertisements that will be appealing. Beauty, wonder, adventure, and money seem to be available just for asking and applying. Want ads serve many real purposes in the world, but readers need to beware of false claims and to proceed with caution and wisdom.

Exercises and paper assignments

The following instructions suggest paper topics and methods of development. The passages should help you think of subjects to write about. Under the guidance of your instructor, your assignment sheet, and your own disposition, choose topics, lengths of papers, methods of development, person and number of pronouns, and tenses of verbs.

Write with references to a passage or about your own ideas independent of the passage but suggested by it.

I

Write a description of one of the following as seen from one stationary position:

A landscape
A room
A small building
A road
A display window
A group of people
A screensaver

II

Narration. Tell a story about an event occurring during a typical or an unusual time.

A trip downtown, to the country, to the beach, to the mountains
A fishing trip or a hunting trip
A ball game
A festival
A ride on the subway

III

A character sketch. What are the sex, age, occupation, and appearance of the person whom you will describe?

IV

One issue or a cause. Choose an economic, political, religious, domestic, marital, educational, or environmental topic.

V

Definition. Choose a belief—religious, political, moral, or philosophical.

VI

Before you slip under the covers each evening, do you run out to the garage to hug your car? And each Saturday morning, before the neighbors have a chance to rise and shine, are you in the driveway scrubbing your vehicle inside and out? If so, the car we sell is not for you. You need a practical machine that puts action ahead of fun, a vehicle for those who don't let a car dictate their life or lifestyle.

Adapted from JIM MATEJAS, Chicago Tribune,
Atlanta Journal/Constitution

POSSIBLE SUBJECTS (NOT TITLES)

    Buying an automobile for the first time
    What you drive shows what you are.
    The necessity of owning a car
    Buying a car for luxury or use

VII

Venus Williams, no longer a curiosity or a teen pumped up by hype, emerged as a legitimate claimant to the future of women's tennis when she advanced to the U.S. Open final and a showdown against Martina Hingis.

    No other final in Grand Slam history has featured two players as young as the seventeen-year-old Williams and the sixteen-year-old

Hingis, and their meeting could presage the direction of the game for years to come.

Adapted from an article based on an Associated Press release,
Atlanta Journal/Constitution

POSSIBLE SUBJECTS (NOT TITLES)

Athletic ability and age
Team sports
Individual sports
Winning and losing
Being a prodigy

VIII

America has become a nation of blabbermouths. Too bad nobody's listening. Overwhelmed by the incessant, intrusive babble of the modern world, the skill of listening has fallen on hard times. People say they are constantly repeating orders, directions, and questions. The word *What?* rings through the halls. People recall only about 25 percent of what they have heard in the past few days.

Adapted from an article by CYNTHIA CROSSEN,
Atlanta Journal/Constitution

POSSIBLE SUBJECTS (NOT TITLES)

A seminar or class discussion
Whispering in class; in a church, mosque, or synagogue; or in a courtroom
Lecturing as opposed to class discussion
Heckling
Not trying to listen

IX

Today, while people throughout the world watch Princess Diana's funeral and mourn her untimely demise in a traffic accident, hundreds of drivers in this state will wreck their cars and injure themselves. And, if averages hold true, five will die.

Drivers are rushing to mayhem on the highways at a frightening pace. While the national injury crash per million miles driven decreased 1 percent since 1990, injuries here actually increased 18 percent.

Adapted from an article by BILL TORPY,
Atlanta Journal/Constitution

POSSIBLE SUBJECTS (NOT TOPICS)

Taking chances
Grief
Speeding and danger

X

The week before the young driver was beaten to death while making a late night pizza delivery, he told his roommate that he wanted to go home to the country of his youth. He had been in this city nearly two years, working two jobs to send his family money each week and banking the remainder for college tuition.

Adapted from an article by R. ROBIN MCDONALD,
Atlanta Journal/Constitution

POSSIBLE SUBJECTS (NOT TITLES)

What the young owe to older generations
Homesickness
Unexpected violence

XI

Lockheed Martin announced late Friday that, weather permitting, it will attempt Sunday to fly the F-22 advanced stealth fighter for the first time. Officials will not allow the flight to take off if visibility is less than five miles, or crosswinds are as great as six miles per hour, or the cloud ceiling is lower than twelve thousand feet. The final decision will be made by the test pilot.

People who usually spot fighter planes overhead may be able to see the F-22 "if they time it just right," said a spokesman." It's going to go by pretty quick," he said.

The cost of a single plane is estimated at one hundred million dollars.

Adapted from an article by JOHN MELVIN,
Atlanta Journal/Constitution

POSSIBLE SUBJECTS (NOT TOPICS)

The effect of one kind of wind on a moving object or person
Experimental testing of a machine by a person
Comparing decisions made by a supervisor and a user
The expensive price of a single thing such as a pair of athletic shoes or
orthopedic shoes
A proper attitude, proceeding with caution

XII

An uneducated person who is deeply rooted in a culture may know legend
and folklore and be oblivious to history; [may have no] concept of progress;
may recognize heritage but have no knowledge of class; may be aware that
people live in cities, but have no comprehension of an urban life.

Adapted from FLOYD C. WATKINS, *Yesterday in the Hills*

POSSIBLE SUBJECTS (NOT TITLES)

*The previous passage is filled with things that are abstract but never-
theless real: folklore and history; earth and progress; heritage, class,
and urban life. Choose one term and narrow it enough that you can
make it real in images and examples.*

XIII

There is a time for everything,
and a lesson for every activity under heaven. . . .
a time to plant and a time to uproot,
a time to kill and a time to heal,
a time to tear down and a time to build,
a time to weep and a time to laugh . . .
a time to keep and a time to throw away . . .

a time to be silent and a time to speak,
a time for war and a time for peace.

Adapted from Ecclesiasles 3

POSSIBLE SUBJECTS (NOT TITLES)

*Choose one of these contrasts (be silent or speak, for example) to write
about, or choose an action (to uproot or to laugh) and write about the
appropriate time for performing it.*

XIV

It seems odd to claim that conversation has declined while popular culture is drenched in talk. Talk radio chatters on. Television talk shows fill
the airwaves. Millions of email exchanges hum over the Internet daily.
Our lives are filled with people yakking.

A conversation involves listening, a willingness to share. Conversation creates community.

Adapted from JOHN BLAKE, "Yakkety-Yak, Why We Don't Talk Back,"
Atlanta Journal/Constitution

POSSIBLE SUBJECTS (NOT TITLES)

A talk with a postal worker
Quiet talk with an intimate friend
Discussion at the dinner table
Debate at a neighborhood meeting

XV

She knew she was a great writer, that she was out of food and ink, that
she had just enough money to buy one—but not both. Which did or
should she buy?

POSSIBLE SUBJECTS (NOT TOPICS)

*Make one of the following changes and then write a paper that ex-
pands upon the previous passage.*

Change the pronoun *she* to *he, you,* or *I.*
Select the plural or the singular.
Change the tense of the verbs as you wish—*knows? is? has? does?*
Use proper nouns, invented or real. *Alice? Bob?*

Alternatively, write about another dilemma:

Job or further education?
Career or marriage?
Having another child or pursuing a career?

You decide on the two areas of choice if your instructor does not assign them.

XVI

A high school teacher is asked to write a confidential recommendation for a former student. She states that she believes the student will make an excellent teacher on the college level but that he should not be employed on the preparatory school level because he might talk intellectually over the heads of young students. Two years later the prep school principal tells the applicant that he did not get the job because of the recommendation.

POSSIBLE SUBJECTS (NOT TITLES)
The need for confidentiality
Honesty in recommendations—pro or con
Respecting honesty and not being too sensitive
Not giving your true opinion or telling the truth

XVII

Describe a process:

Playing a game
Working—mowing a lawn, cutting wood, sorting and delivering, driving a vehicle, rowing, or running a boat

Preparing food, a meal, or a drink
Dining, dancing, or attending a theatrical performance

21 Composing and revising on a computer

Most of the writing techniques discussed in this chapter—for example, freewriting—can be practiced effectively on a personal computer. Computers have become very popular with writers not only because they save time but also because they allow users to generate and record ideas quickly and legibly without seriously interrupting their mental flow. Some writers prefer to begin with pencil and paper and then move to the keyboard once ideas begin to flow; others find it easier to start on a computer, where their thoughts can easily be recorded, reorganized, deleted, or saved.

Perhaps the greatest benefit of composing on a computer is how much easier revision becomes. Writing legible drafts in longhand or on a typewriter requires a huge investment of time and effort and creates a built-in resistance to throwing anything away, to starting over, and to recopying drafts after correcting mistakes. In fact, the hard labor of writing in longhand or on a typewriter often creates a psychological barrier to revision and even to composition itself. The fear of having to start over if your ideas do not immediately emerge in perfect form can prevent your writing anything at all until much too late. With a computer, however, revision is a snap. You can insert words, delete sentences, move paragraphs, change margins, check spelling, and recopy documents almost instantly. Take advantage of these capabilities to cultivate the habit of thorough revision—the best habit a writer can develop. The following is a short list of helpful suggestions.

Save frequently

Use the **Save** command to protect what you have written. A single innocent mistake or circumstance—hitting the wrong key, bumping the power cord, losing power momentarily during a thunderstorm, or the like—can erase hours of hard work. As a general rule, save whenever you stop to think about what to write next. If you are working in a computer lab or on someone else's computer, make sure that you save your work on a floppy disk instead of on the hard drive.

Copy and paste

When you decide to revise a draft, create a separate electronic document for each major revision. Instead of making changes in the original draft document, copy and paste its contents into a new document, save the new document under a new name that clearly identifies what it is ("draft 3," for example), and then begin revising. This technique will enable you to compare your latest draft with earlier ones to see what has or has not been improved. If you prefer an earlier passage, you can easily paste it into the latest version.

Print out

Regularly print copies of drafts as you complete them. Seeing on paper what you have been viewing on the screen creates another perspective that can help you spot errors easily—especially formatting problems, which often are not noticeable until you print out your work. In addition, printing and comparing several different drafts may help you to identify in an early draft valuable material that you can add to the latest one.

Back up

Computers and floppy disks do break down. Ensure yourself against losing everything you have written by using a back-up program (if you have one) or by storing identical copies of important documents in different places. Save one copy on your hard disk and another on a floppy disk, for example, or save copies on two different floppy disks kept in separate places.

Know your tools

Programs and printers possess a vast and fascinating array of functions. Learn as much as you can as early as you can about the ones that you are using. Being thoroughly familiar with your equipment will save you time later on and greatly increase your efficiency.

Take frequent breaks

Sitting and staring at a computer screen for hours without rest can cause physical problems with your eyes, neck, back, and wrists, thus making you a less effective writer. Reward yourself with a short break every half-hour or so to rest your body and wrists and to keep your mind sharp.

Service printers regularly

Turning in a paper with faint type is inconsiderate and sloppy. Change the ribbon or cartridge in your printer regularly so that the appearance of your finished paper will receive the respect it deserves.

Store disks carefully

The life span of a floppy disk can be cut short by exposure to heat, dust, moisture, pressure, and magnetic fields. Store your disks in containers and in areas that will protect them from such hazards.

Paragraphs

3 Writing Paragraphs ¶

A paragraph is a series of sentences usually set off by indentation and grouped together for a specific reason. Paragraphs civilize writing. Without them an essay would be like a wilderness in which it is easy to get lost. They separate, provide direction, and emphasize.

Paragraphs also indicate processes of thought—logical movements from idea to idea. When you begin to develop ideas for a paper, write a page or two without paragraphical separations. Then try separating your ideas into paragraphs as if you were sorting your laundry into different piles.

Paragraphs with specialized functions

Some paragraphs act as signposts by performing functions for an entire essay. They can introduce, provide transitions, or conclude.

Introductions

The first paragraph is often the hardest part of a paper to write. It must capture the reader's attention, introduce the subject, and state the purpose of the essay. A dull, mechanical, or obscure opening paragraph may discourage further reading.

You may begin effectively by presenting a startling fact, by telling a brief anecdote, or by opening with a generalization and then stating a thesis.

In a first paragraph, do not plunge abruptly into an argument, apologize, or discuss your process of writing. The following first paragraph of a paper about a magazine is a poor way to start:

> When I first read this magazine, I was completely bewildered, but then I started to see how it got across the idea of patriotism. After I looked at the articles, advertising, and artwork, I began to see how

much the war was on everyone's mind. *The Woman's Home Companion* from 1943 is very interesting to read.

The paragraph initially establishes no context (which magazine?), then says too much about content and makeup, and wanders without a clear thesis. The next example is a better way to begin the same essay:

> Fifteen cents was the cost of *The Woman's Home Companion* in 1943. In articles, advertisements, and photos, this inexpensive but colorful magazine painted a vivid picture of the people of that era. As World War II raged, Americans banded together to support their country. Consequently, in bold advertisements, many companies challenged readers to fulfill their patriotic duties.

This introduction immediately establishes a context by providing the name and date of the magazine and then narrows down to its thesis: the use of patriotism in advertisements.

Conclusions

The concluding paragraph of a paper should be forceful and climactic. It should not repeat in detail the information presented previously. Instead, it should briefly restate or refer to the thesis and make a final assessment of the importance and originality of the assessment argument.

Transitions

A transitional paragraph usually occurs in longer essays to indicate that the author has finished discussing one major point and is now moving to another. Transitional paragraphs can be relatively brief, as the following example illustrates:

> The women of some ancient tribes exercise a great deal of control in the family unit even though they have little political power in the tribe as a whole. The men, on the other hand, may rule the tribe but lack power in the domestic aspects of life.

3a Write a clear statement of a paragraph's central thought in the topic sentence.

A **topic sentence** usually comes at the beginning of a paragraph and provides a focus for what follows. The rest of the paragraph's sentences may develop that main idea.

topic sentence   Young children have no sense of wonder. They bewilder well, but few things surprise them. All of it is new to young children, after all, and equally gratuitous. Their parents pause at the unnecessary beauty of an ice storm coating the trees; the children look for something to throw. The children who tape colorful fall leaves to the schoolroom windows and walls are humoring the teacher. The busy teacher halts on her walk to school and stoops to pick up fine bright leaves "to show the children"—but it is she, now in her sixties, who is increasingly stunned by the leaves, their brightness all so much trash that litters the gutter.

body of paragraph

ANNIE DILLARD
An American Childhood

Effective topic sentences can appear anywhere in a paragraph. For example, if you want to create a sense of suspense before you introduce the main subject, your topic sentence may not appear until the second or third sentence of a paragraph.

Biologists may be accustomed to working on obscure beasts—ugly horseshoe crabs, prickly sea urchins, slimy algae. But anthropologist Grover Krantz of Washington State University has a problem of a different sort. He is studying, or trying to study, a creature no scientist has ever seen: the mysterious Sasquatch, or Bigfoot. [The rest of the paragraph discusses the nature of the research.]

"TRACKING THE SASQUATCH"
Newsweek

When you have several examples that you intend to use to prove a point, it is sometimes effective to present the evidence first and then to end the paragraph with your central idea. In the following paragraph, the topic sentence comes at the end.

> Farmers no longer have cows, pigs, chickens, or other animals on their farms; according to the U.S. Department of Agriculture, farmers have "grain-consuming animal units" (which, according to the Tax Reform Act of 1986, are kept in "single-purpose agricultural structures," not pig pens and chicken coops). Attentive observers of the English language also learned recently that the multibillion dollar market crash of 1987 was simply a "fourth quarter equity retreat"; that airplanes do not crash—they just have "uncontrolled contact with the ground"; that janitors are really "environmental technicians"; that it was a "diagnostic misadventure of a high magnitude" which caused the death of a patient in a Philadelphia hospital, not medical malpractice; and that President Reagan was not really unconscious while he underwent minor surgery; he was just in a "non-decisionmaking form." In other words, double-speak continues to spread as the official language of public discourse.
>
> WILLIAM LUTZ
> "The World of Doublespeak"

By placing topic sentences at various places in paragraphs, you can skillfully avoid creating automatic and monotonous patterns in your writing.

■ Exercise 1

Underline the topic sentences in the following paragraphs and be prepared to discuss the effectiveness of their placement.

1. The Polish Jewish community was entirely regulated by its rabbis in all religious, moral, and cultural matters. Its school system began with the child in elementary school and continued on up to academies of learning where masters and disciples spent their lives with the Talmud and its commentaries. In 1721 twelve years of such higher learning were required in Lithuania after

marriage before one could become a teacher of the law and a judge. Jewish presses published prayer books, Bibles, the Talmud, books of Talmudic legends for light readings, and a translation of the Pentateuch into Yiddish with a commentary woven of tales and moral teachings that was enormously appealing to women. Rabbinic civilization reached its zenith with the Jewish world of Poland and Lithuania.

CHAIM POTOK
Wanderings

2. The weeks until graduation were filled with heady activities. A group of small children were to be presented in a play about buttercups and daisies and bunny rabbits. They could be heard throughout the building practicing their hops and their little songs that sounded like silver bells. The older girls (non-graduates, of course) were assigned the task of making refreshments for the night's festivities. A tangy scent of ginger, cinnamon, nutmeg and chocolate wafted around the home economics building as the budding cooks made samples for themselves and their teachers.

MAYA ANGELOU
I Know Why the Caged Bird Sings

■ Exercise 2

Compose two paragraphs, one with the topic sentence at the beginning and the other with the topic sentence in another position. Be prepared to justify the placement of the topic sentences.

3b Unify a paragraph by relating each sentence to the central idea.

In an effective paragraph each sentence is directly related to the main point. Do not make readers strain to find connections. Even slightly irrelevant material can throw an entire paragraph out of focus and lead to confusion about its direction. Stick to the subject stated in the topic sentence.

The following paragraph compares secrecy to fire, but after beginning with a good topic sentence, it includes three sentences (in italics) that stray from the main point.

> Secrecy is as indispensable to human beings as fire, and as greatly feared. *Of course, we all know that fear can be a terrible barrier to communication and is itself generally destructive. Nothing is more important to society than communication.* Both *fire* and *secrecy* enhance and protect life, yet both can stifle, lay waste, spread out of all control. *Naturally, gossip is also to be feared as one of the negative aspects of civilization.* Fire and secrecy each can be turned against itself; barriers of secrecy are set up to guard against secret plots and surreptitious prying, just as fire is used to fight fire.
>
> Adapted from SISSELA BOK, *Secrets.*
> [Additions made here are italicized.]

What starts out as a thoughtful and original comparison between secrecy and fire soon sprawls into a commentary on fear, communication, and gossip. What follows is the paragraph as it was actually written. Notice its effective unity.

> Secrecy is as indispensable to human beings as fire, and as greatly feared. Both enhance and protect life, yet both can stifle, lay waste, spread out of all control. Both may be used to guard intimacy or to invade it, to nurture or to consume. And each can be turned against itself: barriers of secrecy are set up to guard against secret plots and surreptitious prying, just as fire is used to fight fire.
>
> SISSELA BOK,
> *Secrets*

The next paragraph attempts to develop the central idea of preserving our forests, but about halfway through, the writer abruptly changes to the topic of beauty and thus destroys the coherence of the paragraph.

An encouraging sign in management of national resources is the planting of trees systematically to replace those harvested. Large timber companies have learned that it is in their best interests to look to the future and not merely to get what they can at the moment from the land. *Besides that, trees are beautiful and add much to the pleasure of being in nature. Only God, as the poet so aptly put it, can make a tree.* With modern tools and methods, whole forests can be destroyed in a fraction of the time that lumberjacks with their axes and handsaws attacked the woods. It is more necessary than ever, therefore, that conservation be a primary concern not only of the general citizenry but also of industry.

If the two digressive sentences printed in italics were deleted, the paragraph would be coherent and would communicate, as it should, a single, well-argued point.

Often it is not that easy to make a good paragraph from a flawed one. Without planning and care, a paragraph can be merely a random collection of thoughts with only a vague central idea.

■ Exercise 3

Study the following paragraph; then delete all extraneous material.

Many American couples today have chosen not to follow the traditional way of being parents, in which the mother serves as the primary caregiver. Both mother and father take family leave when the baby is born, and both feed and change the newborn. ~~During its first year, a baby is very demanding. Some children suffer from colic, which makes them cry for long hours and refuse to go to sleep. The first year can be a tiring time for parents.~~ When the child is older, coparents both participate in the daily routines of caregiving: cooking, feeding, bathing, entertaining, and disciplining. Consequently, the child bonds with both the mother and the father.

3c   Develop paragraphs adequately.

Good paragraphs provide enough information to demonstrate the ideas in their topic sentences. To develop a paragraph, provide specific details, examples, or explanations that support the generalization given in the topic sentence. Skilled writers move back and forth between generalizations and the specific details that flesh out those generalizations.

Starting a new paragraph after every two or three sentences, without regard to development, is nearly as distracting as having no paragraph divisions at all. Underdeveloped paragraphs are like undernourished people: they are weak, unable to carry out their assigned tasks. Make sure your paragraph divisions come with new units of thought and that you have fleshed out an idea appropriately before going on to another idea.

The following paragraphs on George Washington are ineffectively developed:

> In many ways, the version of George Washington we grew up on is accurate. He was an honest and personally unambitious politician.
>
> But history teachers rarely tell us about the complex character of the man.
>
> Most historians feel that he was not a great soldier, yet he was the luckiest man alive.
>
> He even survived the attacks of his mother. When he was president, she went so far as to state publicly that he was starving and neglecting her, neither of which was true.

Though interesting, these paragraphs are too underdeveloped to do their jobs. They are just strong enough to state the points. Contrast them with the following paragraphs:

> In many ways, the version of George Washington we grew up on is accurate. He was an honest and personally unambitious politician, a devout patriot, and a fearless soldier. Through circumstance, he became the lodestar for the swift-sailing Revolution. Even his enemies conceded that national success would have been impossible without him.
>
> But history teachers rarely tell us about the complex character of the man. Often moody and bleak, he did not like to be touched. When he became president, he required so much ritual and formality that it caused one observer to quip: "I fear we may have exchanged George the Third for George the First." Though he drank hard with the enlisted

men, he was a tough disciplinarian, describing himself as a man "who always walked on a straight line."

Most historians feel that he was not a great soldier, yet he was the luckiest man alive. He had two horses shot out from under him; felt bullets rip through his clothes and hat; and survived attacks by Indians, French and English troops, hard winters, cunning political opponents, and smallpox.

He even survived the attacks of his mother. When he was president, she went so far as to state publicly that he was starving and neglecting her, neither of which was true. Then, to twist the emotional knife, she tried to persuade the new government to pass a law that future presidents not be allowed to neglect their mothers.

Adapted from DIANE ACKERMAN,
"The Real George Washington"

In some kinds of writing, short paragraphs are acceptable and even preferred. Newspapers, for example, generally use brief paragraphs because their articles require few details and little exposition.

Sometimes it is effective to insert a short paragraph amid longer ones for emphasis and variety. The length of an essay or a paper may influence the length of its paragraphs. A paper of one thousand words provides more room to develop full paragraphs than a short one does.

■ Exercise 4

Seven broad subjects for paragraphs are listed next. Choose the two that you like best, and select one aspect of each topic. On each subject, first write a skimpy paragraph. Then write a paragraph of 125 to 175 words with fuller development of the subject.

1. diets
2. email
3. television soap operas
4. condominiums

5. the volunteer army
6. college sports
7. national health care

3d Trim, tighten, or divide sprawling paragraphs.

A sprawling paragraph is the opposite of an underdeveloped one: it needs trimming. As you write, keep alert to the length of your paragraphs. One that extends over several pages is obviously too long. To reduce excessive length, you may need to reduce the scope of the topic sentence or divide the material into smaller units. Sometimes you can produce a better paragraph by simply discarding material. For example, all your details may be pertinent and interesting, but you may not need ten examples to illustrate your point; four or five may do it more efficiently.

3e Develop each paragraph by a method appropriate to its content.

Often the topic sentence will suggest a method for writing a paragraph. Some paragraphs use more than one kind of pattern. A paragraph of comparison and contrast, for example, may offer definitions, and a paragraph describing a process may involve narration. Plan patterns that will most effectively help you to develop your ideas.

Narration

Narrative writing unfolds events over time and sometimes across space. In many ways, this is the simplest pattern because we tend to think in chronological order. Narratives usually begin with the first event and end with the last. In some instances, however, it is effective to describe a later event first and then go back to the beginning (employing a flashback).

The following two paragraphs describe events in chronological order:

> The taxi was almost upon her before she noticed it. As it slowed down for the gate, she identified it by its lights, and stepped on to the roadway. It slid to a halt in the gravel, beside her; she stepped in before the driver could come to assist her, slammed the door, and said: "Wooford's Drugstore, on Manchester Street."
>
> He was waiting in front of the drugstore. Almost a block before they got there, she could see him pacing back and forth with his almost prinking, elastic step, his shoulders in the slight slouch which he affected, a hat crushed on his head, and his old raincoat swinging free from the shoulders with the loose belt trailing at both ends. He looked around when the cab pulled to a stop at the corner, and strolled over to her, and watched critically while she paid off the driver. As she turned to face him, he said: "You tipped him far too much."
>
> ROBERT PENN WARREN
> *At Heaven's Gate*

In the previous paragraphs, the writer describes the events as they happened.

Description

Descriptive writing appeals to the five senses: sight, hearing, smell, taste, and touch. Descriptive paragraphs can follow a chronological, spatial, least-to-most-important, or most-to-least-important pattern. In describing a scene or a person, move from detail to detail in a logical order.

The following paragraph guides the reader's eyes around a house under construction. The author also arranges the description in climactic order, ending the scene with the most important person present.

> Inside the house, carpenters, electricians, and plumbers were busily at work. Plywood covered the floor, and everything was shrouded in a thin film of white dust. A plasterer on a ladder was touching up a molding; an older man in overalls stood at a table saw, cutting

strips of wood flooring; two other workers—electricians, to judge from the tool belts slung around their waists—were conferring over a set of blueprints spread out on a makeshift trestle table. A well-dressed woman—obviously the owner—surveyed this activity with what appeared to be a mixture of pride and trepidation.

WITOLD RYBCZNSKI
Looking Around: A Journey Through Architecture

NOTE: Paragraphs of **narration** and **description** sometimes do not have conventional topic sentences.

Example

Many topic sentences state generalizations that gain force with evidence and illustration. Proof can be provided by an extended example or by several short examples. A well-chosen example like the one used in the following paragraph can add interest and vividness as well as proof:

Ours was once a forested planet. The rocky hillsides of Greece were covered with trees. Syria was known for its forests, not its deserts. Lebanon had vast cedar forests, from which the navies of Phoenicia, Persia, and Macedonia took their ship timber, and which provided the wood that Solomon used to build the temple at Jerusalem. Oak and beech forests dominated the landscapes of England and Ireland. In Germany and Sweden, bears and wolves roamed through wild forests where manicured tree farms now stand. Columbus saw the moonscape that we call Haiti "filled with trees of a thousand kinds." Exploring the east coast of North America in 1524, Verrazano wrote of "a land full of the largest forests . . . with as much beauty and delectable appearance as it would be possible to express."

CATHERINE CAUFIELD
"The Ancient Forest"

Definition

Whether you are using a new word or a new meaning for an old one, a definition explains a concept. It avoids the problems that arise when two persons use the same term for different things. Effective definitions use specifics or examples to demonstrate abstractions. A definition in a paragraph may be much more elaborate than one given in a dictionary.

> "Whistleblower" is a recent label for those who make revelations meant to call attention to negligence, abuses, or dangers that threaten the public interest. They sound an alarm based on their expertise or inside knowledge, often from within the very organization in which they work. With as much resonance as they can muster, they strive to breach secrecy, or else arouse an apathetic public to dangers everyone knows about but does not fully acknowledge.
>
> SISSELA BOK
> *Secrets: On the Ethics of Concealment and Revelation*

Analogy

Analogies are figurative comparisons that explain one thing in terms of another. They are most effective when you show a resemblance between two things with so many differences that they are not ordinarily compared. The following paragraph, for example, reveals an analogy between landing an airplane on autopilot and the clotting of blood:

> The landing of an airplane is just one example of a system that has to work within very tight restrictions to avoid disaster. Even the Wright brothers had to worry about landing properly. A little too short or a little too high, and the plane and passengers are in big trouble. But imagine the greater difficulty of landing a plane on autopilot—with no conscious agent to guide it! Blood clotting is on autopilot, and blood clotting requires extreme precision. When a pressurized blood circulation system is punctured, a clot must form quickly or the animal will bleed to death. If blood congeals at the wrong time or place, though, then the clot may block circulation as it does in heart attacks and strokes. Furthermore, the clot has to stop bleeding all along the length of the cut, sealing it completely. Yet blood clotting must be confined to the cut or the entire blood system of the animal might solidify, killing

it. Consequently, the clotting of blood must be tightly controlled so that the clot forms only when and where it is required.

MICHAEL J. BEHE
Darwin's Black Box

Comparison and contrast

Comparisons show similarities; contrasts present differences. The ratio of comparison to contrast can vary greatly from one paragraph to another. You might write, for example, that two things have five likenesses but only one or two differences. Or the reverse could be true.

The following paragraph on Thomas Jefferson and Abraham Lincoln begins by briefly contrasting the two men and then moves on to point out three similarities in their early lives.

> As one would expect, the formative years of Jefferson and Lincoln represent a study in contrasts, for the two men began life at opposite ends of the social and economic spectrum. There are, however, some intriguing parallels. Both men suffered the devastating loss of a parent at an early age. Jefferson's father, an able and active man to whom his son was deeply devoted, died when his son was fourteen, and Thomas was left to the care of his mother. His adolescent misogyny and his subsequent glacial silence on the subject of his mother strongly suggest that their relationship was strained. Conversely, Lincoln suffered the loss of his mother at the age of nine, and while he adored his father's second wife, he seems to have grown increasingly unable to regard his father with affection or perhaps even respect. Both Jefferson and Lincoln had the painful misfortune to experience in their youth the death of a favorite sister. And both were marked for distinction early by being elected to their respective legislatures at the age of twenty-five.

DOUGLAS L. WILSON
"What Jefferson and Lincoln Read"

NOTE: Sometimes entire paragraphs may consist of either comparisons or contrasts rather than of both.

Paragraphs using comparison and contrast can follow an **alternating structure,** which moves back and forth between the subjects being discussed, or a **block structure,** which discusses one subject completely and then moves to the next. In the following paragraph, the author uses an alternating structure to contrast Jefferson and Lincoln.

Jefferson

Lincoln

Jefferson

Lincoln

> In the matter of education the contrasts are equally great. Jefferson received a superb education, even by the standards of his class. It included formal schooling from the age of five, expert instruction in classical languages, two years of college, and a legal apprenticeship. Along the way he had the benefit of conspicuously learned men as his teachers. . . . Lincoln had almost no formal education. Growing up with nearly illiterate parents and in an atmosphere that had, as he wrote, "nothing to excite ambition for education," Lincoln was essentially self-taught. The backwoods schools he attended very sporadically were conducted by teachers with meager qualifications. . . . Jefferson read Latin from an early age and, after mastering classical languages and French, was able to teach himself Italian; Lincoln at about the same age was teaching himself grammar in order to be able to speak and write standard English.

If the author had used the block structure for the same paragraph, it would read as follows:

Jefferson

Lincoln

> In the matter of education the contrasts are equally great. Jefferson received a superb education, even by the standards of his class. It included formal schooling from the age of five, expert instruction in classical languages, two years of college, and a legal apprenticeship. Along the way he had the benefit of conspicuously learned men as his teachers. He read Latin from an early age and, after mastering classical languages and French, was able to teach himself Italian. Lincoln had almost no formal education. Growing up in an atmosphere that had, as he wrote, "nothing to excite ambition for education," Lincoln was essentially self-taught. The backwoods schools he attended very sporadically were conducted by teachers with

meager qualifications. Lincoln taught himself grammar in order to be able to speak and write standard English.

Adapted from DOUGLAS L. WILSON,
"What Jefferson and Lincoln Read"

Cause and effect

Generally a paragraph of this kind states a condition or effect and then proceeds by listing and explaining the causes. However, the first sentences may list a cause or causes and then conclude with the consequence, the effect. In either method, the paragraph usually begins with a phenomenon that is generally known and then moves on to the unknowns.

The following paragraph begins with an effect and proceeds to examine the causes.

This close-knit fabric [of the city] was blown apart by the automobile, and by the postwar middle-class exodus to suburbia which the mass-ownership of automobiles made possible. The automobile itself was not to blame for this development, nor was the desire for suburban living, which is obviously a genuine aspiration of many Americans. The fault lay in our failure, right up to the present time, to fashion new policies to minimize the disruptive effects of the automobile revolution. We have failed not only to tame the automobile itself, but to overhaul a property-tax system that tends to foster automotive-age sprawl, and to institute coordinated planning in the politically fragmented suburbs that have caught the brunt of the postwar building boom.

EDMUND K. FALTERMAYER
Redoing America

Classification and analysis

Classification stresses similarities or common denominators; **analysis** stresses differences. To show how two or more things are related, despite their differences, and then to label that grouping is to classify. To show how despite being part of the same group or class, two or more things are distinctive is to analyze (or divide).

The following paragraph classifies several famous people, assigning each to either of two categories: extroverts and introverts.

> Most people can be classified as either extroverts or introverts. William Shakespeare, Franz Schubert, George Armstrong Custer, and Charles Dickens form a disparate group indeed, but they had one important characteristic in common: the communal urge. They sought to find their identity in relation to other people and thus can be termed extroverts. On the other hand, Emily Dickinson, Joseph Stalin, Herbert Hoover, and Geronimo exhibited strong proclivities toward inwardness and constantly had to struggle with the urge to exclude others from their activities and interests. Different as they were, they shared the distinction of being introverts.

Contrast the previous paragraph, which illustrates a method of classification, with the following paragraph, in which the writer breaks down one of the categories—that of introverts—into component parts and then analyzes them.

> Although introverts share broad characteristics, they differ greatly among themselves. Aggressive introverts, such as Joseph Stalin, find their tendency toward privacy disturbing and attempt to deal with it, indeed to obliterate it, by forcing themselves into positions of power and authority. Creative introverts, like Emily Dickinson, tend to possess greater self-knowledge and to accept themselves for what they are. They become adjusted to themselves (though never to society), and that leads to a high potential for creativity.

Process

A writer may use several methods to describe a process. Most processes are given in chronological order, step by step. The simplest kind perhaps is the type used in a recipe, usually written in the second person or imperative mood. The necessity here is to get the steps in order and to state each step very clearly. This process is instruction; it tells *how to do* something.

Another kind is the exposition of *how something works* (a clock, the human nervous system). Here the writer should avoid technical terms and intricate or incomprehensible steps. This kind of process is explanation.

Still another kind of process, usually written in the past tense, tells *how something happened* (how oil was formed in the earth, how a celebration or a riot began). Usually a paragraph of this type is written in the third person. It is designed to reveal how something developed (once in a single time period or on separate occasions). Its purpose is to explain and instruct.

The following paragraph explains one theory about the process that formed the moon. Distinct steps are necessary for explanation here just as they are for instruction in a paragraph that tells how to do something.

There were tides in the new earth long before there was an ocean. In response to the pull of the sun the molten liquids of the earth's whole surface rose in tides that rolled unhindered around the globe and only gradually slackened and diminished as the earthly shell cooled, congealed, and hardened. Those who believe that the moon is a child of earth say that during an early stage of the earth's development something happened that caused this rolling, viscid tide to gather speed and momentum and to rise to unimaginable heights. Apparently the force that created these greatest tides the earth has ever known was the force of resonance, for at this time the period of the solar tides had come to approach, then equal, the period of the free oscillation of the liquid earth. And so every sun tide was given increased momentum by the push of the earth's oscillation, and each of the twice-daily tides was larger than the one before it. Physicists have calculated that, after 500 years of such monstrous, steadily increasing tides, those on the side toward the sun became too high for stability, and a great wave was torn away and hurled into space. But immediately, of course, the newly created satellite became subject to physical laws that sent it spinning in an orbit of its own about the earth. This is what we call the moon.

RACHEL CARSON
The Sea Around Us

3f Use transitional devices to show the relationships between the parts of your writing. *tr*

Transitional devices are connectors and direction-givers. They connect words to other words, sentences to sentences, paragraphs to paragraphs. Writings without transitions are like a strange land with no road signs. Practiced writers assume that they should give clear signs as to where a paragraph and a paper are going.

The beginnings of paragraphs can contribute materially to clarity, coherence, and the movement of the discussion. Some writers meticulously guide readers with a connector at the beginning of almost every paragraph. H. J. Muller, for example, begins a sequence of paragraphs about science as follows:

> In this summary, science . . .
> Yet science does . . .
> Similarly, the basic interests of science . . .
> In other words, they are not . . .
> This demonstration that even the scientist . . .
> This idea will concern us . . .
> In other words, facts and figures . . .

CONNECTIVE WORDS AND EXPRESSIONS

but	indeed	likewise
and	in fact	consequently
however	meanwhile	first
moreover	afterward	next
furthermore	then	in brief
on the other hand	so	to summarize
nevertheless	still	to conclude
for example	after all	similarly

DEMONSTRATIVE PRONOUNS

this	that	these	those

References to demonstratives must be clear (see p. 85).

OTHER PRONOUNS

many	each	some	others	such	either

Repeated key words, phrases, and synonyms

Repetitions and synonyms guide the reader from sentence to sentence and from paragraph to paragraph.

Parallel structures

Repeating similar structural forms of a sentence can show how certain ideas within a paragraph are alike in content as well as in structure. A sequence of sentences beginning with a noun subject or with the same kind of pronoun subject, a series of clauses beginning with *that* or *which,* a series of clauses beginning with a similar kind of subordinating conjunction (like *because*)—devices like these can achieve transition and show connection.

Excessive use of parallelism, however, is likely to be too oratorical, too dramatic. Used with restraint, parallel structures are excellent transitional devices.

The following paragraph on the subject of emotions illustrates how various transitional devices can help create direction and coherence.

Emotions are part of our genetic heritage. Fish swim, birds fly,

repeated words

and people feel. Sometimes we are happy; sometimes we are not.

connective word: But

But sometimes in our life we are sure to feel anger and fear, sadness

and joy, greed and guilt, lust and scorn, delight and disgust. While

we are not free to choose the emotions that arise in us, we are free

to choose how and when to express them, provided we know what

demonstrative: That

they are. That is the crux of the problem. Many people have been

parallel structure

educated out of knowing what their feelings are. When they hated, they were told it was only dislike. When they were afraid, they were told there was nothing to be afraid of. When they felt pain, they were advised to be brave and smile. Many of our popular songs tell us "pretend you are happy when you are not."

HAIM G. GINOTT
Between Parent and Child:
New Solutions to Old Problems

General exercises

■ Exercise 5

Write one paragraph each on three of the following subjects. Use a different primary method of development for each. Name the various methods you use in each paragraph.

1. good manners
2. autumn
3. cooking
4. farms
5. wealth
6. political campaigns
7. the International Space Station
8. tennis

■ Exercise 6

Find three good paragraphs from three different kinds of writing: from a book of nonfiction, an essay, a review, or a newspaper article. Discuss how effective paragraphs differ in various kinds of writing.

Grammar

4 Grammar

Anyone who uses language, who puts words together to communicate ideas, knows something about grammar. The word *grammar* refers to the often unconscious principles that guide people as they use language. It also can refer to the formal study of a grammatical system and its rules. For example, the person who says, "They are" is using grammar. A person who says, "*They* is a plural pronoun and therefore takes the plural verb *are*" is using grammatical terms and rules to explain how Standard English works. The technical study of grammar can be conducted in great detail, but this book presents only basic elements of the grammatical system—what you need in order to communicate effectively in writing and speech.

The Parts of Speech

A basic aspect of grammar is knowing the parts of speech. This gives you a vocabulary for identifying words and talking about how language works.

The eight parts of speech are **nouns, pronouns, verbs, adjectives, adverbs, conjunctions, prepositions,** and **interjections.** Each of these is explained next.

The function of a word within a sentence determines what part of speech that word is. For example, a word may be a **noun** in one sentence but an **adjective** in another.

noun
↓
She teaches in a *college*.

adjective
↓
She teaches several *college* courses.

4a Nouns

Nouns are words that name. They also have various forms that indicate **gender** (masculine, feminine, neuter), **number** (singular, plural), and **case** (see **Glossary of Terms**). Nouns are classified as follows:

(a) **Proper nouns** name specific groups, people, places, or things. They usually begin with a capital letter *(Toni Morrison, London, Knicks)*.

Thomas Jefferson built *Monticello* in *Virginia*.

(b) **Common nouns** name general groups, people, places, or things *(reader, city, players)*.

Few *authors* write anonymously.

(c) **Collective nouns** name a whole group but are singular in form *(navy, family, choir)*. (See **11f**.)

The *jury* is weighing the evidence.

(d) **Abstract nouns** name concepts, beliefs, or qualities that cannot be perceived with the five senses *(faith, honor, joy)*.

Her *love* of *freedom* was as obvious as her *courage*.

(e) **Concrete nouns** name things that can be perceived with the five senses *(rain, desk, heat)*.

After a shower of rain, the *white blooms* were *crumpled* and *brown*.

4b Pronouns

Most **pronouns** take the place of a noun. Some pronouns (such as *something, none, anyone*) have general or broad references and do not take the place of a particular noun.

The following categories classify pronouns and tell how they function in a sentence. Some words that function as pronouns can also function as other parts of speech:

The red apple is his [pronoun].

His [adjective] apple is not very red.

(a) **Personal pronouns** usually refer to a person but sometimes to a thing. They have many forms, which depend on their grammatical function.

	SINGULAR	PLURAL
First person	I, me, mine	we, us, ours
Second person	you, yours	you, yours
Third person	he, she, it	they, them, theirs
	his, hers, its	

(b) **Indefinite pronouns** do not refer to a particular person or thing. Some of the most common are *some, any, each, everyone, everybody, anyone, anybody, one, neither* (see **12f**).

indefinite pronoun
↓
Everyone likes praise.

(c) **Reflexive pronouns** end in *-self* or *-selves* and indicate that the subject acts upon itself.

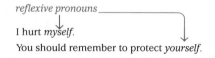

reflexive pronouns
↓
I hurt *myself*.

You should remember to protect *yourself*.

(d) **Intensive pronouns** also end in *-self* or *-selves*. An intensive pronoun emphasizes a noun that precedes it in the sentence.

intensive pronoun
↓
I *myself* will carry the message.

intensive pronoun

Julie *herself* will eat the frozen yogurt.

(e) **Demonstrative pronouns**—*this, that* [singular]; *these, those* [plural]—point to and stand for specific objects or people. (See **demonstrative adjectives,** p. 89.)

demonstrative pronoun

Many varieties of apples are grown here. *These* are winesaps.

(f) **Interrogative pronouns** ask questions: *what, who, whom, whose, which* (see **13f**).

interrogative pronoun

Who was chosen?

(g) **Relative pronouns** (*who, whoever, whom, whomever, that, what, which, whose*) generally introduce dependent adjective clauses (see p. 105) and refer to noun or pronoun antecedents in independent clauses. They serve as connectives between dependent and independent clauses.

adjective clause
relative pronoun

Special rooms are provided for guests *who* need quiet rest.

Relative pronouns also introduce noun clauses (see p. 105), and in this function they do not refer to a definite noun or pronoun.

noun clause
relative pronoun

Whoever wins friends will have great riches.

■ **Exercise 1**

Identify nouns and pronouns.

       N   **N**   **N**

1. Amelia Earhart was a famous aviator in the thirties; almost

     P   **N**   **N**

    everyone in the United States could identify her.

       N   **N** **P**

2. George Palmer Putnam was a brash publicist who managed the

    N   **N**

    career of Earhart.

    N   **P**   **P**   **N**

3. Earhart herself was shy, but she possessed great courage.

    P   **N**   **N**

4. She was sometimes called "Lady Lindy" after Charles A. Lindbergh,

    P   **N**   **N**   **N**

    who made the first solo flight across the Atlantic Ocean in 1927.

                             N   **N**

5. Always an unconventional dresser, Earhart became famous for

                   N **P** **P**

    the white silk scarf that she often wore with a brown bomber

    N   **N**   **N**

    jacket and a pair of trousers.

4c Verbs

Verbs assert an action or express a condition (see **7**).

                 action
                  ↓

Tall sunflowers *sway* gracefully.

               condition
                 ↓

The tall plants *are* sunflowers.

Main verbs may have helpers, called **auxiliary verbs,** such as *are, have, will be, do, did.*

auxiliary verb   *main verb*

The strong wind *will bend* the sunflowers.

auxiliary verbs   *main verb*

Leif Ericson *may have preceded* Columbus to America.

Linking verbs express condition: *appear, become, feel, look, seem, smell, sound, taste.* The most common linking verbs are forms of the verb *to be,* such as *is, are, was, were, be, being, been* (see p. 477).

linking verb

The woman with the plastic fruit on her hat *is* an acrobat.

linking verb

In the presence of so many toys, the child *appeared* joyful.

The **mood** (or mode) of a verb indicates whether an action is to be thought of as a fact, command, wish, or condition contrary to fact. Modern English has three moods: the indicative, for ordinary statements and questions; the imperative, for commands and entreaty; and the subjunctive, for certain idiomatic expressions of wish, command, or condition contrary to fact.

INDICATIVE

    Does she *play* the guitar?

    She *does.*

IMPERATIVE

    Stay with me.

    Let him stay.

The imperative is formed like the plural present indicative without -s.

SUBJUNCTIVE

> If I *were* you, I would go.
>
> I wish he *were* going with you.
>
> I move that the meeting *be* adjourned.
>
> It is necessary that he *stay* absolutely quiet.
>
> If this *be* true, no man ever loved.

The most common subjunctive forms are *were* and *be*. All others are formed like the present-tense plural form without -s.

Verbs are either **transitive** or **intransitive** (see pp. 120, 483). (For **verb tenses**, see **8**. For **verbals**, see pp. 102–103, 483).

■ Exercise 2

Identify verbs.

1. The aroma of fresh popcorn <u>wafted</u> through the building.

2. The flight attendant <u>walked</u> among the passengers and <u>looked</u> for the ring.

3. The symphony <u>was performed</u> by a distinguished orchestra, and the audience <u>was</u> enthusiastic.

4. Hercules <u>performed</u> the twelve labors that Hera <u>demanded</u>.

5. A chance encounter with a celebrity <u>can be</u> an exciting experience.

4d Adjectives

Adjectives modify a noun or a pronoun by describing, qualifying, or limiting. Most adjectives appear before the word they modify (see **14**).

The three **articles** *(a, an,* and *the)* are classified as adjectives.

adjective
↓
Beautiful music soothes the soul.

Predicate adjectives follow linking verbs and modify the noun or pronoun that is the subject of the sentence.

subject   *predicate adjective*
↓   ↓
The wild blackberries in the fresh pie tasted *delicious.*

The words *his, its, her, our, your,* and *their* are possessive adjective forms. Adding an *-s* to the last four words of the list changes these adjectives into possessive pronouns: *hers, ours, yours,* and *theirs.*

Demonstrative adjectives, which have exactly the same forms as demonstrative pronouns, are used before the nouns they modify.

this dog, *that* dog; *these* dogs, *those* dogs

Indefinite adjectives such as *any, each, every,* and *some* have the same form as indefinite pronouns.

4e Adverbs

Adverbs (like adjectives) describe, qualify, or limit other elements in the sentence. They modify verbs (and verbals), adjectives, and other adverbs.

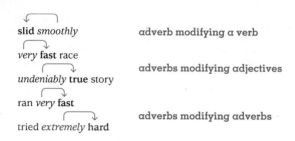

slid *smoothly*   adverb modifying a verb

very **fast** race   adverbs modifying adjectives
undeniably **true** story

ran *very* **fast**
tried *extremely* **hard**   adverbs modifying adverbs

Sometimes adverbs modify an entire clause or sentence.

> *Apparently,* this kind of plastic is stronger than steel.

Conjunctive adverbs show the relationship between a sentence or an independent clause and an earlier sentence or clause. Conjunctive adverbs show relationships of addition *(furthermore, moreover),* contrast *(however, nonetheless),* comparison *(similarly),* result *(therefore, thus),* and time *(meanwhile).*

> She found a job; *therefore,* she could buy a car.
> *However,* she still could not afford to buy a house.

Many adverbs end in *-ly (effectively, curiously),* but not all words that end in *-ly* are adverbs *(lovely, friendly).*

Adverbs often tell how *(slowly, well),* how much *(profusely, somewhat),* how often *(frequently, always),* when *(late, before),* or where *(there, here).* You cannot memorize a list of words which are always adverbs. One form of some words may function as more than one part of speech.

■ Exercise 3

Identify adverbs and adjectives. Then identify the single word that each one modifies. (Remember that a, an, *and* the *are adjectives.)*

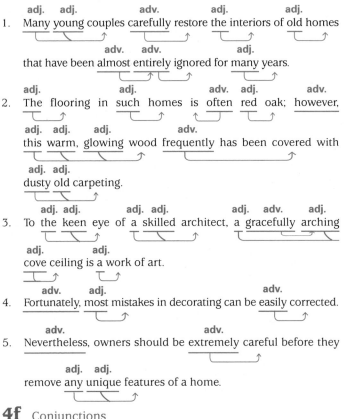

      adj.   adj.   adv.   adj.   adj.

1. Many young couples carefully restore the interiors of old homes

                     adv.   adv.   adj.

   that have been almost entirely ignored for many years.

  adj.   adj.   adv. adj.   adv.

2. The flooring in such homes is often red oak; however,

  adj. adj.   adj.   adv.

  this warm, glowing wood frequently has been covered with

  adj. adj.

  dusty old carpeting.

      adj. adj.   adj. adj.   adj. adv.   adj.

3. To the keen eye of a skilled architect, a gracefully arching

  adj.   adj.

  cove ceiling is a work of art.

     adv.   adj.   adv.

4. Fortunately, most mistakes in decorating can be easily corrected.

     adv.   adv.

5. Nevertheless, owners should be extremely careful before they

       adj. adj.

  remove any unique features of a home.

4f Conjunctions

Conjunctions used effectively connect words to words, phrases to phrases, and clauses to clauses. They are classified as **coordinating, correlative,** or **subordinating.**

    Coordinating conjunctions—*and, but, for, nor, or, so,* and *yet*—connect elements of equal grammatical rank or importance.

coordinating conjunction

The orchestra played selections from *Brahms, Bach,* **and** *Wagner.*

coordinating conjunction

The conductor left the stage, **and** *he did not return.*

Correlative conjunctions are pairs of words that join equal elements (see **22b**). Examples are *both . . . and, either . . . or, not only . . . but also,* and *neither . . . nor.*

correlative conjunctions

An athlete needs **not only** *strength* **but also** *discipline.*

Subordinating conjunctions introduce a subordinate or dependent clause and connect that clause to an independent clause. Examples are *after, although, as, because, before, even though, if, since, so that, though, unless, until, when, where,* and *while.*

subordinating conjunction

Before *many painters sell their work,* they labor for years.

Some words (such as *before* or *after*) may function as conjunctions and also as other parts of speech.

preposition

The artist paused before the door.

■ Exercise 4

Identify conjunctions and tell whether each is coordinating, correlative, or subordinating.

subordinating

1. After the Great Depression had ended, Americans were eager to

   coordinating

   escape to a glamorous world, and elaborate musical motion

   coordinating

   pictures provided such an escape and a release.

subordinating

2. When the curtain went up in the theater, the world looked

   coordinating

   entirely new, so thoughts of unemployment could be left

   behind.

   coordinating

3. The plots of these films were predictable, but the costumes

   coordinating

   were elaborate, and the full orchestras were inspiring.

4. Inevitably, the story involved a spirited couple who were sepa-

   correlative

   rated either by outside forces or by their own stubbornness

   subordinating

   before they were happily reunited.

   correlative

5. Both Ginger Rogers and Fred Astaire were accomplished

   dancers who often starred in these films.

4g Prepositions

Prepositions connect a noun or pronoun to another word in the sentence and show a relationship, often one of time or direction.

the fox *in* the box

(The preposition *in* connects the word *fox* to the word *box*.)

Some of the most common prepositions are *above, across, after, against, along, among, at, before, behind, below, beneath, beside, between, by, from, in, into, of, on, over, through, up, upon, with, without.* Groups of words can also serve as prepositions: *along with, according to, in spite of.*

A preposition introduces a word group called a **prepositional phrase** (see p. 101), which is made up of the preposition, the **object of the preposition,** and **adjectival modifiers** (see p. 100).

preposition   object of the preposition

The butterfly hovered **above** the brilliant **sunflower.**

preposition   object of the preposition

Along with the **milk,** she ordered a cheese sandwich.

(See **41h** for a discussion of the idiomatic use of prepositions.)

■ Exercise 5

Identify prepositions, objects of prepositions, and prepositional phrases.

1. The soprano delivered the aria with supreme effectiveness, a combination of sweetness and sorrow that greatly moved the audience.

2. According to the rules of the game, the contestant at the front of the line must turn quickly and race toward the rear.

3. There on the shelf was the book that the historian had borrowed from a friend.

       P   O   P   O

4. Never in the history of the province had so fortunate an event

occurred.

     P   O   P   O   P   O

5. After a fast stroll along the deck, the passenger fell into a chair

          P   O

and slept for an hour.

4h Interjections

Interjections express surprise or strong emotion. They may stand alone or serve as part of a sentence.

> *Ouch!*
>
> *Ah,* I understand the problem.

Because of their nature, interjections are used more often in speech than in writing, which is generally more deliberate than exclamatory.

■ **Exercise 6**

Name the part of speech of each word underlined and numbered.

   1   *2*   *3* *4*   *5*   *6*   *7* *8* *9*

Oh, people are not always kind, but that is not justification for

bitterness.

     10   *11*   *12*   *13*

Successful athletes and recognizable politicians mingled

14   *15*   *16*   *17*   *18*

with famous writers and prominent actors at the opera

19   *20*

that opened last night.

	9. verb	15. adjective
	10. adjective	16. adjective
1. interjection	5. adverb	11. conjunction	17. noun
2. noun	6. adjective	12. adjective	18. noun
3. verb	7. conjunction	13. noun	19. pronoun
4. adverb	8. pronoun	14. preposition	20. verb

The Parts of Sentences

A sentence expresses a complete thought. It must have a subject and a predicate.

A **subject** does something, has something done to·it, or is identified or described.

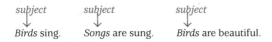

subject   *subject*   *subject*

↓   ↓   ↓

Birds sing.   *Songs* are sung.   *Birds* are beautiful.

A **predicate** expresses what the subject does, what is done to it, or how it is identified or described.

predicate   *predicate*   *predicate*

↓   ↓   ↓

Birds *sing*.   Songs *are sung*.   Birds *are beautiful*.

4i Simple subjects, complete subjects, compound subjects

The **simple subject** may consist of a single word.

simple subject

↓

The large *balloon* burst.

The subject may be understood rather than actually stated. A director of a chorus might say, "Sing," meaning "You sing." In this case, one spoken word would be a complete sentence.

understood subject   *predicate*

↘   ↙

[*You*] Sing.

All the words that form a group and function together as the subject are called the **complete subject.**

> *complete subject*
>
> The large balloon burst.

Compound subjects (that is, two or more subjects joined by a conjunction) function together.

> *compound subject*
>
> Students and *faculty* cheered.

Pronouns as well as nouns may make up compound subjects.

> *compound pronoun subject*
>
> He and *I* took a stroll.

■ Exercise 7

Identify the complete subjects. Tell whether each sentence has a simple subject or a compound subject.

C 1. The secretary and the administrative assistant discussed the error on the spreadsheet.

S 2. The new computer network has proven a useful but frustrating tool.

C 3. Both teachers and students can benefit from using new technology.

C   4.   The user-friendly <u>desktop</u> and a properly adjusted <u>keyboard</u>

help the operator to feel comfortable.

S   5.   A speedy <u>printer</u> can turn out ten pages every minute.

4j Simple predicates, complete predicates, compound predicates

The single verb (or the main verb and its auxiliary verbs) is the **simple predicate.**

The simple predicate, its modifiers, and any complements (see pp. 99–100) form a group that is called the **complete predicate.**

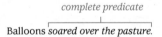

When two verbs in the predicate express actions or conditions of a subject, they are a **compound predicate**—just as two nouns may be a **compound subject.**

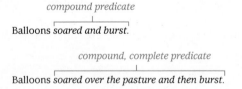

(For errors in predication, see **19b.**)

■ Exercise 8

Identify the verbs (including auxiliaries) and the complete predicates. Tell whether each sentence has a simple predicate or a compound predicate.

S   1.   The profit margin on the item <u>was</u> unusually slim.

S   2.   All day long the caravan <u>moved</u> through long valleys and over

steep hills.

S   3.   <u>Plan</u> for a bright and meaningful future.

C   4.   Playgoers <u>arrived</u> at the theater early and <u>waited</u> eagerly for the

box office to open.

C   5.   Children at the picnic <u>played</u> softball, <u>swam</u> in the pool, and

<u>rowed</u> on the lake.

4k Complements

Complements complete the meaning of the sentence and are usually part of the predicate. They are nouns, pronouns, or adjectives. With linking verbs (see p. 87), they function as **predicate adjectives** or **subjective complements.** With transitive verbs, they function as **direct** or **indirect objects** and are always in the objective case (see **13**).

A **predicate adjective** is an adjective that follows a linking verb (see p. 88) and modifies the subject of the sentence, not the verb.

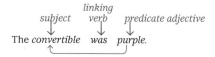

A **subjective complement** (which is also called a **predicate nominative**) follows a linking verb and renames the subject.

$$\text{subjective complement}$$
$$\downarrow$$

Georgia O'Keefe was a *painter.*

A **direct object** receives the action of a transitive verb. (See p. 128).

$$\text{verb} \qquad \text{direct object}$$
$$\downarrow \qquad\qquad \downarrow$$

The board *appointed* a new *president.*

An **indirect object** receives the action of the verb indirectly. It comes between the verb and the direct object and tells to whom or for whom something is done.

$$\qquad\qquad \text{indirect} \quad \text{direct}$$
$$\text{verb} \qquad \text{object} \quad \text{object}$$
$$\downarrow \qquad\quad \downarrow \qquad \downarrow$$

The guest *gave* the *hostess flowers.*

To identify an indirect object, rearrange the sentence by using the preposition *to* or *for:*

$$\qquad\qquad \text{direct} \qquad \text{prepositional}$$
$$\text{verb} \qquad \text{object} \qquad\quad \text{phrase}$$
$$\downarrow \qquad\quad \downarrow \qquad\qquad \downarrow$$

The guest *gave   flowers   to the hostess.*

(Now *hostess* functions not as the indirect object but as the object of the preposition *to.*)

Objective complements accompany direct objects. They modify the object or rename it. To identify an objective complement, mentally insert *to be* before it:

The editor considered the manuscript *publishable.*

The corporation named a former clerk its *president.*

■ **Exercise 9**

Underline and identify predicate adjectives (PA), predicate nominatives (PN), direct objects (DO), and indirect objects (IO). (Start by finding the verbs and their complements.)

          PN
1. Venice will always be a beautiful place.

     DO   DO
2. Those who love art should visit the city.

        PA   PA
3. The famous canals are busy and picturesque.

    IO   DO   DO
4. Give the gondoliers a good tip and a hearty handshake.

          PA
5. The sea vistas are especially stunning, but I was pleasantly sur-

          DO
  prised when my guide directed my gaze toward the shore.

41 Phrases

A **phrase** is a group of words that does not have both a subject and a predicate. Some important kinds of phrases are **prepositional phrases, verb phrases,** and **verbal phrases.**

Prepositional phrases

Prepositional phrases function as adjectives or adverbs.

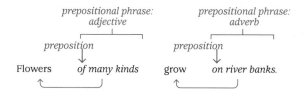

Verb phrases

Verb phrases are made up of the main verb and its auxiliaries: *were sitting, shall be going, are broken, may be considered.* Common auxiliary verbs, or "helping" verbs, include *were, shall be, are,* and *may be.*

verb phrase

The metaphor *may be considered* an essential tool for writing.

Verbal phrases

Verbal phrases are made up of verbals and the words associated with them. A **verbal** is a verb form that does not function as a verb but rather as a noun, an adjective, or an adverb. There are three kinds of verbals: **gerunds, participles,** and **infinitives.**

GERUNDS AND GERUND PHRASES

Gerunds always end in *-ing* and function as nouns.

*gerund phrase as noun
(complete subject)*

gerund

Riding a bicycle is good exercise.

PARTICIPLES AND PARTICIPIAL PHRASES

Participles always function as adjectives. **Present participles** end in *-ing* (*sailing, watching*); **past participles** usually end in *-ed* (*hopped, skipped*), but some follow irregular forms (*swum, brought*).

participle ending in -ing (*modifies* she)

Swimming steadily, she reached the shore.

participial phrase as adjective

participle ending in -ed *(modifies* bread*)*

Overbaked, the bread was hard.

NOTE: Both gerunds and present participles end in *-ing.* Distinguish between them by identifying their functions in a sentence. (Gerunds are nouns; present participles are adjectives.)

INFINITIVES AND INFINITIVE PHRASES

Infinitives begin with *to,* which is sometimes understood rather than actually stated. They can be used as nouns, adjectives, or adverbs.

USED AS NOUN

infinitive phrase used as subject

infinitive

To operate the machine was simple.

USED AS ADJECTIVE

infinitive phrase modifies book *(noun)*

infinitive

Charlotte's Web is a good book *to read to a child.*

USED AS ADVERB

infinitive phrase modifies reluctant *(adjective)*

infinitive

A true hero is reluctant *to boast of accomplishments.*

TO UNDERSTOOD

Someone must go [*to*] *buy* a tire.

■ Exercise 10

Identify phrases and tell what kind each is—infinitive, gerund, participial, prepositional, or verb.

      gerund

1. <u>Taking the census</u> is not as simple as it was two thousand

    years ago.

          prepositional   **verb**

2. Candidates <u>for local office</u> <u>will be attending</u> the Parent-Teacher

                  infinitive   **infinitive**

    Association meeting <u>to make themselves known</u> and <u>to express</u>

    <u>their views.</u>

              participial

3. <u>Perceiving his opponent's strategy,</u> the world-famous chess

              infinitive   **infinitive**   **prepositional**

    player managed <u>to win the game</u> and <u>to do so</u> <u>in record time.</u>

       participial   **prepositional**

4. <u>Speaking strangely,</u> the young man <u>from the audience</u> said that

                  prepositional   **infinitive**

    his will was too strong <u>for him</u> <u>to be hypnotized,</u> but neverthe-

              verb

    less he <u>was doing</u> whatever the hypnotist commanded.

              participial

5. <u>Insisting that his vegetables were fresh,</u> the gardener refused

         infinitive

    <u>to lower the price.</u>

4m Clauses

A **clause** is a group of words containing a subject and a predicate. Clauses are either **independent** or **dependent (subordinate)**.

Independent clauses

An **independent clause** can stand alone grammatically and form a complete sentence. Two or more independent clauses in one sentence can be joined by coordinating conjunctions, conjunctive adverbs, semicolons, or other grammatical devices or punctuation marks.

> *independent clause*   *independent clause*
> *Coral snakes are beautiful,* but *they are deadly.*

> *independent clause*   *independent clause*
> *Coral snakes are beautiful; they are also deadly.*

Dependent clauses

A **dependent clause** has a subject and a predicate, but it cannot stand alone grammatically because it begins with a subordinating word. Like verbals, dependent clauses function as nouns, adjectives, and adverbs.

USED AS NOUN (usually subject or object)
> *That the little child could read rapidly* was well known.
>   *(noun clause used as subject)*
> The other students knew *that the little child could read rapidly.*
>   *(noun clause used as direct object)*

USED AS ADJECTIVE
> Everyone *who completed the race* won a shirt.
> *(modifying pronoun subject* Everyone)

USED AS ADVERB
> *When dusk comes* the landscape seems to hold its breath.
> *(modifying verb* seems)

4n   The Kinds of Sentences

A **simple sentence** has only one independent clause (but no dependent clause). A simple sentence is not necessarily short; it may contain several phrases.

> Birds sing.
>
> The bird began to warble a sustained and beautiful song after a long silence.

A **compound sentence** has two or more independent clauses (but no dependent clause).

> *independent clause*   *independent clause*
>
> *Birds sing,* and *bees hum.*

A **complex sentence** has both an independent clause and one or more dependent clauses.

> ┌───────────*dependent clauses*───────────┐ ┌*independent* ─
>
> When spring comes and [when] new leaves grow, *migratory birds*
>
> ─*clause*─┐
>
> *return north.*

A **compound-complex sentence** has at least two independent clauses and at least one dependent clause. The dependent clause can be part of an independent clause.

> *dependent adverb*   *independent*
>
> ┌──── *clause* ────┐ ┌──*clause*──┐   ┌*independent*-
>
> When heavy rains come, *the streams rise, and farmers know*

*dependent noun clause
used as object*

┌──────────────┐
├──── *clause* ────┤
└──────────────┘

that there will be floods.

■ Exercise 11

Underline each clause. Tell whether it is dependent or independent. Identify whether each sentence is simple (S), compound (C), complex (X), or compound-complex (CC).

independent
S   1.   Arriving at college for the first time can be an unsettling

experience.

dependent
X   2.   Although I was eager to leave home and be on my own, the

independent
prospect of sharing a room with a stranger did not appeal to me.

dependent   **independent**
CC   3.   Since I was the oldest child in my family, I had always had the

independent
luxury of my own room, and I valued the privacy that my

privileged status earned me.

independent
S   4.   I arrived at school, found my way to the dormitory, and met

my roommate.

dependent   **independent**   **dependent**
X   5.   When I first met her, I was amazed to discover how much we

had in common.

Sentence
Errors

109

5 Sentence Fragments *frag*

Write complete sentences.

Knowledge of what makes up a sentence (and what does not) is necessary for producing clear writing. A sentence fragment written as a complete sentence can be a serious error and can cause confusion.

Notice how the following fragments are revised and made into complete sentences.

FRAGMENT (phrase)
    Genealogy, the study of family history.

COMPLETE SENTENCE (verb added)
    Genealogy is the study of family history.

FRAGMENT (dependent clause)
    Although several large rivers have been cleaned up.

COMPLETE SENTENCE (subordinating conjunction *although* omitted)
    Several large rivers have been cleaned up.

FRAGMENT (noun and phrase—no main verb)
    The green fields humming with sounds of insects.

COMPLETE SENTENCE (modifier *humming* changed to verb *hummed*)
    The green fields hummed with sounds of insects.

Fragments are often permissible in dialogue when the meaning is clear.

    "See the geese."
    "Where?" [fragment]
    "Flying north." [fragment]

Fragments are occasionally used for special effects or emphasis.

> The long journey down the river was especially pleasant. A time of rest and tranquillity.

■ Exercise 1

Write F *by fragments,* C *by complete sentences.*

F   1. Looking forward to a prosperous and fulfilling career.
C   2. Increasingly, educators use computers for instructional purposes.
F   3. Sixty miles from the nearest town.
C   4. Do not be late.
F   5. Florida and California, two states that boast of almost constant sunshine.
C   6. How did people ever do without transparent tape?
F   7. Not really concerned about the plight of migrant workers.
C   8. Travel enlightens.
F   9. Lightning not striking twice in the same place.
F 10. "Where the deer and the antelope play."

■ Exercise 2

Underline all fragments in the following passage.

> Students of Franklin D. Roosevelt are agreed that the polio attack of 1921 profoundly changed him. He might have become President without having had to surmount that obstacle, but it is unlikely that he would have been a great President. Or even a good one. Before he was crippled, Roosevelt had been a genial glad-hander. An acceptable politician. Considered lightweight by the pros (men like Al Smith). Too anxious to please. Clumsily ingratiating. His caustic cousin, Alice Roosevelt Longworth, called him a sissy. A mama's boy. He had been sheltered from hardship. Cushioned in privilege. At the least, then, the struggle to

walk again—always defeated but never quite given up—toughened Roosevelt. Some say that the suffering deepened his sympathy with others. Who were afflicted.

Adapted from GARRY WILLS,
"What Makes A Good Leader?"

6 Comma Splices and Fused Sentences *cs/fus*

Join two independent clauses appropriately, or write two separate sentences.

A **comma splice,** or **comma fault,** occurs when a comma is used between two independent clauses without a coordinating conjunction.

SPLICE OR FAULT

> Human nature is seldom as simple as it appears, hasty judgments are often wrong.

A **fused sentence,** or **run-on sentence,** occurs when the independent clauses have neither punctuation nor coordinating conjunctions between them.

FUSED OR RUN-ON

> Human nature is seldom as simple as it appears hasty judgments are often wrong.

Writers of comma splices and fused sentences fail to indicate the break between independent clauses. Revise in one of the following ways:

1. Use a *period* and write two sentences.

↓

Human nature is seldom as simple as it appears. Hasty judgments are often wrong.

2. Use a *semicolon* (see also **26**).

↓

Human nature is seldom as simple as it appears; hasty judgments are often wrong.

NOTE: Before *conjunctive adverbs* (see **24f** and **26a**), use a *semicolon* to join *independent clauses,* or use a *period* and *begin a new sentence.*

↓

Production of the item has greatly increased; *therefore,* the cost has come down.

⎍↓

Production of the item has greatly increased. *Therefore,* the cost has come down.

3. Use a *comma* and a *coordinating conjunction (and, but, for, nor, or, so, yet)* (see also **24a**).

⎍↓

Human nature is seldom as simple as it appears, *so* hasty judgments are often wrong.

4. Use a *subordinating conjunction* (see pp. 91–92, 483) and a *dependent clause.*

Because *human nature is seldom as simple as it appears,* hasty judgments are often wrong.

■ Exercise 3

Identify comma splices and fused sentences with CS *or* FUS. *Then correct them. Write C by sentences that are already correct.*

CS   1. Russian music flowered late; however, it has developed rapidly
            ∧
during the past two centuries.

C   2. Few people realize that Sigmund Freud was born in what later be-

came Czechoslovakia, where he spent his early years in poverty.

                       ; *or* .N

FUS   3. Conflicts almost always exist within a family nevertheless, it is

                                      ∧

still the most enduring of social units.

                        ;   ;

FUS   4. The bread stuck in the toaster the smoke detector went off the

                             ∧   ∧

smell of burned toast permeated the apartment.

CS   5. Signs warning about riptides and the undertow were posted on

                 so

the beach, no one ventured into the water.

             ∧

■ Exercise 4

Identify each of the following as correct (C), *a comma splice* (CS), *a fused sentence* (FUS), *or a fragment* (F).

CS   1. The *Savannah* was launched in 1958, it was the first ship to be propelled by nuclear power.

C   2. Vitamins are necessary for health; however, excessive amounts of some of them are dangerous.

F   3. Vitamins are necessary for health. Excessive amounts of some of them, however, dangerous.

C   4. Nearly every student of the classical guitar admires the playing of Andrés Segovia, who was essentially self-taught and who gave his first public performance when he was sixteen.

FUS   5. The magnitudes of earthquakes are measured by instruments called seismographs they record movements in the earth's crust.

■ Exercise 5

Identify fragments (F), *comma splices* (CS), *or fused sentences* (FUS) *and correct them. Write C by correct sentences.*

CS 1. Some students do not look forward to studying poetry, they ^{; or . T} ∧

probably have not had much experience with it.

C 2. Pleasure does seem to make time go faster.

FUS 3. Jane Addams was a famous social reformer she won the Nobel ^{; or . S} ∧

Prize in 1931.

F 4. All over the city, new buildings and the skyline rapidly changing. **are appearing** ∧   **is** ∧

CS 5. Lighthouses are fascinating, many people travel around the ; or . M ∧

country to visit them.

F 6. An impressive lighthouse in Florida, tall and stately and painted **is** ∧

red.

F 7. Continual snowfall, increasing the likelihood that classes will **is** ∧

be canceled.

C 8. For many, swimming is more pleasant than jogging, especially

in hot weather.

CS 9. The clothing of former times appears strange and comical, that
      of the present seems appropriate and smart, why is that?

FUS 10. Learning to play a musical instrument is difficult when one is
      young there are often many distractions.

■ Exercise 6

Follow the instructions for Exercise 5.

F 1. Autumn leaves are especially vivid this year, Leaves of bright red
    and gold.

FUS 2. A relatively new kind of surgery is helping many nearsighted
      people not everyone, though, is a good candidate for the
      procedure.

F 3. St. John's is the capital and the port of Newfoundland, An island
    off the east coast of Canada.

CS 4. Many generous people are naive, they simply do not realize
    when they are being imposed upon.

CS 5. The Statue of Liberty, a gift from France, is made of copper, it is
    situated on an island in New York harbor.

C   6. Microwave ovens are in wide use today.

CS   7. After all, the student argued, any imbecile can use periods and

                                       ; *or* . S

       commas, studying punctuation is a complete waste of time.
           ∧

FUS   8. Some families agreed that for two weeks they would keep

                                       ; *or* . T

       their television sets turned off the children were surprisingly
                              ∧

       cooperative.

FUS   9. Why anyone would want to go over Niagara Falls in a barrel is

                          ; *or* . M

       puzzling many people have tried it, however.
          ∧

F   10. The tortoises on the Galápagos Islands often weigh great

               , s

       amounts, Some as much as five hundred pounds.
        ∧

7 Verb Forms *vf*

Use the correct form of the verb.

All verbs have five different forms:

BASE FORM (present infinitive)	walk
PAST TENSE	walked
PAST PARTICIPLE	walked
PRESENT TENSE WITH -*S* (third person singular)	walks
PRESENT PARTICIPLE	walking

Most verbs are **regular;** they form the past tense and the past participle by adding *-d* or *-ed* to the base form. Sometimes you double the final consonant of the base verb before adding the *-d* or *-ed.* The dictionary lists only one form, the base (or infinitive) form, when the verb is regular.

BASE	PAST TENSE	PAST PARTICIPLE
help	helped	helped
smile	smiled	smiled
scan	scanned	scanned
talk	talked	talked

Over two hundred verbs in English are **irregular:** they do not follow the standard formula to produce past tense and past participles. For irregular verbs, a dictionary gives four forms: the base (infinitive), past tense, past participle, and present participle.

BASE	PAST TENSE	PAST PARTICIPLE	PRESENT PARTICIPLE
see	saw	seen	seeing
think	thought	thought	thinking
freeze	froze	frozen	freezing

The following list contains the forms of many irregular verbs. You probably already know most of them. Learn the ones unfamiliar to you. For the rest of your life, check a dictionary when you're in doubt. (See also the list of irregular verbs on pp. 466–467.)

BASE	PAST TENSE	PAST PARTICIPLE
awake	awoke, awaked	awoke, awaked
be	was	been
begin	began	begun
bid (to offer as a price or to make a bid in playing cards)	bid	bid
bid (to command, order)	bade, bid	bidden, bid
blow	blew	blown

BASE	PAST TENSE	PAST PARTICIPLE
break	broke	broken
bring	brought	brought
build	built	built
burst	burst	burst
buy	bought	bought
choose	chose	chosen
come	came	come
deal	dealt	dealt
dig	dug	dug
dive	dived, dove	dived
do	did	done
drag	dragged	dragged
draw	drew	drawn
drink	drank	drunk
drive	drove	driven
drown	drowned	drowned
eat	ate	eaten
fly	flew	flown
freeze	froze	frozen
get	got	gotten, got
give	gave	given
go	went	gone
grow	grew	grown
know	knew	known
lead	led	led
lend	lent	lent
lose	lost	lost
ring	rang	rung
run	ran	run
see	saw	seen
sing	sang	sung
sink	sank, sunk	sunk
slay	slew	slain
sting	stung	stung
swim	swam	swum
swing	swung	swung
take	took	taken
teach	taught	taught
think	thought	thought
throw	threw	thrown
wear	wore	worn
write	wrote	written

Some verb forms are especially troublesome. *Lie* is confused with *lay;* *sit* with *set;* and *rise* with *raise.* *Lie, sit,* and *rise* are intransitive (do not take objects) and have the vowel *i* in the infinitive form and the present tense. *Lay, set,* and *raise* are transitive (take objects) and have *a, e,* or *ai* as vowels in the infinitive form and the present tense.

TRANSITIVE	lay (to place)	laid	laid
INTRANSITIVE	lie (to recline)	lay	lain
TRANSITIVE	set (to place)	set	set
INTRANSITIVE	sit (to be seated)	sat	sat

In special meanings the verb *set* is intransitive (a hen *sets;* the sun *sets,* and so forth).

TRANSITIVE	raise (to lift)	raised	raised
INTRANSITIVE	rise (to get up)	rose	risen

■ Exercise 7

Underline the incorrect verb and write the correct form above it. Write C by correct sentences.

         threw
1. The tourist <u>throwed</u> quarters into the sea, and several islanders

   dived for them.

             saw   **ran**
2. When Virginia was four, she <u>seen</u> a parade and <u>run</u> along the

   street to keep up with it.

3. Although the most recently appointed member of the board <u>came</u>come

   in late to the meeting, she <u>did</u>done right when she apologized.

4. Before the Bebo family bought a car, they <u>took</u>taken few trips; but

   now that they are <u>used</u>use to traveling, they seldom stay home in the

   summer.

5. The builder <u>led</u>lead the owner of the property to the back of the lot

   and showed him where someone had <u>dragged</u>drug old cars onto his

   land and had left them there as eyesores.

6. The passenger <u>gave</u>give a small tip to the cabdriver, who frowned

   and glared.

7. Abigail <u>set</u>sat the potted plant in the window and <u>took</u>taken the dog for

   a walk.

C 8. The artist laid the brush on the stand after he painted the por-

   trait, and it has been lying there ever since.

9. The carpenter promised to <u>set</u>sit the bucket on the tile, but it has

   been <u>sitting</u>setting on the carpet for a week.

10. The balloon that <u>hung</u>hanged over the doorway suddenly <u>burst</u>busted.

■ **Exercise 8**

Follow the instructions for Exercise 7.

          lay
1. Murray layed around the house all day and then wondered
              gone
where his time had went.

           come   **written**
2. The fall had came and gone, and still he had not wrote his parents.

          sat
3. Often he just set in front of his television watching old films that
       seen
he had saw before.

              ate   **frozen**
4. Now and then he eat a candy bar that he had froze in the

refrigerator.

   had
5. He been that way for about a month when someone rung his
    ∧   **rang**

doorbell.

      did   **gave**
6. It done no good to ring the bell, however, for Murray give no

heed.

7. Then, when the visitor just opened the door and walked in,
            took
Murray taken one look at him and jumped up in surprise.

    was   **burst**
8. This were not just any visitor who had busted in but his boy-
                          flown
hood hero, his brother, who had flew there from overseas to

see him.

C   9. They talked well into the night, and Murray suddenly seemed to

       see things much more clearly than he had previously.

                                            broken   **began**
   10. In a few days, Murray's terrible spell was broke, and he begun

       to put his life back together.

8 Tense and Sequence of Tenses   *t/shift*

Use appropriate forms of verbs to express time sequences.
Avoid incorrect shifts in tense.

Tense expresses the time of an action or a condition.

8a Use the **present tense** to express an action or a
condition that is occurring currently, that occurs regularly,
that is consistently true, or that refers to events in a work
of art.

> The word processor *is printing* the letter in red. [currently occurring]
>
> After the name of the month is typed, a word processor automatically *shows* the day and the year. [regularly occurring]
>
> In 1997, scientists discovered that El Niño *controls* the currents in the Pacific. [consistently true]
>
> *Cold Mountain* tells how a soldier *escapes* from prison, *flees,* and then *dies* before he gets home. [in a work of art]

8b Use the **past tense** to express an action that was completed before the time of writing.

> Sometimes the word processor *refused* to obey orders. [completed action]
>
> Ancient Greeks believed that the earth was motionless. [Once believed, now disproved; compare with the previous sentence, about El Niño.]

8c Use the **future tense** to express an action expected to occur after the time of writing.

The most common form of the future tense combines *will* or *shall* with the base form of the verb.

> The meek *shall* inherit the earth.

In strictly formal English, *shall* is conventional in the first person (I *shall;* we *shall);* *will,* in the second and third persons (you *will;* he *will;* they *will).* To indicate determination, duty, or necessity, *will* is formal in the first person (I *will;* we *will); shall,* in the second and third persons (you *shall;* he *shall;* they *shall).* These distinctions are weaker than they used to be, and *will* is increasingly used in all persons.

8d Use **progressive tenses** to show that an action or a condition is ongoing.

The three progressive tenses are **present progressive, past progressive,** and **future progressive.** Progressive forms use the present participle form of the verb (the *-ing* form) with auxiliary verbs. (See p. 87.)

PRESENT PROGRESSIVE
> The computer *is printing* a perpendicular bar instead of quotation marks. [action currently taking place]

PAST PROGRESSIVE

The computer *was printing* many errors all last week. [action ongoing during a certain time frame in the past]

FUTURE PROGRESSIVE

Because more professors are building their own web sites, students *will be expecting* to receive responses and grades on the Web. [future action that will be ongoing]

8e Use **perfect tenses** to indicate one time or action completed before another.

The three perfect tenses are **present perfect, past perfect,** and **future perfect.**

PRESENT PERFECT WITH PRESENT

I *have paid* the rent; therefore, **I am moving** in.

The controlling time word sometimes is not a verb.

I *have paid* the rent **already.**

PAST PERFECT WITH PAST

I *had paid* the rent; therefore, I **moved** in.
I *had bought* my ticket before the bus **came.**

CAUTION: Do not use the past perfect tense when the past tense will suffice.

NOT

I *had ordered* the shrimp, and I asked to see the wine list.

BUT

I *ordered the shrimp,* and I asked to see the wine list.

FUTURE PERFECT WITH FUTURE

> I *shall have eaten* by the time we go. [The controlling time word, *go,* is present tense in form but future in meaning.]

> I *shall have eaten* by **one o'clock.** [Note that the controlling time words do not include a verb.]

The future perfect is rare. Usually the simple future tense is used with an adverb phrase or clause.

RARE

> I shall have eaten before you go.

MORE COMMON

> I shall eat before you go.

NOTE: The perfect participle also expresses an action that precedes another action.

> *Having laughed* at length, the audience finally quieted down.

8f   Use the **present infinitive** (*to* and the base form of a verb) to express action that occurs at the same time as that of the controlling verb.

NOT

> I wanted *to have gone.*

BUT

> I wanted *to go.*

NOT

> I had expected *to have met* my friends at the game.

BUT

> I had expected *to meet* my friends at the game.

NOT

    I would have preferred *to have waited* until they came.

BUT

    I would have preferred *to wait* until they came.

8g Be consistent in the use of tenses. Do not shift tenses within a sentence or a paragraph without good cause.

TWO PAST ACTIONS

    The furniture maker *sanded* each piece with thorough care and only then *applied* [not *applies*] the stain.

    The child *smiled* broadly when she *saw* the clown approaching her.

TWO PRESENT ACTIONS

    As the child *smiles,* the photographer *takes* the picture.

■ Exercise 9

Underline incorrect verbs or verbals, and write the corrections above them. Write C by correct sentences.

                        made

  1. The judge listened to attorneys for both sides and then <u>makes</u>

     his ruling.

C   2. North Americans are said to have originated the game of

     lacrosse.

                       discovers

  3. In novels by Charles Dickens, a young man sometimes <u>discovered</u>

     that his birthright is far more advantageous than he had imagined.

4. Having composed a rough draft on his computer, the author sat
   stared
   back in his chair and stares at the ceiling.

5. The horses rushed out of the starting gate and head for the
   headed
   first turn.

6. In looking back, public officials almost always say they would
   to remain
   have preferred to have remained private citizens.

7. The soprano met with the civic group, agreed to sing a solo at
   began
   the Christmas concert, and begins to search for suitable music.

8. The periodic table shows that the symbol for the element mer-
   is
   cury was Hg, not Me.

9. At one time, many people thought that the world is flat.
   was

10. In Gérôme's painting *The Cadet,* the young man had a slight
    has
    sneer on his face.

9 Voice   *v·o*

Use the active voice for conciseness and emphasis.

A transitive verb (see p. 120) is in either the active or the passive
voice. (An intransitive verb does not have voice.) When the subject

acts, the verb is **active.** In most sentences the actor is more important than the receiver.

PASSIVE	A positive impression *was made* on the employees by the new chief executive officer.
USE ACTIVE	The new chief executive officer *made* a positive impression on the employees.
PASSIVE	A brief but highly effective speech *was delivered* by the valedictorian.
USE ACTIVE	The valedictorian *delivered* a brief but highly effective speech.

In the previous sentences, the **active voice** creates a more vigorous style.

When the subject is acted upon, the verb is passive. A **passive verb** is useful when the performer of an action is unknown or unimportant.

The book about herbs *was misplaced* among books about cosmetics.

The **passive voice** can also be effective when the emphasis is on the receiver, the verb, or even a modifier.

The police *were* totally *misled.*

In most situations, however, active verbs are more forceful and concise.

■ Exercise 10

Rewrite the following sentences. Change from passive to active voice.

The white-handed gibbon quickly climbed the tree
1. ~~The tree was quickly climbed by the white handed gibbon, and~~ and glared at the lions below.
~~the lions below were glared at.~~

2.   The three children watched a television program as their mother
~~A television program was watched by the three children as~~
brought them cake.
~~cake was brought to them by their mother.~~

3.   The ~~road~~ reporter had been traveled many times ~~by the reporter,~~ but
she the road
~~the old house~~ had never before been noticed ~~by her.~~ the old house

4.   The shipwrecked sailors witnessed a beautiful sunset,
~~A beautiful sunrise was witnessed by the shipwrecked sailors,~~
and at that very moment they spotted a ship dispatched
~~and at that very moment a ship dispatched to rescue them was~~
to rescue them.
~~spotted by them.~~

5.   The leaders of the tribe destroyed the   used
~~The~~ cameras that ~~were used~~ by the anthropologists to take

pictures of the ancient village. ~~were destroyed by the leaders~~

~~of the tribe.~~

■ Exercise 11

Change the voice of the verb when it is ineffective. Rewrite the sentence if necessary. Write E by sentences in which the verb is effective.

Mowing the grass and pruning the hedges
1. ~~The appearance of the yard was~~ dramatically improved ~~by~~
~~the appearance of the yard.~~
mowing the grass and pruning the hedges.

E   2. Both passengers were thrown clear, and they walked away un-

injured.

E   3.   The horse lost the race because the shoe was improperly nailed

to the hoof.

        scuba-diving instructor told his students that they could
    4.   The ~~students were told by their scuba-diving instructor that a~~
        all have a good time
        ~~good time could be had by all~~ if they simply took proper

precautions.

        Cooking shows on television make some
    5.   ~~Some~~ people ~~are made~~ hungry ~~by cooking shows on television.~~

10   Subjunctive Mood   *MO*

Use the **subjunctive mood** to express wishes, orders, and
conditions contrary to fact (see **Mood,** p. 478).

WISHES

    I wish that tomorrow *were* here.

ORDERS

    The instructions are that ten sentences *be* revised.

CONDITIONS CONTRARY TO FACT

    If I *were* a little child, I would have no responsibilities.

    If I *were* you, I would not go.

    Had the weather *been* good, we would have gone to the top of the
    mountain.

In modern English the subjunctive survives mainly as a custom in
some expressions.

SUBJUNCTIVE

The new manager requested that ten apartments *be* remodeled.

SUBJUNCTIVE NOT USED

The new manager decided to have ten apartments remodeled.

■ Exercise 12

Change verbs to the subjunctive mood when appropriate.

                                  were

1. This house would sell at a higher price if it ~~was~~ not painted

   purple.

                                      be

2. Let us stipulate in our will that our children are ~~well~~ cared for.

    were

3. If it ~~was~~ not for the ozone layer, ultraviolet rays would be more

   destructive.

                         be

4. I demand that my money ~~is~~ refunded!

                              were

5. Many people wish that the entire world ~~was~~ at peace.

11 Subject and Verb: Agreement *agr*

Make subjects and verbs agree.

Subjects and verbs must agree in number. A singular subject takes a singular verb. A plural subject takes a plural verb.

11a Use a singular verb with a singular subject.

Use an *-s* or *-es* ending for a singular verb with a third person subject, in the present tense (she *talks,* he *wishes).*

      singular
       ↓   ↓
The *door* **opens.**

      singular
       ↓   ↓
The *noise* **disturbs** the sleepers.

11b Use a plural verb with a plural subject.

      plural
       ↓   ↓
The *doors* **open.**

      plural
       ↓   ↓
The *noises* **disturb** the sleepers.

11c Use a plural verb ordinarily with a compound subject (see p. 97).

Work and play **are** not equally rewarding.
Golf and polo **are** usually outdoor sports.

EXCEPTION: Compound subjects connected by *and* but expressing a singular idea take a singular verb.

The rise and fall of waves **draws** a sailor back to the sea.

When the children are in bed, *the tumult and shouting* **dies.**

The coach and history teacher **is** Ms. Silvo.

11d After a compound subject with *or, nor, either . . . or, neither . . . nor, not . . . but, or, not only . . . but also,* the verb agrees in number and person with the nearer subject (see **12d**).

NUMBER

Neither the *photographs* nor the *camera* **was** damaged by the fire.

Either *fans* or an *air conditioner* **is** necessary.

Either an *air conditioner* or *fans* **are** necessary.

PERSON

Neither *you* nor your *successor* **is** affected by the new regulation.

11e Do not allow phrases or clauses between a subject and a verb to affect the number of a verb.

After singular subjects, intervening prepositional phrases with plural objects do not make the subject or the verb plural.

Some words and phrases of this kind that may cause mistakes are *along with, as well as, in addition to, including, with,* and *together with.*

SINGULAR SUBJECT, INTERVENING PHRASE, SINGULAR VERB

A mother *skunk* with three *babies* **was** prowling nearby.

Rewritten with a coordinating conjunction, the sentence requires a plural verb:

A mother *skunk* and her three *babies* **were** prowling nearby.

NOTE: Do not be confused by inversion.

From kind acts **grows** [not *grow*] *friendship.*

11f Use a singular verb with a collective noun that refers to a group as a unit; use a plural verb when the members of a group are thought of individually.

A collective noun names a class or group: *congregation, family, flock, jury.* When the group is regarded as a unit, use the singular.

> The *audience* at a concert sometimes **determines** the length of the performance.

When the group is regarded as separate individuals, use the plural.

> The *audience* at a concert **vary** in their reactions to the music.

11g Use a singular verb with most nouns that are plural in form but singular in meaning.

Economics and *news* (and other words like *genetics, linguistics,* etc.) are considered singular.

> *Economics* **is** often thought of as a science.

> The *news* of a cure **is** encouraging.

Scissors and *trousers* are treated as plural except when used after *pair.*

> The *scissors* **are** dull.

> That *pair* of scissors **is** dull.

> The *trousers* **are** pressed and ready to wear.

> An old *pair* of trousers **is** sometimes stylish.

Other nouns that cause problems are *athletics, measles,* and *politics.* When in doubt, consult a dictionary.

11h Use singular verbs with indefinite pronouns (*anybody, anyone, each, either, everybody, everyone, neither, no one, nobody, one, somebody, someone*).

Neither of the explanations **was** satisfactory.

Everybody **has** trouble choosing a subject for a paper.

Each of the students **has** chosen a subject.

11i Use a singular or a plural verb with words such as *all, some, part, half* (and other fractions), depending on the noun or pronoun that follows. If the indefinite pronoun refers to something countable (apples), it takes a plural verb. If it refers to a whole entity (sugar, rain), it takes a singular verb.

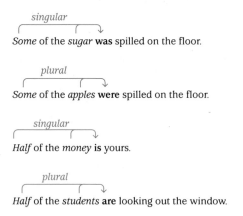

singular

Some of the *sugar* **was** spilled on the floor.

plural

Some of the *apples* **were** spilled on the floor.

singular

Half of the *money* **is** yours.

plural

Half of the *students* **are** looking out the window.

The number is singular.

>   *singular*
> *The number* of *translations* **was** never determined.

A number (meaning "some") is always plural.

>   *plural*
> *A number* of translations of the phrase **were** suggested.

11j After *there* or *here,* the number of the verb (singular or plural) is the same as the number of the subject.

There and *here*, which can function as **expletives,** are never used as subjects.

>   *verb*   *subject*
> There **was** a long *interval* between the two discoveries.
>
> There **were** thirteen *blackbirds* perched on the fence.
>
> Here **is** a *principle* to remember.
>
> Here **are** two *principles* to remember.

After an expletive, the singular (*is, was*) may be used when the next noun is singular.

> There **is** *a swing and a footbridge* in the garden.

NOTE: In sentences beginning with *It* (a pronoun), the verb is always singular.

> *It* **was** many years ago.

11k   Make a verb agree with its subject, not with a subjective complement/predicate nominative.

NO

His horse and *his dog* **are** his main source of pleasure.

NO

His main *source* of pleasure **is** his horse and his dog.

11l   After a relative pronoun (*who, which, that*), use a verb with the same person and number as the antecedent.

antecedent   *relative pronoun* → **verb of relative pronoun**

Those who → **were** invited came.

We who → **are** about to die salute you.

The *costumes that* → **were** worn in the ballet were dazzling.

He was the *candidate who* → **was** able to carry out his pledges.

He was one of the *candidates who* → **were** able to carry out their pledges.

BUT

He was the only *one* of the candidates *who* → **was** able to carry out his pledges.

11m   Use singular verbs with titles and with words used as words.

T. S. Eliot's *Four Quartets* **demands** careful study.

The Grapes of Wrath **tells** about the great troubles of farm workers in Oklahoma and California.

"Hints from Heloise" **is** a syndicated newspaper column.

Oodles **is** an informal word.

11n   Use singular verbs with expressions of time, money, measurement, weight, and volume and with fractions (*half, quarter, part*) when the amount is considered a unit.

Two tons **is** a heavy load for a small truck.

Forty-eight hours **is** a long time to go without sleep.

■ Exercise 13

Correct any verb that does not agree with its subject. Write C by any correct sentence.

1. A ship and an airplane affords different ways of crossing the At-

   lantic Ocean.

   has
2. "Jingle Bells" ~~have~~ given many children pleasure in the

   wintertime.

   mingles
3. The screech of seagulls ~~mingle~~ with the sound of the waves.

C 4. Several different careers are now open to those who major in

   the humanities.

5. A book on statistical methods in the social sciences together

   is
   with several essays ~~are~~ required reading in the course.

was
6. Molasses ~~were~~ used in a great number of early New England

recipes.

is
7. Childish sentences or dull writing ~~are~~ not improved by a sprin-

kling of dashes.

wants
8. Neither of the senator's two daughters ~~want~~ a career in politics,

has
which ~~have~~ always attracted other members of the family.

is
9. Either cash or credit card ~~are~~ acceptable when paying for the

tickets to the concert.

brings
10. The breaking of laws ~~bring~~ penalties.

■ Exercise 14

Correct any verb that does not agree with its subject. Mark C by any correct sentence.

recounts
1. Garrison Keillor's *Lake Wobegon Days* ~~recount~~ the history of a

mythical Minnesota town.

2. The stories from this humorous book capture$ small-town

American life.

C 3. A number of the characters have been developed from Keillor's

PBS radio program, "A Prairie Home Companion."

4. In the printed version of the stories, Keillor's warm voice and in-
   are
   fectious laugh ~~is~~ missing, his infrequent verbal slips do not oc-

   cur, and the sound effects are missing.

5. Dorothy of the Chatterbox Cafe together with Ralph of Ralph's
   appears
   Pretty Good Grocery ~~appear~~ in the book.
                                      serves
6. Neither Dorothy nor Ralph ~~serve~~ customers with modern

   efficiency.

7. One of the daily specials at the Chatterbox often is tuna hot-
                          drifts
   dish, the odor of which ~~drift~~ across Main Street.
                                                     are
8. Neither the codfish nor the pork loins at Ralph's ~~is~~ very fresh.

9. At Christmastime, smelly tubs of dried cod soaked in lye and

   called *lutefisk* appears at Ralph's meat counter.
        was
10. Politics ~~were~~ always less important in Lake Wobegon than

    sports and religion were.

■ Exercise 15

Correct any verb that does not agree with its subject.

                          deals
1. The novel *Glittering Images* ~~deal~~ with leaders in the Anglican

   Church in the 1930s.

2. The difference between illusion and reality ~~play~~ **plays** a major role in

   the story.

3. The title refers to illusions that ~~has~~ **have** to be abandoned as reality
   ~~intrude~~ **intrudes**.

4. Susan Howatch is one of those novelists who ~~has~~ **have** been trained

   in law.

5. Some of her characters (the exact number of them ~~are~~ **is** not important) ~~is~~ **are** based on real people.

6. The author, along with her husband, ~~live~~ **lives** in Surrey, England.

7. Each of the pages ~~were~~ **was** carefully written and revised.

8. Neither superficiality nor verbosity ~~damage~~ **damages** her writing.

9. Great technical skill and philosophical depth ~~is~~ **are** rare in a popu-

   lar novelist.

10. Four hundred pages ~~are~~ **is** a substantial amount to read, but the
    plot ~~move~~ **moves** along swiftly.

12 Pronouns and Antecedents: Agreement, Reference, and Usage *agr/ref*

Make pronouns agree with antecedents and refer to antecedents clearly.

A singular pronoun refers to a singular **antecedent** (see p. 470); a plural pronoun refers to a plural antecedent. A pronoun should refer clearly to a definite antecedent.

12a Use a singular pronoun with a singular antecedent.

The *debater* made **her** point eloquently.

Water finds **its** own level.

12b Use a plural pronoun with a plural antecedent.

The *debaters* made **their** points eloquently.

Three *rivers* spread beyond **their** banks.

12c In general, use a plural pronoun to refer to a compound antecedent linked with *and.*

The *owner* and the *captain* refused to leave **their** distressed ship.

If two nouns designate the same person, the pronoun is singular.

The *owner and captain* refused to leave **his** distressed ship.

12d After a compound antecedent linked with *or, nor,
either . . . or, neither . . . nor, not . . . but,* or *not only . . . but
also,* make a pronoun agree with the nearer part of the
antecedent (see **11d**).

> Neither the chess *pieces* nor the *board* had been placed in **its** proper
> position.
> Neither the *board* nor the chess *pieces* had been placed in **their** proper
> positions.

A sentence like this written with *and* is less artificial and stilted.

> The chess *pieces* **and** the *board* had not been placed in **their** proper
> positions.

12e Use a singular pronoun with a collective noun
antecedent when the members act as a unit; use a plural
pronoun when they act individually.

A UNIT

> The *committee* presented *its* report.

INDIVIDUALS

> The *committee,* some of *them* smiling, filed into the room and
> took *their* seats.

12f Use singular pronouns with such singular antecedents
as *each, either, neither, one, no one, everyone, someone, anyone,
nobody, everybody, somebody,* and *anybody.*

> Not *one* of the linemen felt that **he** had played well.

Be consistent in number within the same sentence.

INCONSISTENT

singular   *plural*

Everyone takes **their** seats.

CONSISTENT

Everyone who is a mother sometimes wonders how **she** will survive the day.

Once the pronouns *he* and *his* were used to refer to females as well as to males when the sex of the person was not specified or was not known.

Each person must face *his* own destiny.

Today the masculine pronoun alone generally is not used to represent both sexes. The following are three alternatives to using only the masculine pronoun.

1.   Make the sentence plural.

All *persons* have to face *their* own destinies.

2.   Use *he or she* (or *his or her*).

Each person has to face *his or her* own destiny.

3.   Use a neutral third person construction instead. Whenever possible avoid using *his or her*.

Each person must face *the* future.
Each person must face destiny.

12g Make pronouns refer clearly to definite
antecedents—not to an entire sentence, to a clause, or to
unidentified persons.

VAGUE

> Some people worry about wakefulness but actually need little sleep.
> *This* is one reason why they have so much trouble sleeping.

This could refer to the worry, to the need for little sleep, or to psychological problems or other traits that have not even been mentioned.

CLEAR

> Some people have trouble sleeping because they lie awake and worry
> about their inability to sleep.

Avoid using *it, them, they,* and *you* as vague references to people and
conditions that need more precise identification.

VAGUE

> *They* always get *you* in the end.

Here the pronouns *they* and *you* and the sentence itself are so vague
that the writer could mean almost anything pessimistic. The sentence could refer to teachers, deans, government officials, or even
all of life.

NOTE: The words *this, which,* and *it* may refer to the whole idea
stated in a previous clause or phrase when no misunderstanding is
likely.

> The grumbler heard that his boss had called him incompetent. *This*
> made him resign.

A pronoun should refer clearly to one antecedent, not uncer-
tainly to two.

UNCERTAIN

The agent visited her client before she went to the party.

CLEAR

Before the client went to the party, the agent visited her.

■ Exercise 16

Revise sentences in which pronouns do not agree with their antecedents. Write C by any correct sentence.

1. At the roadblock, each motorist had to show ~~their~~ **his or her** driver's

   license.

2. The jury reached ~~their~~ **its** verdict after four hours.

3. The drifter, along with his irresponsible relatives, never paid

   back a cent ~~they~~ **he** borrowed.

4. Neither my mother nor my aunt could start ~~their~~ **her** car on that

   cold morning.

5. Candy and cookies are not known for ~~its~~ **their** nutritional value.

C 6. Search the field for either a daisy or a dandelion so that we can

   observe it.

7. Everyone must pay ~~their~~ **her or his** income taxes.

8. The League of Nations failed because ~~they~~ *it* never received full

   support from member countries.

9. None of the bridesmaids believed that ~~they~~ *she* would have occasion to wear ~~their~~ *her* lavender dress again.

10. In the early days of the West, almost every man could ride ~~their~~ *his*

    horse skillfully.

■ Exercise 17

*Revise sentences in which pronouns do not refer clearly to one definite
antecedent.*

1. On the night of July 14, the patriots stormed the doors of the
   prison, and ~~they were~~ smashed *them.*

2. There was a rumor going around that worms constituted part of
   the hamburger meat, *nasty* ~~and it was nasty.~~

3. Cattle egrets are so named because they are frequently seen
   with cows, but ~~they~~ *the cows* do not seem to mind them.

4. ~~It says in today's~~ *Today's* paper *indicates* that a cure is being sought for laziness.

5. ~~They tell~~ *The government tells* us that we must pay taxes whether we want to or not.

6. The poet is famous, but ~~it~~ *poetry or fame* does not put food on the table.

7. The professor did not push his point further with the stu-
   , who
   dent ~~because he~~ was embarrassed.

   mints
8. According to dealers in rare coins, ~~they~~ do not put as much sil-

   ver in coins as they used to.

9. Some photographers have a talent for getting small children to
   children *or* photographers
   sit quietly; still, ~~they~~ can be impatient.

10. Garth's little sister threw his CD player against the mirror with
    the player *or* the mirror
    such force that ~~it~~ broke.

12h Use *which* to refer to animals and things, *who* and
whom to refer to persons and sometimes to animals or
things called by name, and *that* to refer to animals or things
and sometimes to persons.

The *man* **who** was taking photographs is my uncle.

The *dog,* **which** sat beside him, looked happy.

Secretariat, **who** won the Kentucky Derby, will be remembered as one
of the most beautiful horses of all time.

Sometimes *that* and *who* are interchangeable.

A *mechanic that (who)* does good work stays busy.

A *person that (who)* giggles is often revealing embarrassment.

NOTE: *Whose* (the possessive form of *who*) may be less awkward
than *of which,* even in referring to animals and things.

The *car* **whose** right front tire blew out came to a stop.

12i Do not use intensive or reflexive pronouns for
personal pronouns in the **nominative** or **objective case.**

Use intensive and reflexive pronouns ending in *-self* or *-selves (myself, yourself, himself, herself, itself, themselves)* only in sentences
containing antecedents for such pronouns. These words are not the
equivalents of *I, me, you, he, she, him, her, it, they,* or *them.*

FAULTY
> My brother and *myself* helped Father cut the wheat.

USE
> My brother and *I* helped Father cut the wheat.

INTENSIVE
> I *myself* helped Father cut the wheat.

REFLEXIVE
> I helped Father cut the wheat *myself.*

FAULTY
> The antiques dealer sold the ancient chair to my roommate and *myself.*

USE
> The antiques dealer sold the ancient chair to my roommate and *me.*

■ Exercise 18

Revise sentences that contain errors in usage of pronouns.

               who
1. The early navigator ~~which~~ discovered the island thought that he

   had found a new continent.

2. Was the first section of the essay written by your coauthor or by
you
~~yourself~~?

me
3. Our son bought tickets for my husband and ~~myself.~~

who
4. That woman in the red dress is the one ~~which~~ inherited a for-

tune and gave it away.

its
5. The green frog uses ~~his~~ tongue to catch insects.

13 Case   *C*

Use correct case forms.

Case expresses the relationship of a pronoun or a noun to other
words in a clause by the use of different forms (such as *I* or *me* for the
first person singular). Case is determined by the function of the word
in a clause. Decide how a word is being used in a particular clause—
for example, whether it is functioning as a **subject,** a **subjective complement,** or an **object.** Pronouns used as **subjects** or **subjective
complements/predicate nominatives** (*I, they;* see pp. 99–100) are in
the **subjective case.** Those used as **objects** (*me, them*) are in the **objective case.** Those showing possession are in the **possessive case**
(*ours, yours*).

    Nouns also have case, but they change form only for the pos-
sessive case (*child, child's*).

The following is a chart of the cases of pronouns:

PERSONAL PRONOUNS

Singular	*Subjective*	*Possessive*	*Objective*
First person	I	my, mine	me
Second person	you	your, yours	you
Third person	he, she, it	his, her, hers, its	him, her, it

Plural	*Subjective*	*Possessive*	*Objective*
First person	we	our, ours	us
Second person	you	your, yours	you
Third person	they	their, theirs	them

RELATIVE OR INTERROGATIVE PRONOUNS

Number	*Subjective*	*Possessive*	*Objective*
Singular	who	whose	whom
Plural	who	whose	whom

13a Use the subjective case for subjects and for subjective complements (predicate nominatives).

SUBJECT

After seven years, my former *roommate* and *I* [not *me*] had much to talk about.

It looked as if my *friend* and *I* [not *me*] were going to be roommates again.

SUBJECTIVE COMPLEMENT

The fortunate ones were *you* and *I*.

In speech, *it's me, it's us, it's him,* and *it's her* are sometimes used. These forms are not appropriate for formal writing.

13b Use the objective case for a direct object, an indirect object, or the object of a preposition.

DIRECT OBJECT
> The magician *amazed* Yolanda and **me** [not **I**].

INDIRECT OBJECT
> Mozart *gave* **us** great music.

OBJECT OF PREPOSITION
> The director had to choose *between* **her** and **me** [not **she** and **I**].

NOTE: Be careful about the case of *we* or *us* before a noun.

FAULTY
> A few *of* **we campers** learned to cook.

CORRECT
> A few *of* **us campers** learned to cook.

When in doubt, test the usage by dropping the noun:

> A few *of* **us** learned to cook.

CORRECT (when pronoun is subject)
> *We* campers learned to look.

13c Use the objective case for subjects and objects of infinitives.

> *subject of infinitive*
> The editors considered **her** *to be* the best reporter on the staff.

objective of infinitive

To show **her** our new office took time.

13d Use the same case for an appositive and the word to which it refers (see **27c**).

SUBJECTIVE

Two delegates—Esther Giner and **I**—were appointed by the president.

OBJECTIVE

The president appointed two *delegates*—Esther Giner and **me**.

13e After *than* or *as* in an **elliptical** (incomplete) **clause**, use the same case that you would use if the clause were completely expressed.

subject of understood verb

No one else in the play was as versatile as **she** (*was*).

object of understood subject and verb

Her fellow actors respected no one more than (*they respected*) **her**.

13f Use *who* for the subjective case and *whom* for the objective case.

In formal writing, it is still important to use *whom* in the objective case. In conversation these days, however, *who* is used more frequently for the objective case.

IN QUESTIONS
subjective case

subject verb   object

Who conceived the idea of a committee?

When words intervene between the pronoun and the main verb, determining the case can be more difficult.

[*Who* or *Whom?*] do they say conceived the idea of a committee?

Mentally cancel the intervening words:

Who ~~do they say~~ conceived the idea of a committee?

objective case

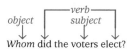

object   ——verb——
                subject
Whom did the voters elect?

To choose the correct pronoun in a dependent clause, first identify the clause; then determine the function of the pronoun **within that clause.** If the pronoun serves as a subject or subjective complement within the clause, use *who* (or *whoever*); if it serves as an object, use *whom* (or *whomever*). Do not confuse the function of the relative pronoun within its clause with the function of the clause as a whole in the complete sentence.

IN DEPENDENT CLAUSES
subjective case

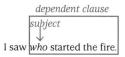

dependent clause
subject

I saw *who* started the fire.

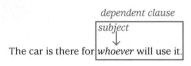

The car is there for *whoever* will use it.

objective case

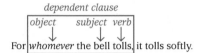

Make an appointment with your English professor, *whom* you will like.

dependent clause

For *whomever* the bell tolls, it tolls softly.

13g   Use an apostrophe with a noun in forming the possessive case. (See **37**.)

> The motto of the club was written in Latin.
> The *club's* motto was written in Latin.

13h   Use the possessive case for pronouns and nouns preceding a gerund.

> *gerund*
> None of my friends had heard about **my** [not **me**] *leaving*.

> *gerund*
> The baby's *crying* could be heard throughout the building.

BUT

A noun before a gerund (see p. 102) need not be possessive when the noun is **plural**:

> There is no rule against **people** *working* overtime.

when the noun is **abstract:**

> I object to **emotion** *overruling* judgment.

or when the noun denotes an **inanimate object:**

> The police officer did not like the **car** *being* parked in the street.

When a verbal is a participle (see p. 102) and not a gerund, a noun or pronoun preceding it is in the objective case. The verbal functions as an adjective.

> No one saw **anyone** *running* from the scene.

■ **Exercise 19**

Underline the correct word.

1. Serve a free meal to (whoever, whomever) is hungry.

2. Margo did not tell her mother (who, whom) she had invited to dinner.

3. Will the delegate from the Virgin Islands please indicate (who, whom) is to receive her delegation's votes?

4. (Who, Whom) do historians believe invented ink?

5. The Muses were supposed to be the nine daughters of Zeus, each of (who, whom) reigned over a different art or science.

6. (Whoever, Whomever) is elected will have to deal with the
   problem.

7. There was in those days in Paris a singer (who, whom) the secret police knew was a double agent.

8. On the platform stood the man (who, whom) they all believed
   had practiced witchcraft.

9. On the platform stood the man (who, whom) they all accused
   of practicing witchcraft.

10. The speaker defended his right to talk critically about (whoever,
    whomever) he pleased.

■ Exercise 20

*Cross out the incorrect forms of pronouns and nouns, and write in the
correct forms.*

                                          she
1. No one was a better sales manager than her.
   Hers
2. Her's was a rare talent for dealing with people.
                                          me
3. She was always kind to my mother and I.
                     me who
4. Just between you and I, whom is it that the judges are favoring?

5. Evan and ~~him~~ **he** appeared just before sunset in that old car, waving and shouting at Eileen and me.

6. The physician said that he had not objected to the ~~employee~~ **employee's** returning to work.

7. It was plain to ~~we~~ **us** students that the professor was delivering the same lecture that we had heard the week before.

8. If the ordinance were passed granting a right of way to you and ~~I,~~ **me** whose responsibility would it be to make sure that we are allowed access?

9. Between ~~she~~ **her** and ~~I~~ **me** there never were any secrets; at least, that is what she told me.

10. I decided to allow nothing to interfere with ~~me~~ **my** studying.

14 Adjectives and Adverbs   *adj/adv*

Use adjectives to modify nouns and pronouns; use adverbs to modify verbs, adjectives, and other adverbs.

Most adverbs end in *-ly*. Only a few adjectives (such as *lovely, holy, manly, friendly*) end in *-ly*.

Some adverbs have two forms, one with *-ly* and one without: *slow* and *slowly, loud* and *loudly.* Most adverbs are formed by adding *-ly* to adjectives: *warm, warmly; pretty, prettily.*

14a Use an adverb, not an adjective, to modify a verb, an adjective, or another adverb.

Choosing correctly between adverbs and adjectives in some sentences is simple.

> They stood *close.* [adverb, modifies verb *stood*]
> She was a *close* relative. [adjective, modifies noun *relative*]

Adjectives do not modify verbs, adverbs, or other adjectives. Distinguish between *sure* (adjective) and *surely* (adverb); *easy* and *easily; good* and *well; real* and *really.*

    surely
You ~~sure~~ cannot count on an alarm clock.

               easily
I could have passed the examination ~~easy~~.

    well
Allen did ~~good~~ on his final examination.

         really
The fireworks were ~~real~~ impressive.

14b Use a predicate adjective, not an adverb, after a linking verb (see p. 89) such as *appear, be, become, feel, look, seem, smell, sound,* or *taste.*

ADJECTIVE

He feels **bad.** [He is ill or depressed. An adjective modifies a pronoun.]

ADVERB

He *reads* **badly.** [*Reads* is not a linking verb. An adverb modifies a verb.]

ADJECTIVE

The *tea* tasted **sweet.** [*Sweet* describes the tea.]

ADVERB

She *tasted* the tea **daintily.** [*Daintily* tells how she tasted the tea.]

14c Use an adjective, not an adverb, after a verb
and its object when the modifier refers to the object,
not to the verb.

Verbs like *keep, build, hold, dig, make,* and *think* are followed by a direct object and a modifier. After verbs of this kind, choose the adjective or the adverb form carefully.

ADJECTIVES—MODIFY OBJECTS

Keep your *clothes* **neat.**
Make the *line* **straight.**

ADVERBS—MODIFY VERBS

Arrange your clothes **neatly** in the closet.
Draw the line **carefully.**

14d For adjectives and adverbs, use the positive degree to describe one thing or concept, the comparative to describe and compare two things or concepts, and the superlative to describe one thing as compared with two or more. (See pp. 89–90.)

The **comparative** and **superlative degrees** of most short adjectives or adverbs are formed by adding *-er* or *-est* to the positive.

	POSITIVE	COMPARATIVE	SUPERLATIVE
Adjective	slow	slower	slowest
Adverb	slow	slower	slowest
	slowly	more slowly	most slowly

For longer modifiers use *more* and *most* (or *less* and *least*) instead of adding *-er* and *-est*.

ADJECTIVE	expensive	more expensive	most expensive
		less expensive	least expensive

NOTE: Adding *-er* or *-est* to a longer modifier would be bad usage:

ADJECTIVE	*avoid* →	pitifuller	pitifullest
ADVERB	*avoid* →	*slowlier*	*slowliest*

Some adjectives and adverbs have irregular forms: *good, better, best; well, better, best; little, less, least; bad, worse, worst.* Consult a dictionary.

14e Avoid using **double comparatives** and **superlatives**.

Using *more* with *-er* and *most* with *-est* would be extravagant and illogical.

                               earlier
Five o'clock is ~~more earlier~~ than most people wish to get up.

> earliest

Three o'clock is the ~~most earliest~~ that I have ever gotten up.

14f Do not apply comparative and superlative degrees to modifiers that describe **absolute concepts.**

Dead, unique, and *perfect* are examples of **absolute modifiers.**

A being can be *dead* but not *deader.*

ILLOGICAL

Denise is the *most unique* person of my acquaintance.

Unique is an **absolute concept,** meaning "one of a kind":

Among my acquaintances, Denise is *unique.*

Experts who judge the perfection of a diamond use the terms *imperfect, nearly perfect,* and *perfect.* A diamond may be any of these three but not *more perfect.*

ILLOGICAL

The small diamond is *more perfect* than the large one.

ACCEPTABLE

The small diamond is *nearly perfect,* but the large one is *perfect.*

14g Avoid using double negatives.

Double negatives actually mean the opposite of what is intended. One negative is sufficient; two, unacceptable.

NOT

She could *not hardly* keep from screaming.

BUT

> She could *hardly* keep from screaming.

NOT

> I was *not* doing *nothing* to her.

BUT

> I was doing *nothing* to her.

OR

> I was *not* doing anything to her.

NOTE: Some **double negatives** that emphasize the positive are allowable (but often are showy and artificial):

> It was *not for nothing* that she spent so many years in medical training.

■ Exercise 21

Underline unacceptable forms of adjectives and adverbs, and write the correct forms. Write C by any correct sentence.

                                  sweet
1. The night was beautiful, and she smelled sweetly.

                                frantically
2. During that cold winter, birds sought frantic for food.

      surely
3. Computers sure are complicated.

                       awkwardly   **tentatively**
4. Both actors performed awkward and tentative during the first act.

C   5. Then, toward the final scenes of the play, they acted their parts

      convincingly.

           really
6. I was real pleased with their performance overall.

    logically
7. Think <u>logical</u> in times of confusion and pressure.

            scarcely
8. The acoustical situation was so bad that we could <u>scarce</u> hear

   the speaker.

    bad
9. We felt <u>badly</u> that we had to leave before the lecture was over.

10. Jennifer did volunteer work at the nursing home gladly and
   frequently
   <u>frequent</u>.

■ Exercise 22

Cross out unnecessary or incorrect words. Write the correct forms.
Write C *by any correct sentence.*

1. Pluto is ~~more~~ further from the sun than is Earth.

               smaller
2. When compared with Earth, Pluto is the ~~smallest~~.

3. As far as scientists have determined, there is ~~not~~ nobody on

   Pluto.

4. Sir Malcolm Campbell's Blue Bird had a ~~more~~ unique design
      for a
   ~~than any other~~ racing car.

5. Katherine was the youngest of three daughters born into one of

   the ~~most~~ noblest families in England.

least
6. Of the four tours, the one to Brazil is the ~~less~~ expensive.

7. If you have to choose between being safe and being sorry, be-
   better
   ing safe is ~~best~~.

C 8. Though several candidates are running, Leon seems the most

   qualified for the office.
                                                      less
9. Compared with, say, accounting, teaching offers ~~the least~~ pay.
                                     noticed
10. You ~~did not~~ hardly even ~~notice~~ me.

Sentence
Structure

15 Choppy Sentences and Excessive Coordination *chop/coor*

Use phrases and dependent clauses to express connections between ideas and to create a varied style.

Choppy sentences or strings of independent clauses connected by coordinating conjunctions *(and, but, or, nor, for, yet, so)* may be repetitious and monotonous. The resulting jerkiness prevents a paragraph from having smoothness and rhythm. Excessive coordination does not show precise relationships between thoughts.

NOTE: Avoid beginning consecutive sentences with the same word or with pronouns that stand for it.

CHOPPY SENTENCES

Mount Vesuvius is a volcano. It is in Italy. Perhaps it is the most famous volcano in the world. It has erupted several times. It has caused great devastation. Also, it is famous in a more positive way. Its slopes are extremely fertile. The best Italian wine comes from the grapes that grow there.

CHOPPY INDEPENDENT CLAUSES WITH COORDINATING
CONJUNCTIONS (SAME SUBJECT)

Mount Vesuvius is a volcano, and it is in Italy, and it is perhaps the most famous volcano in the world, for it has erupted several times, and it has caused great devastation, but it is also famous in a more positive way, for its slopes are extremely fertile, and some of the best Italian wine comes from the grapes that grow there.

IMPROVED

Italy's Mount Vesuvius, perhaps the most famous volcano in the world, has erupted several times with devastating results. In spite of the destruction, it is famous for wine made from grapes that grow on its fertile slopes.

■ Exercise 1

Rewrite the following to avoid choppy sentences and series of independent clauses.

Also called a devilfish, the graceful manta ray has a

1. The manta ray has a wide body, and it is flat, and it is also called

   wide, flat body.

   a devilfish, and it is graceful.

   Although some kinds of sharks are ferocious and attack many

2. Some kinds of sharks are ferocious. And they attack many bathers

   bathers each year, they are just seeking food and seldom kill.

   each year, but they are just seeking food, and they seldom kill.

   Having fallen most of the day, the rain suddenly stopped,

3. Rain fell most of the day. The rain suddenly stopped. The sun

   the sun came out, and it shone brightly. Enjoying the clear

   came out. It shone brightly. The little girl enjoyed the clear day.

   day, the little girl said the rain had washed the sun.

   She said the rain had washed the sun.

   Leaving the city in search of quiet and knowing that

4. Some vacationers leave the city in search of quiet, so they look

   parks become crowded with trailers and tents, some

   for a remote camping place, and they want almost complete

   vacationers look for a remote, even isolated, camping

   isolation, and for a time they do not wish for a telephone or

   place where they do not miss a telephone or even

   even electricity, but parks become crowded also, and they are

   electricity.

   filled with trailers and tents.

   In early times, the intrinsic value of coins was the value

5. In early times, coins had intrinsic value. They were worth what-

   of the metal in them; thus, merchants and bankers

   ever the metal in them was worth at the moment. They had to

   were kept busy weighing coins to determine their value.

   be weighed. Merchants and bankers were kept busy weighing

   coins. They had to be constantly determining the value of coins.

16 Subordination *sub*

Subordinate for emphasis and for effective, varied sentence construction.

Putting the less important idea of a sentence in a dependent clause emphasizes the more important thought expressed in the independent clause. Also, piling one dependent clause on top of another stretches out sentences awkwardly and obscures their meaning.

16a Express main ideas in independent clauses and less important ideas in dependent clauses.

An optimistic sociologist wishing to stress progress despite crime would write:

> Although the crime rate is high, society has progressed in some ways.

A pessimistic sociologist might use the opposite emphasis:

> Although society has progressed in some ways, the crime rate is high.

Upside-down subordination results from placing the main idea of a sentence in a dependent clause. The writer of the following sentence wished to stress the insight and wisdom possessed by a young woman despite her youth.

────────────dependent clause──────────── ┐┌ *independent*
Although she possessed unusual insight and wisdom, she was still

clause ┐
young.

Unintentionally, the writer of the previous sentence emphasized the person's youth. For the proper stress, the sentence should read:

> ┌────── *dependent clause* ──────┐┌─────────── *independent clause* ───────────┐
> Although she was still young, she possessed unusual insight and wisdom.

16b Avoid excessive overlapping of dependent clauses.

Monotony and confusion can result from a series of clauses in which each depends on the previous one.

OVERLAPPING

Pianos are instruments
      ↲
      that contain metal strings
        ↲
        that make sounds when struck by felt-covered hammers
          ↲
          that are operated by keys.

IMPROVED

Pianos are instruments containing metal strings that make sounds when struck by felt-covered hammers operated by keys.

■ Exercise 2

Explain differences in meaning or emphasis in the following pairs of sentences.

1. Because he took time to help the stranded cat, the children thought their uncle was a hero.
   Because the children thought their uncle was a hero, he took time to help the stranded cat.
2. Although she played the cello poorly, she was an effective legislator.

Although she was an effective legislator, she played the cello poorly.

3. If pitching fails, hitting and fielding may sparkle.
   If hitting and fielding sparkle, pitching may fail.

4. Even though the movie was tiresome, the lead actress brilliantly portrayed an aging dancer.
   Even though the lead actress brilliantly portrayed an aging dancer, the movie was tiresome.

5. Although insects lead short lives, they are ecologically vital.
   Although they are ecologically vital, insects lead short lives.

■ Exercise 3

Rewrite the following sentences to avoid excessive subordination.

1. Numerous ~~people who love animals~~ [animal lovers] are volunteering their time, ~~which is precious,~~ [precious] [help] to their local humane societies ~~that are trying~~ to find homes for cats and dogs ~~that are currently homeless.~~

2. ~~A controversy that is raging centers on~~ [C]ollege football players who [illegally] accept money and gifts ~~that are illegal~~ from [unscrupulous] agents ~~who are unscrupulous.~~ [have created a raging controversy.]

3. ~~In a discovery that took place in~~ [In] 1939, construction workers ~~found~~ [discovered] a cave ~~that is~~ near Monte Circeo, Italy, that had been sealed for fifty thousand years.

4. Inside the cave ~~was~~ a circle ~~that was made~~ of rocks ~~that~~ sur-

   the

   rounded ⱥ broken skull ~~which was that~~ of an ancient man.

5. Lobster Newburg is ~~a dish that consists of~~ cooked lobster meat,

   with

   ~~which is~~ heated in a chafing dish ~~that contains~~ a special cream

   sauce.

17 Completeness   *compl*

Make your sentences complete in structure and thought.

Include all necessary words to make the parts of a sentence consistent and the meaning clear.

17a Do not omit a verb or a preposition that is necessary to the structure of the sentence.

OMITTED PREPOSITION

> The apes were both attracted and suspicious **of** the stuffed animal placed in their midst. [The apes were attracted **of**?]

IMPROVED

> The apes were both attracted **to** and suspicious **of** the stuffed animal placed in their midst.

BETTER

> The apes were both attracted **to** the stuffed animal placed in their midst and suspicious **of** it.

OMITTED VERB

> The cabinet *drawers* **were** open and the glass *door* shattered. [The door **were** shattered?]

VERB STATED

> The cabinet *drawers* **were** open, and the glass *door* **was** shattered.

NOTE: When the same verb form is called for in both elements, it need not be repeated.

> To err is human; to forgive, divine.

17b   Omission of *that* sometimes obscures meaning.

INCOMPLETE

> The labor leader reported a strike was not likely.

COMPLETE

> The labor leader reported **that** a strike was not likely.

18 Comparisons   *comp*

Comparisons must be logical and clear.

18a   Compare only similar terms.

The following sentence mistakenly compares vegetation and a volcano.

> Notice the difference between the vegetation here and the crater of the volcano.

Use similar constructions in order to make a more logical comparison of similar terms.

> Notice the difference between the vegetation here and that at the crater of the volcano.

18b Use the word *other* to exclude the first object from the group with which it is being compared.

INCOMPLETE AND ILLOGICAL
> Alaska is larger in land area than any state.

Any state must include Alaska itself.

COMPLETE
> Alaska is larger in land area than any *other* state.

18c Avoid awkward and incomplete comparisons.

AWKWARD AND INCOMPLETE
> The new cars appear to be as small if not smaller than last year's models. [*As small* requires *as,* not *than.*]

BETTER
> The new cars appear to be as small as last year's models, if not smaller.

AWKWARD AND INCOMPLETE
> Queen Elizabeth I was one of the most powerful if not the most powerful woman in the world. [After *one of the most powerful,* the plural form *women* is required.]

BETTER
> Queen Elizabeth I was one of the most powerful women in the world, if not the most powerful.

AMBIGUOUS

> A year after the trial, the judge remembered me better than the defendant. [Better than he remembered the defendant, or better than the defendant remembered me?]

CLEAR

> A year after the trial, the judge remembered me better than the defendant did.

OR

> A year after the trial, the judge remembered me better than he did the defendant.

■ Exercise 4

Correct any errors in completeness and comparisons.

               that
1. The adventurer found ⋀ the buried treasure was but a myth.

                        as
2. Some wildflowers are as beautiful ⋀ if not more beautiful than

   hothouse varieties.

                  other
3. The aorta is larger than any ⋀ artery in the body.

                            in
4. Taxes are usually higher in urban areas than ⋀ the country.

      been
5. I have always ⋀ and will always be true to you.

                             as
6. For good health, plain water is as good ~~if not better than~~ most

   if not better. ⋀
other liquids, ⋀

                        of
7. The lighthouse stood as a symbol and guide to safety. ⋀

                                do. or . . . than they do mice.

8. Cats eat more cheese than mice.
                                    Λ

9. Statistics reveal that the average age of our nation's populace
      increasing *or* increasing and will continue to do so.
      is and will continue to increase.
      Λ
                                        was
10. The king's daughters were ugly, but the prince handsome.
                                          Λ

■ Exercise 5

Follow the instructions for Exercise 4.

                     that
1. Some people believe the Bermuda triangle is more dangerous
        other   Λ
     than any part of the world.
          Λ   **that**
2. Copernicus discovered the sun is at the center of our solar
                              Λ

     system.

3. Birds seem to sing more beautifully in the early morning than
      in
     the afternoon.
   Λ

4. The editors say that the headlines have been written and the
           has been
     type set.
      Λ

5. Shoppers standing in the checkout line are sometimes both
          about *or* about the tabloids on the display racks and
     curious and disapproving of the tabloids on the display racks.
         Λ
      disapproving of them.

19 Consistency   *cons*

Write sentences that maintain consistency in form and meaning.

19a Avoid confusing or awkward shifts in grammatical forms.

Shift in tense

PRESENT AND PAST

> The actors *rehearsed* and rehearsed, and then they finally *perform*. [Use *rehearsed . . . performed* or *rehearse . . . perform*.]

CONDITIONAL FORMS *(SHOULD, WOULD, COULD)*

> Exhaustion after a vacation *could* be avoided if a family *can* plan better. [Use *could . . . would* or *can . . . can*.]

Shift in person

> In department stores, *good salespersons* [**3rd person**] first ask whether a customer needs help or has questions. Then *they* [**3rd person**] do not hover around. If *you* [**2nd person**] do, *you* [**2nd person**] run the risk of making the customer uncomfortable or even angry. [The third sentence should read, "If *they* do, *they* run. . . ."]

Shift in number

> A *witness* may see an accident one way when it happens, and then *they* remember it an entirely different way when *they* testify. [Use *witness* and a singular pronoun or *witnesses* and *they . . . they*.]

Shift in mood

                 indicative   *imperative*
                     ↓   ↓

> First the job-seeker *mails* an application; then *go* for an interview. [Use *mails* and *he or she goes* or *job-seekers mail . . .* then *they go*.]

Shift in voice

The chef *cooks* [**active**] the shrimp casserole for thirty minutes, and then it *is allowed* [**passive**] to cool. [Use *cooks* and *allows*. See **9**.]

Shift in connectors

RELATIVE PRONOUNS

She went to the chest of drawers *that* leaned perilously forward and *which* always resisted every attempt to open it. [Use *that . . . that.*]

CONJUNCTIONS

The guests came *since* the food was good and *because* the music was soothing. [Use *since . . . since* or *because . . . because.*]

Shift in use of direct and indirect discourse

MIXED

The swimmer says that the sea is calm and why would anyone fear it?

CONSISTENT

The swimmer says that the sea is calm and asks why anyone would fear it.

■ Exercise 6

Correct shifts in the following sentences.

1. Customers no longer seem to chat with each other in laundro-
   they
   mats; ~~you~~ have to be more careful than in the past.

2. Success in the experiments will be achieved this time if the as-
   will
   sistants ~~would~~ follow the instructions precisely.

3. Contact lenses that are well fitted and ~~which~~ are well cared for
     (that)

usually cause few problems.

4. Ulysses S. Grant was looking forward to the day of Lee's sur-
render, but when that day came, he ~~experiences~~ a migraine
     (experienced)
headache and ~~suffers~~ through the ceremony.
     (suffered)

5. The smiling actor backed carefully down the steps, jumped on
his horse, and ~~rides~~ off, leaving a cloud of dust behind.
     (rode)

6. Enthusiastic runners like to get out every day, but occasionally
the weather in this region ~~would be~~ too bad even for the most
     (is)

dedicated.

7. ~~A lawyer does~~ not always enjoy a good reputation, for they are
     (Lawyers do)

the subjects of many jokes.

8. Before one purchases an electrical appliance, ~~you~~ should find
     *(one *or* he or she)*

out how expensive it will be to operate.

9. ~~It is wise to start~~ a fire with a wood like pine and then a heavier
     (Start)   *(use)* ∧

wood like oak ∧ ~~is used~~.

10. Use pine first to start a fire ~~since~~ it ignites easily and because it
     (because)

will then make the oak burn.

19b Make subjects and predicates fit together logically. Avoid faulty predication.

Test a sentence by mentally placing the subject and predicate side by side. If they do not fit together (faulty predication), rewrite for clarity and logic.

FAULTY

After eating a large meal *is a bad time* to go swimming. [*Eating* is not a time.]

LOGICAL

The *period* just after eating a large meal *is a bad time* to go swimming. [*Period* and *time* match.]

FAULTY

When crime statistics decrease *causes* some people to become careless. [*When* does not cause the carelessness.]

LOGICAL

A *decrease* in crime statistics *causes* some people to become careless.

19c Avoid the constructions *is when, is where,* and *the reason . . . is because.*

Constructions with *is when, is where,* or *the reason . . . is because* are both illogical and ungrammatical.

FAULTY

Tragedy is *where* a person of high standing falls to a low estate. [Tragedy is not *where.*]

LOGICAL

Tragedy *occurs* when a person of high standing falls to a low estate.

FAULTY   ✗

The *reason* why Macbeth falls is *because* he is overly ambitious.

LOGICAL   ✔

The *reason* why Macbeth falls *is that* he is overly ambitious.

■ Exercise 7

Correct any faulty constructions in the following sentences.

                   occurs when

1. Faulty predication ~~is when~~ the subject and verb do not fit to-

   gether logically.

2. Because she was always late ~~explains why~~ she was fired.

          P   **∧**   **only when**

3. ~~The only time~~ people should be late ~~is if~~ they cannot possibly

   avoid it.

4. The reason why so many houses in coastal Florida have flat

            that

   roofs is ~~because~~ they endure the strong winds of hurricanes.

            the reason

5. Volcanic action is ∧ why many islands in the South Seas have

   beaches with dark sand.

                                      and

6. A pretzel is ~~where~~ a slender roll of dough sprinkled with salt ~~is~~

   baked into the shape of a knot.

             number of

7. Some years ago, the ~~growth in~~ applications to graduate schools

     increased because of a recession.

               what   **feels**

8. An example of confusion is a bewildered person in a house
                                 Λ   Λ

     of mirrors.

             results in the inability to

9. Confusion ~~is when you cannot~~ think straight.

10. Apologetically, Edgar explained that the reason why he had not

                     that
     called was simply ~~because~~ he had been too busy.

20 Position of Modifiers   *dg/mod*

Attach modifiers clearly to the right word or element in the sentence.

A misplaced modifier can cause confusion or misunderstanding.

20a Avoid dangling modifiers.

A verbal phrase at the beginning of a sentence should modify the subject.

DANGLING PARTICIPLE   **✗**

     Speeding down the hill, several slalom *poles* were knocked down by the skier.

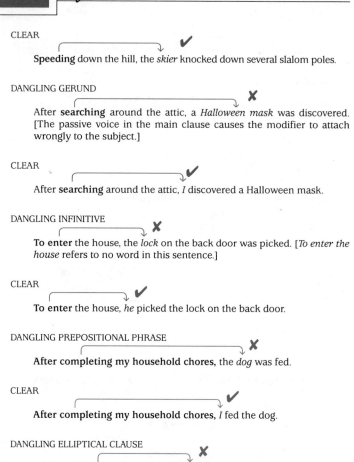

CLEAR

Speeding down the hill, the *skier* knocked down several slalom poles.

DANGLING GERUND

After **searching** around the attic, a *Halloween mask* was discovered. [The passive voice in the main clause causes the modifier to attach wrongly to the subject.]

CLEAR

After **searching** around the attic, *I* discovered a Halloween mask.

DANGLING INFINITIVE

To enter the house, the *lock* on the back door was picked. [*To enter the house* refers to no word in this sentence.]

CLEAR

To enter the house, *he* picked the lock on the back door.

DANGLING PREPOSITIONAL PHRASE

After completing my household chores, the *dog* was fed.

CLEAR

After completing my household chores, *I* fed the dog.

DANGLING ELLIPTICAL CLAUSE

While still sleepy and tired, the *counselor* lectured me on breaking rules.

CLEAR

While I was still sleepy and tired, the counselor lectured me on breaking rules.

NOTE: Loosely attaching a verbal phrase to the end of a sentence is unemphatic.

UNEMPHATIC

Tomatoes are a relatively recent addition to our tables, having been widely cultivated only in the last hundred years or so.

BETTER

Tomatoes are a relatively recent addition to our tables; they have been widely cultivated only in the last hundred years or so.

Some verbal phrases that are **sentence modifiers** do not need to refer to a specific word:

Strictly speaking, does this sentence contain a dangling construction? *To tell the truth,* it does not.

20b Avoid misplaced modifiers.

Placement of a modifier in a sentence affects meaning.

He enlisted after he married *again.*
He enlisted *again* after he married.

To prevent awkwardness or misreading, keep words, phrases, and clauses close to the words they modify.

MISLEADING

Even on a *meager* sheriff's salary, a family may have some comforts.

CLEAR

Even on a sheriff's *meager* salary, a family may have some comforts.

PUZZLING

He admitted that he was the anonymous donor *in the letter.*

CLEAR
> He admitted *in the letter* that he was the anonymous donor.

20c   Place limiting modifiers (words like *only, just, even, almost,* and *hardly*) directly before the words that they modify.

Careless placement of **limiting modifiers** can cause awkwardness, create confusion, or convey wrong meanings. Notice the different meanings of the following two sentences:

> *Just* a word of encouragement is adequate.
> A word of encouragement is *just* adequate.

In the following sentences, notice how limiting modifiers are misplaced.

> Mary *only* attended college for one reason: to meet boys.

> She *almost* failed all her subjects the first term.

> She *only* passed Orientation.

> *Even* she neglected to write home.

> Then she reformed and *merely* socialized on occasion until she im-

> proved her grades.

20d   Avoid squinting modifiers.

A modifier placed between two words so that it can modify either word is said to squint.

SQUINTING
> Persons who exercise *frequently* will live longer.

CLEAR

    Frequently persons who exercise will live longer.

OR

    Persons who *frequently* exercise will live longer.

■ Exercise 8

Correct faulty modifiers in the following sentences.

          only

1. A pessimist ~~only~~ thinks of the dark side of life.
        ∧   **while still in pajamas,**

2. Early one morning in Kenya, the photographer saw a white ele-
               ∧

   phant.~~while still in pajamas.~~
        often *or* **People who read will often . . .**

3. People who read ~~often~~ will develop a good vocabulary.
     T ∧

4. ~~Looking~~ through a magnifying glass, the flaw in the diamond

   appeared to be a dark spot.
       who have strange beliefs

5. Listeners often call in to radio talk shows. ~~who have strange~~
        ∧

   ~~beliefs.~~
             three boys discovered

6. While strolling near a railroad track, a satchel of money. ~~was~~
                 ∧

   ~~discovered by three boys.~~
          even

7. The review did not even include a brief summary of the novel's
          ∧

   plot.
   Frequently t *or* **frequently**

8. Those who lose sleep ~~frequently~~ cannot function properly.
     ∧

          with sophisticated programs   **problems**

9. Computers can solve ~~problems~~ in minutes ~~with sophisticated~~

   ~~programs~~ that used to take months.

   Before sawing, t

10. ~~T~~he carpenter inspected the board ~~before sawing~~ for nails.

■ Exercise 9

Follow the instructions for Exercise 8.

           inexpensive

1. The restaurant offers meals for children.~~that are inexpensive.~~

         one must count

2. To diet effectively, calories.~~must be counted.~~

                 only

3. Visitors can ~~only~~ enter some countries if they have the proper

   credentials.

              the Pilgrims signed

4. Before landing at Plymouth, the Mayflower Compact.~~was signed~~

   ~~by the Pilgrims.~~

                     in the refrigerator

5. Serve some of the sandwiches now; keep the rest for the picnic.

   ~~in the refrigerator.~~

             T

6. ~~Deliberately and deviously,~~ ~~t~~he reporter said the senator had

   deliberately and deviously
   misled the press.

       one can often follow

7. Without thinking, a daily routine.~~can often be followed.~~

                the captain made
8. Desiring to calm the passengers, a witty remark.~~was made by~~

~~the captain~~.

    Frequently, e *or* **Experiencing failure leads frequently . . .**
9. ~~E~~xperiencing failure ~~frequently~~ leads to success.

                 the diver entered
10. Wishing to prevent the bends, the decompression chamber.~~was~~

~~entered by the diver~~.

21   Separation of Elements   *sep*

Do not needlessly separate closely related elements of a sentence.

21a   Separation of a subject and a verb, parts of a verb phrase, or a verb and an object can result in awkwardness and confusion.

AWKWARD SEPARATION OF SUBJECT AND VERB

> Former Senator John Glenn, because he is the oldest person ever to orbit the earth, has become a symbol of enduring vitality to elderly Americans.

IMPROVED

> Because former Senator John Glenn is the oldest person ever to orbit the earth, he has become a symbol of enduring vitality to elderly Americans.

PUZZLING POSSESSIVE

She is the man who owns the restaurant's wife.

CLEAR

She is the wife of the man who owns the restaurant.

21b Do not divide the parts of a sentence with a quotation long enough to cause excessive separation.

SEPARATION OF VERB AND SUBJECT BY A LONG QUOTATION

The candidate's opinion that "no citizen ever deserves free health care, even in advanced years" probably caused him to lose the election.

BETTER

The candidate probably lost the election because of his opinion that "no citizen ever deserves free health care, even in advanced years."

21c Generally, avoid using split infinitives.

A verbal with a modifier between *to* and the verb form is called a **split infinitive.** Some writers and readers object to split infinitives almost without exception. Others accept them when they are not noticeably awkward. Often it is easier to avoid using them than it is to defend them.

SPLIT

⌜ *splits the infinitive* ⌝
The nurse vowed to **strongly and bravely** *face* the disease.

BETTER

The nurse vowed to *face* the disease strongly and bravely.

■ **Exercise 10**

Revise separations in the following sentences.

1. Some early geographers failed to **see** clearly and without bias ~~see~~
   ∧

   that the earth could not be flat.

2. Paul Christopher's finding on grave-robbings—**is correct:** "Most resurrec-

   tionists [body snatchers] in the United States avoided grave-

   yards in highly populated areas in favor of paupers' plots."—~~is~~

   ~~correct.~~

3. ~~The Bible,~~ **B** because of its appeal to so many people over such a

   long period of time, has sold more copies than any another **the Bible**
   ∧

   book in America.

4. ~~Some infants have~~ **B** by the time they say their first words **, some infants have** already
   ∧

   cut several teeth.

5. ~~Members~~ **A** at the first meeting of the aerobics class **, members** were
   ∧

   asked to honestly and fairly ~~estimate~~ **estimate** what their body weight
   ∧

   should be.

22 Parallelism   *paral*

Use parallel grammatical forms to express parallel thoughts.

Elements in a sentence are *parallel* when one construction (or one part of speech) matches another: a phrase and a phrase, a clause and a clause, a verb and a verb, a noun and a noun, a verbal and a verbal, and so forth.

22a   Use parallel constructions with coordinating conjunctions *(and, but, for,* etc.).

NOT PARALLEL

          adjective   *verb*
            ↓   ↓

    Sailing ships were *stately* and *made* little noise.

PARALLEL

           adjectives
          ↙   ↘

    Sailing ships were *stately* and *quiet*.

NOT PARALLEL

                       nouns   *pronoun*
                     ↙   ↘   ↓

    Young Lincoln read widely for *understanding, knowledge,* and *he* just liked books.

PARALLEL

                            —— *nouns* ——
                               ↓

    Young Lincoln read widely for *understanding, knowledge,* and *pleasure*.

NOTE: Repeat an article *(a, an, the),* a preposition *(by, in, on,* etc.), the sign of an infinitive *(to),* or other key words to make parallelism clear.

UNCLEAR

The artist was *a* painter and sculptor of marble.

CLEAR

The artist was *a* painter and *a* sculptor of marble.

UNCLEAR

They passed the evening *by* eating and observing the crowds.

CLEAR

They passed the evening *by* eating and *by* observing the crowds.

22b Use parallel constructions with correlative conjunctions *(not only . . . but also, either . . . or,* etc.).

NOT PARALLEL

$$\overset{\textit{infinitive}}{\downarrow} \qquad \overset{\textit{preposition}}{\downarrow}$$

Petroleum is used **not only** *to make* fuels **but also** *in* plastics.

NOT PARALLEL

$$\overset{\textit{verb}}{\downarrow} \qquad \overset{\textit{preposition}}{\downarrow}$$

Not only *is* petroleum used in fuels **but also** *in* plastics.

PARALLEL

$$\overset{\textit{prepositions}}{\swarrow \qquad \searrow}$$

Petroleum is used **not only** *in* fuels **but also** *in* plastics.

NOT PARALLEL

$$\overset{\textit{adverb}}{\downarrow} \quad \overset{\textit{pronoun}}{\downarrow}$$

The speeches were **either** *too* long, **or** *they* were not long enough.

NOT PARALLEL

>   *article*   *adverb*
>   ↓   ↓
> **Either** *the* speeches were too long **or** *too* short.

PARALLEL

>   *adverbs*
>   ↙   ↘
> The speeches were **either** *too* long **or** *too* short.

PARALLEL

> **Either** the speeches were too long, **or** they were too short.

22c   Use parallel constructions with *and who* and with *and which.*

Avoid using *and who, and which,* or *and that* unless they are preceded by a matching *who, which,* or *that.*

NOT PARALLEL

> The position calls for a person with an open mind *and who* is coolheaded.

PARALLEL

> The position calls for a person *who* is open-minded *and who* is coolheaded.

PARALLEL

> The position calls for a person with an open mind and a cool head.

NOT PARALLEL

> A new dam was built to control floods *and that* would furnish recreation.

PARALLEL

> A new dam was built to control floods and to furnish recreation.

■ **Exercise 11**

Revise sentences with faulty parallelism. Write C by any correct sentence.

1. Lawrence of Arabia was a soldier, an adventurer, and ~~he wrote a book~~. **an author.**

2. From an early age, the aspiring astronomer believed that his mission was to look farther into space than anyone else had looked and ~~making~~ **to make** new discoveries about distances in the universe.

3. Floppy disks are coated with magnetic material, covered by a protective jacket, and are ~~for use~~ **used** in microcomputers.

4. At the time it appeared ~~either~~ impossible **either** ∧ to get around the crowd or to go through it.

5. Children generally like bubble gum because it is appealingly packaged, sweet, and ~~it lasts a long time~~. **long lasting.**

6. The archaeologists decided to move to another site after spending three months digging, sifting, and ~~unable to find~~ **finding** ~~anything~~ **nothing** of significance.

7. A young ballerina must practice long hours, give up pleasures, and ~~one has to~~ be able to take severe criticism.

8. The ~~performance was~~ **performance** long, boring, ~~and~~ made everyone in the
   ∧
   audience restless.

C   9. Roaming through the great north woods, camping by a lake, and getting away from crowds are good ways to forget the cares of civilization.

10. The common cold brings on the following symptoms: a scratchy throat, a running nose, and ~~you are generally fatigued.~~ **general fatigue.**

23 Variety *var*

Vary sentences in structure, order, and length.

An unbroken series of short sentences may become monotonous and may fail to indicate intricate relationships among ideas (see **15**).

Structure and pattern

Write simple, compound, and complex sentences (see p. 167). Write loose, periodic, and balanced sentences. A **loose sentence,** the most common kind, makes a main point early and then adds further comments and details.

LOOSE

> There are only two or three human stories, and they go on repeating
> themselves as fiercely as if they had never happened before.
>
> WILLA CATHER

> Conversation is necessary because it is a means by which people com-
> municate ideas and ideals.

PERIODIC

A **periodic sentence** withholds an element of the main thought until the end to create suspense and emphasis.

> Three people may keep a secret if two of them are dead.
>
> BENJAMIN FRANKLIN

> Under a government which imprisons any unjustly, the true place for a
> just man is also a prison.
>
> HENRY DAVID THOREAU

Balanced sentences

A **balanced sentence** has parallel parts that are similar in structure,
length, and thought. Indeed, *balance* is simply a word for a kind of
parallelism (see **22**).

BALANCED

> Knowledge comes, but wisdom lingers.
>
> ALFRED, LORD TENNYSON

> That which is bitter to endure may be sweet to remember.
>
> THOMAS FULLER

> It is as easy to deceive oneself without perceiving it as it is difficult to
> deceive others without their perceiving it.
>
> LA ROCHEFOUCAULD

A sentence can be balanced even if only parts of it are symmetrical. The balance in the next sentence consists of nouns in one group that are parallel to adjectives in the other.

> Thus the Puritan was made up of two different men, the one all self-abasement, penitence, gratitude, passion; the other proud, calm, inflexible, sagacious.
>
> THOMAS BABINGTON MACAULAY

Thus
the Puritan
was made up
of two different men,

the one – – – – – – – – – the other
all self-abasement, – – – – – – proud,
penitence, – – – – – – – – calm,
gratitude, – – – – – – – – inflexible,
passion; – – – – – – – – sagacious.

The following passage dealing with the use of the live oak tree in shipbuilding is monotonous because of its unrelenting use of loose sentences.

> The wood from live oak trees was ideal for building sailing ships because of many characteristics. The shape of the tree's trunk and branches was one characteristic. The wood was also ideal for shipbuilding because it is dense, hard, strong, tough, and heavy. It is the heaviest of American woods. It is close-grained and therefore durable when in contact with soil and water. It has no characteristic odor. It did not cause nausea among people confined to the holds of ships. Other kinds of wood are subject to fungus attacks. The fungi rot the wood and cause a foul odor. This rotting odor became intolerable for anyone forced to stay below when the hatches were battened down.

Study the difference between the preceding paragraph and the one following, which exhibits variety in sentence structure.

> In the building of sailing ships, several kinds of wood were acceptable, but that of the live oak tree was ideal. Many characteristics contributed

to its suitability: the shape of the trunk and branches, its density, its hardness, its strength, and its heaviness. In fact, of all American woods, it is the heaviest. Since it is close-grained, it proved to be durable when in contact with soil and water. Because it has no characteristic odor and resists fungi, it did not cause nausea in people confined to the holds of ships with the hatches battened down. The timber of ships made of other woods rotted from the fungus attacks that produced foul odors, but the wood of the live oak tree remained free of fungi and odorless.

Adapted from LAURENCE C. WALKER,
Trees

Order and sequence in sentences

The most common order for a sentence is SUBJECT—VERB—OBJECT. This is a natural pattern in English, and it is fundamental to the language.

USUAL ORDER

    subject verb   *object*   *modifiers* —————————————→
     ↓   ↓   ↓
    She attributed these defects in her son's character to the general weak-
    nesses of humankind.

If several consecutive sentences follow this order, however, they can become monotonous and reduce reader interest. Change the order occasionally. Study the following ways to create variety in word order.

SENTENCE BEGINNING WITH ADVERB
    Quickly the swordfish broke the surface of the water.

INVERTED SENTENCE BEGINNING WITH CLAUSE USED AS OBJECT
    That the engineer tried to stop the train, none would deny.

SENTENCE BEGINNING WITH PARTICIPIAL PHRASE
    Flying low over the water, the plane searched for the reef.

SENTENCE BEGINNING WITH DIRECT OBJECT
    These *defects* in her son's character she attributed to the general weak-
    nesses of humanity.

SENTENCE BEGINNING WITH PREPOSITIONAL PHRASE

> *To the general weaknesses of humanity* she attributed the defects in her son's character.

■ **Exercise 12**

Rewrite the following sentences and make them periodic. If you consider a sentence already periodic, write P *by it.*

1. ~~Very~~ **A** ~~is~~ a word much overused in the English language **is *very*.**

P 2. The story that Sir Isaac Newton formulated the law of gravity after watching an apple fall can be traced to one man, Voltaire.

3. ~~A sense of humor is one quality that~~ **N** no great leader can be without **one quality: a sense of humor.**

4. Virginia Woolf was the daughter of ~~Leslie Stephen,~~ a well-known English writer **, Leslie Stephen.**

5. One machine, ~~the computer,~~ is revolutionizing science, streamlining business practice, and influencing profoundly the writing habits of many authors **: the computer.**

■ **Exercise 13**

Rewrite the following sentences to give them balanced constructions.
Place a B by any sentence that is already balanced.

        Wanting   **is wise;**

1. ~~It is wise to want~~ to bring one's weight down to normal, ~~but~~
   wanting to bring it far below normal   ∧
   ~~when the desire goes far beyond that, it~~ is dangerous.

2. The highest peak in North America is Mount McKinley; ~~Mount~~
                                    is Mount Everest.
   ~~Everest is~~ the highest peak in the world, ∧

3. A trained ear hears many separate instruments in an orchestra,
        an untutored ear hears only
   but the melody. ~~is often all that is herd by the untutored.~~
      ∧

B 4. Realists know their limitations; romantics know only what

      they want.

B 5. Our moods affect our perception of nature as our perception

      of nature affects our moods.

Punctuation

---

24 Commas ,

Use commas to separate parts of sentences and to assure clarity.

Use **commas** (1) to separate equal elements such as independent clauses and items in a series and (2) to set off modifiers or parenthetical words, phrases, and clauses within a sentence. Use a comma *before* and *after* to set off an element.

before ---- & ---- *after*

The new bridge, a triumph of engineering, is attracting much attention.

24a Use a comma to separate independent clauses joined by a coordinating conjunction (see p. 91–92).

coordinating conjunction

Most children dislike coffee, yet many of them like it as they grow older.

coordinating conjunction

Computers are useful and effective, but they will never replace books.

NOTE: The comma is sometimes omitted before a coordinating conjunction between the clauses when they are brief and there is no danger of misreading.

The weather cleared and the aircraft departed.

24b Use commas between words, phrases, or clauses in a series.

The closet contained worn clothes, old shoes, and dusty hats.

The final comma before *and* in a series is sometimes omitted, as in journalistic styles.

> The closet contained worn clothes, old shoes and dusty hats.

But the comma must be used when *and* is omitted.

> The closet contained worn clothes, old shoes, dusty hats.

And it must be used to avoid misreading.

> An old chest in the corner was filled with nails, hammers, a hacksaw and blades, and a brace and bit.

Series of phrases or of dependent or independent clauses are also separated by commas.

PHRASES

> We hunted for the letter in the album, in the old trunks, and even under the rug.

DEPENDENT CLAUSES

> Finally we concluded that the letter had been burned, that someone had taken it, or that it had never been written.

INDEPENDENT CLAUSES

> We left the attic, Father locked the door, and Mother suggested that we never unlock it again.

In a series of independent clauses, the comma is not omitted before the final element.

■ Exercise 1

Insert commas where necessary.

1. Pets may prevent anxiety, or so it has been argued.

2. A good speaker should organize her subject carefully ʌ enunciate

clearly to be understood ʌ and practice effective timing.

3. Quilts were once made slowly by hand ʌ but now they are mass-

produced.

4. The sales manager ʌ the trainee ʌ and a secretary visited branch

offices in Pittsburgh ʌ in Dallas ʌ and in San Diego.

5. Rest is often necessary ʌ for the body needs time to recuperate.

6. The sensitive child knew that the earth was round ʌ but she

thought that she was on the inside of it.

7. The reporter wrote that the students were exuberant ʌ that the

parents were sedate ʌ that the teachers were reticent ʌ and that the

police were bored and sleepy.

8. For breakfast the menu offered only bacon and eggs ʌ toast and

jelly ʌ and hot coffee.

9. Careless driving may include speeding ʌ stopping suddenly ʌ turn-

ing from the wrong lane ʌ going through red lights ʌ and failing to

yield the right of way.

10. Do not underestimate your enemies⌃for to do so could be a

grave mistake.

24c Use a comma between coordinate adjectives not joined by *and*. Do not use a comma between cumulative adjectives.

Coordinate adjectives modify a noun independently.

COORDINATE

We entered a forest of tall, slender, straight pines.

Ferocious, alert, loyal dogs were essential to safety in the Middle Ages.

Cumulative adjectives modify a whole cluster of subsequent adjectives and a noun.

CUMULATIVE

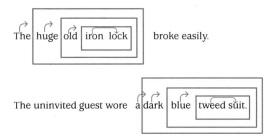

The huge old iron lock broke easily.

The uninvited guest wore a dark blue tweed suit.

Two tests are helpful.

Test One

And is natural only between coordinate adjectives.

> tall *and* slender *and* straight pines
> ferocious *and* alert *and* loyal dogs

BUT NOT
> dark *and* blue *and* tweed suit
> huge *and* old *and* iron lock

Test Two

Coordinate adjectives are easily reversible.

> straight, slender, tall pines
> loyal, alert, ferocious dogs

BUT NOT
> tweed blue dark suit
> iron old huge lock

The distinction is not always clear-cut, however, and the sense of the cluster must be the deciding factor.

She was wearing a full-skirted,  low-cut velvet gown.

[a velvet gown that was full skirted and low cut, not a gown that was full skirted and low cut and velvet]

■ Exercise 2

Insert commas where necessary. When in doubt, apply the previously described tests. Write C by sentences that require no commas.

C 1. Lhasa apso dogs have coarse straight hair.

2. From the ancient castle issued a shrill, prolonged, weird sound.

3. A prosecuting attorney needs a steady, penetrating, stern eye.

C 4. A red fox often has dusky reddish-brown fur.

C 5. The torn brown paper bag contained a fortune in cash.

6. Sarah Bernhardt was a beautiful, talented, creative actress.

7. That bitterly cold, dark, snowy day was etched in his memory.

C 8. The toga was a large loose outer garment worn by Roman

citizens.   **optional**

9. Ancient Rome was a dauntless, highly organized, widely feared

power in ancient times.

10. A slight, delicate, agreeable scent arose from the garden.

24d Use a comma after an introductory phrase
or clause.

PHRASE

> With the most difficult part of the trek behind him, the traveler felt
> more confident.

CLAUSE

> When the most difficult part of the trek was behind him, the traveler
> felt more confident.

NOTE: A comma is always correct after introductory elements, but if the phrase or clause is short and cannot be misread, the comma may be omitted.

SHORT PHRASE
> After the ordeal the traveler felt more confident.

SHORT CLAUSE
> When day came the traveler felt more confident.

BUT

               comma needed to prevent misreading
                   ↓
> When sixty-five, people often consider retirement.

Introductory verbal phrases are usually set off by commas.

PARTICIPLE
> Living for centuries, redwoods often reach great heights.

INFINITIVE
> To verify a hypothesis, a scientist performs an experiment.

24e Use commas to set off nonessential elements.

A **nonessential (nonrestrictive) element** adds information that describes but does not alter the essential meaning of the sentence. When the modifier is omitted, the sentence loses some meaning but does not change radically.

NONESSENTIAL
> The painter's latest work, *a landscape,* has achieved wide acclaim.
> Salt, *which is plentiful in this country,* is inexpensive.
> Languages contain abstract words, *which do not convey concrete images.*

NOTE: *That* should never introduce a nonessential clause. *That* or *which* may, however, introduce an essential clause.

NOT

Salt**,** *that* is plentiful in this country**,** is inexpensive.

BUT

Salt**,** *which* is plentiful in this country**,** is inexpensive.

An **essential (restrictive) element** furnishes information that cannot be removed without radically changing the meaning of the sentence.

ESSENTIAL

The Russian ruler *Nicholas* was married to Alexandra.

Huge signs *that are displayed along a stretch of Highway 627* advertise a place called The Hornet's Nest.

Words *that convey images* are important in poetry.

In all these sentences, the italicized expressions identify the words they modify; to remove the modifiers would change the meaning.

Some modifiers can be either essential or nonessential; use or omission of commas changes the sense.

The coin that gleamed in the sunlight was a Spanish doubloon.
[There were several coins.]
The coin**,** which gleamed in the sunlight**,** was a Spanish doubloon.
[There was only one coin.]

■ Exercise 3

The clauses in six of the following sentences are restrictive and require no commas. Write R, No Commas *by each of the six. The clauses in the other four are nonrestrictive. Insert commas at the proper places in those four and write* Nonr.

R, No Commas 1. Do not use commas to set off a clause that is restrictive.

R, No Commas 2. Camels that have two humps come from central Asia.

Nonr 3. Dinosaurs , which had cold blood , were not mammals.

Nonr 4. Few people know that the foul-smelling seeds of ginkgo trees , which originally came from Asia , enclose an edible inner kernel.

R, No Commas 5. Universities usually give the highest rank and the most money to professors who conduct research.

R, No Commas 6. Workers who came from Latin America picked all the oranges.

Nonr 7. Gladiators , who fought animals or other men for the entertainment of the spectators , might have been captives or slaves.

Nonr 8. The church catholic , which is the Christian church as a whole , includes all the Catholic and Protestant churches.

R, No Commas 9. Viewers of television shows who do not hear well need to know that closed captioning is sometimes available.

R, No Commas 10. Baseball fans who do not grasp the game's many rules want a broadcaster's explanations.

■ Exercise 4

The following pairs of sentences illustrate differences in meaning that result from use or omission of commas with modifiers. Answer the questions about each pair of sentences.

1. A. In Allison Long's novel, *Only Once,* the heroine is a doctor.
   B. In Allison Long's novel *Only Once,* the heroine is a doctor.

   In which sentence has Allison Long written only one novel? **A**

2. A. People who have faults should not find fault with others.
   B. People, who have faults, should not find fault with others.

   Which sentence implies that all people have faults? **B**

3. A. The winter, which is mild in Virginia, seems to pass rapidly.
   B. The winter that is mild in Virginia seems to pass rapidly.

   Which sentence describes what winters are generally like in **A**
   Virginia?

4. A. The moviegoers who did not understand Japanese welcomed
      the English subtitles.
   B. The moviegoers, who did not understand Japanese, welcomed the English subtitles.

   Which sentence suggests that some moviegoers did not de- **A**
   pend on English subtitles?

5. A. Anthropologists, who respect native ways, are welcome among most tribes.
   B. Anthropologists who respect native ways are welcome among most tribes.

   Which sentence reflects confidence in anthropologists? **A**

■ Exercise 5

Write Y by sentences that need commas in the places indicated, N by those that do not.

Y 1. Eric's only brother ⋀ Jason ⋀ decided to move to Australia.

N 2. Barbers ⋀ who are bald ⋀ often recommend cures for baldness.

N 3. The American composer ⋀ George Gershwin ⋀ wrote *Rhapsody in Blue.*

Y 4. Because of the extremely hot climate in the tropics ⋀ many of the citizens wear large straw hats.

Y 5. The most beautiful photograph ⋀ a white bird against a darkening sky ⋀ was made on a small island.

Y 6. According to the latest national survey of gender in our country ⋀ women outnumber men.

N 7. All lawyers ⋀ who are dishonest ⋀ should be disbarred.

N 8. Only those ⋀ who have the price of admission ⋀ may enter.

Y 9. Throughout a period of about twenty minutes ⋀ the candidate never stopped talking.

Y 10. During those long days of waiting and watching Elvin Grotte a
                                                    ∧   ∧
teacher at the local community college never gave up hope that
                                              ∧
his wife would be found.

24f Use commas to set off sentence modifiers,
conjunctive adverbs, and sentence elements out of normal
word order.

Modifiers like *on the other hand, for example, in fact, in the first place, I
believe, in my opinion, fortunately,* and *certainly* are set off by commas.

> Some poets, fortunately, do make a living by writing.
> Thomas Hardy's poems, I believe, raise probing questions.

Commas are frequently used with **conjunctive adverbs** such as *accordingly, anyhow, besides, consequently, furthermore, hence, however, indeed, instead, likewise, meanwhile, moreover, nevertheless,
otherwise, still, then, therefore, thus.*

BEFORE CLAUSE
> The auditor checked the figures again; therefore, the mistake was dis-
> covered.

WITHIN CLAUSE
> The auditor checked the figures again; the mistake, therefore, was dis-
> covered.

Commas **always** separate the conjunctive adverb *however* from the
rest of the sentence.

> The auditor found the error in the figures; however, the books still did
> not balance.
> The auditor found the error in the figures; the books, however, still did
> not balance.

Commas are not used when *however* is an adverb meaning "no matter how."

> *However* fast the hare ran, it could not catch the tortoise.

Use commas if necessary for clarity or emphasis when part of a sentence is out of normal order.

NOT NORMAL ORDER
> Confident and alert, the young woman invested her own money.

OR
> The young woman, confident and alert, invested her own money.

NORMAL ORDER
> The confident and alert young woman invested her own money.

24g Use commas with degrees and titles and with elements in dates, places, and addresses.

DEGREES AND TITLES
> Sharon Weiss, M.A., applied for the position.
> Louis Ferranti, Jr., owns the tallest building in the city.
> Alphonse Jefferson, chief of police, made the arrest.

DATES
> Sunday, May 31, is her birthday.
> July 1994 was very wet. [Commas around 1994 are also acceptable.]
> July 20, 1969, was the date when a human being first stepped on the moon. [Use commas *before* and *after*.]
> He was born 31 December 1970. [Use no commas.]
> The year 1980 was a time of change. [Essential; use no commas.]

PLACES

Cairo, Illinois, is my hometown. [Use commas *before* and *after*.]

ADDRESSES

Write the editor of *The Atlantic*, 8 Arlington Street, Boston, Massachusetts 02116. [Use no comma before the zip code.]

24h Use commas for contrast or emphasis and with short interrogative elements.

The pilot used an auxiliary landing field, not the city airport.

The field was safe enough, wasn't it?

24i Use commas with mild interjections and with words like *yes* and *no*.

Well, no one thought it was possible.

No, it proved to be simple.

24j Use commas with words in direct address and after the salutation of a personal letter.

Driver, stop the bus.

Dear John,

It has been some time since I've written. . . .

24k Use commas with expressions like *he said, she remarked,* and *she replied* when used with quoted matter.

"I am planning to enroll in Latin," she said, "at the beginning of next term."

He replied, "It's all Greek to me."

24l   Set off an absolute phrase with commas.

An **absolute phrase** consists of a noun followed by a modifier. It modifies the sentence as a whole, not any single element in it.

> ┌─*absolute phrase*─┐
> **Our day's journey over,** we made camp for the night.

> ┌─*absolute phrase*─┐
> **The portrait having dried,** the artist hung it on the wall.

24m   Use commas to prevent misreading or to mark an omission.

> After washing and grooming**,** the poodle looked like a different dog.
> When violently angry**,** elephants trumpet.
> Beyond**,** the open fields sloped gently to the sea.

> *verb omitted*
> ↓
> To err *is* human; to forgive**,** divine. [Note that *is,* the verb omitted, is the same as the one stated.]

■ Exercise 6

Add necessary commas. If a sentence is correct as written, place a C by it.

1. To an ambitious person ‸**,** receiving much fame quickly is dangerous; receiving none at all ‸**,** devastating.

2. Geelong ‸**,** a city with an unusual name, is in South Victoria ‸**,** Australia.

3. A few hours before he was scheduled to leave, the mercenary visited his father, who pleaded with him to change his mind and then finally said quietly, "Good luck."

C 4. Large winglike fins enable flying fish to glide through the air.

5. Inside, the automobile looked almost new; however, it was battered on the outside.

6. History, one would think, ought to teach people not to make the same mistakes again.

7. The Vandyke beard, according to authorities, was named after Sir Anthony Van Dyck, a famous Flemish painter.

C 8. Measles is an acute, infectious viral disease that is recognizable by red circular spots.

9. Moving holidays from the middle of the week to Monday, a recent national practice, gives workers more consecutive days without work.

10. While burning, cedar has a distinct, strong odor.

■ Exercise 7

Follow the instructions for Exercise 6.

1. Seattle Pacific University according to its catalog was founded in Seattle Washington in 1891.

2. A small and affectionate dog of German breed the dachshund has a long body short legs and drooping ears.

3. A woman of spotless reputation and widely admired wisdom, Abigail Lindstrom R.N. will be greatly missed.

C 4. Most visitors who see the White House for the first time are surprised because it seems smaller than expected.

5. Discovered in 1799 the Rosetta stone a black basalt tablet offered the first clue fortunately to the deciphering of Egyptian hieroglyphics.

6. While the mystery writer was composing his last novel *The Tiger's Eye* he received a note warning him not to write about anyone he knew in the Orient.

7. The race being over, the jockey who rode the winning horse turned to the owner and said, "Now, Mrs. Astor, you have the money and the trophy."

8. The Levant is a region that includes Greece, Turkey, and Egypt.

9. Highway 280, known as "the world's most beautiful freeway," connects San Francisco and San Jose.

10. Of late, streets of Hollywood, California, have been undergoing restoration.

■ Exercise 8

Add necessary commas.

1. A set of encyclopedia volumes is helpful, but a good dictionary is indispensable.

2. Yes, I prefer small, economical cars.

3. Attempting to save money as well as time, some shoppers go to the grocery store only once a month; others, however, go almost daily.

4. The guest fell into a chair propped his feet on an ottoman placed his hands behind his head and yawned as the host glared at him.

5. However the travelers followed the worn outdated city map they always returned to the same place.

6. The last selection on the program a waltz by Strauss brought the most applause I believe.

7. Above the sky was peppered with tiny dark birds.

8. Ruth Friar Ph.D. was awarded her honorary degree on June 1 1947 in Fulton Missouri.

9. Yes friends the time has come for pausing not planning.

10. With a major snowstorm on the way people should stock up on bread milk and eggs shouldn't they?

25 Unnecessary Commas   no,

Do not use commas where they do not belong.

Do not sprinkle a page with unneeded commas. Some pauses within a sentence do not require a comma. When in doubt, use no comma.

25a Do not use just one comma to separate a subject and a verb, a verb and an object, or an adjective and the word it modifies. Do not use a comma to separate two compound subjects or two compound verbs joined by *and* except for special emphasis.

incorrect single comma

The driver frustrated by the traffic, closed his eyes and tried to imagine that he was swimming in a mountain stream.

NOTE: A short modifier or appositive between a subject and a verb may be set off by *two* commas.

correct

The driver, frustrated by the traffic, closed his eyes.

incorrect between verb and object

One student had forgotten to read, "Stopping by Woods on a Snowy Evening."

incorrect between adjective and word it modifies

The stubborn, mischievous, child did not hear the music.

not between two subjects with and

For once the umpire, and the coach agreed.

not between two compound predicates with and

The driver agreed to the terms, and signed the contract.

25b Do not use a comma to set off essential (restrictive) clauses, phrases, or appositives.

[essential to the meaning]
Playwrights **,** *who create several failures* **,** cannot find backers.

delete

[essential to the meaning]
Toni Morrison's novel **,** *Beloved* **,** has been highly praised.

delete

25c Do not use a comma between adjectives that are not coordinate, between an adverb and an adjective, or between an adjective and a noun.

no commas
A *dark green canvas* awning gave the cottage a look of comfort.
[cumulative adjectives]

no comma
The badly damaged ship finally reached its destination.
[adverb] [adjective]

no comma
The stubborn, mischievous child would not respond to questions.
[adjective]   [noun]

25d Do not use a comma after a coordinating conjunction.

wrong
All entries must be submitted by Wednesday, and **,** the winner will be announced on Friday.

wrong
↓
Nor, will the judges allow late entries under any circumstances.

25e Do not use a comma before the subordinating conjunction (*after, although, because, before, if, since, unless, until, when, where*) when an adverbial clause follows an independent clause.

no comma
↓
We cannot leave today because the roads are impassable.

no comma
↓
Do not call unless an emergency arises.

25f Do not use a comma after the opening phrase of an inverted sentence (see p. 199).

no comma
↓
Close to the water's edge sits the house with seven gables.

25g Do not use a comma before the first item in a series or after the last.

no commas
The ancient chest contained rubies, emeralds, and pearls in abundance.

25h Do not use a comma before *than* in a comparison.

no comma
↓
The pelican is a larger bird than the seagull.

25i Do not use a comma after *like* or *such as*.

no comma
↓
The coin looked like a Spanish doubloon.

no comma
↓
A language such as Latin is no longer spoken.

25j Do not use a comma with a period, a question mark, a dash, or an exclamation point.

no comma
↓
"Is there a motel nearby?" asked the traveler.

25k Do not use a comma before parentheses.

no comma
↓
The celebration (for the mayor's re-election) lasted all day and all night.

■ Exercise 9

Circle all unnecessary commas; be prepared to explain your decisions.

optional

1. A region in western Canada, the Klondike⊙ once attracted⊙ gold miners, adventurers, and opportunists⊙ in abundance.

2. Tasmanian wolves⊙ were once common⊙ in Australia, but now they are confined to remote parts of Tasmania.

3. Restaurants͵ that serve excellent food at modest prices͵ are always popular among local people, though tourists seldom know about them.

4. In the wintry far north of Scandinavia, means of transportation like͵ snowshoes, skis, and sleds have to be used͵ because vehicles͵ with wheels͵ are impractical.

5. Ticket holders standing at the end of the line͵ worried that they would not find seats͵ or that the only available seats would be too far forward in the theater.

6. Although the composer had indicated that the piece was to be played adagio͵ (slowly), the conductor, sensing the audience's boredom, increased the tempo.

7. Communities͵ near large airports͵ have become increasingly aware that noise pollution can be just as unpleasant as impurities in the air or in streams.

8. Once, huge movie houses were fashionable, but now most of these palaces are like dinosaurs: that is, extinct͵ giants that are curious reminders͵ of the past.

9. The Olympic runner was disqualified, after he ran out of his lane, but he would not have won a gold medal, anyway.

10. The accountant vowed that she would never work for the millionaire again, and that she would go back to her small firm.

■ Exercise 10

Circle all unnecessary commas. Write C by any correct sentence.

1. The markup on handbags, was much more, than on shoes, on which the profit margin was slim.

2. Sales on sandals were seasonal, and unprofitable.

3. The most famous of all labyrinths, was that built by, Daedalus, for King Minos of Crete.

4. A filmy, cobweb wafted on the air, until a brisk wind carried it away.

C 5. The prairie dog is a small, quick rodent with a barking cry.

6. Marie Hautbois, who had just joined the orchestra, found an oboe in an antique shop, and, she discovered that it was made in the seventeenth century.

7. She purchased the instrument⊙ and told her conductor, Augustine Sey, of her great⊙ fortune.

8. Upon first gazing at the Great Pyramid of Khufu, the tourist said that it was "prodigious⊙" and that it was "inspiring beyond measure."

9. He found it grander⊙ than the falls⊙ that he had visited on the Zambezi River in Africa⊙ or the Grand Canyon⊙ (which he had seen the previous year), a popular tourist attraction in the United States.

10. Mammals such as⊙ whales⊙ and dolphins have flippers.

26 Semicolons ;

Use a semicolon between independent clauses not joined by coordinating conjunctions (*and, but, for, nor, or, so, yet*) and between coordinate elements with internal commas.

Omitting a semicolon between independent clauses may result in a comma splice or a fused sentence (see **6**).

26a Use a semicolon between independent clauses not connected by a coordinating conjunction.

WITH NO CONNECTIVE

For fifteen years the painting was stored in the attic; even the artist forgot about it.

WITH A CONJUNCTIVE ADVERB

A specialist from the museum arrived and asked to examine it; *then* all the family became excited.

See **24f** for use of commas with conjunctive adverbs.

WITH A SENTENCE MODIFIER

The painting was valuable; *in fact,* the museum offered one hundred thousand dollars for it.

See **24f** for use of commas with sentence modifiers, such as *on the other hand, for example, in fact,* or *in the first place.*

Notice the use of semicolons in the following paragraph, a light-hearted treatment of semicolons.

The semicolon tells you that there is still some question about the preceding full sentence; something needs to be added; it reminds you sometimes of the Greek usage. It is almost always a greater pleasure to come across a semicolon than a period. The period tells you that that is that; if you did not get all the meaning you wanted or expected, anyway you got all the writer intended to parcel out and now you have to move along. But with a semicolon there you get a pleasant little feeling of expectancy; there is more to come; read on; it will get clearer.

LEWIS THOMAS
The Medusa and the Snail

26b Use a semicolon to separate independent clauses that are long and complex or that have internal punctuation.

In many compound sentences either a semicolon or a comma can be used.

COMMA OR SEMICOLON

Moby-Dick, by Melville, is an adventure story **,** [*or* **;**] and it is also one of the world's greatest philosophical novels.

SEMICOLON PREFERRED

Ishmael, the narrator, goes to sea, he says, "whenever it is a damp, drizzly November" in his soul **;** and Ahab, the captain of the ship, goes to sea because of his obsession to hunt and kill the great white whale, Moby Dick.

26c Use semicolons in a series between items that have internal punctuation.

The small reference library included a few current periodicals, those most often read **;** a set of encyclopedia volumes (the *Americana,* I believe) **;** several dictionaries, both abridged and unabridged **;** and various bibliographical tools.

26d Do not use a semicolon between elements that are not grammatically equal.

```
┌──────────dependent clauses──────────┐
After the rains increased and the winds blew hard;

┌──────independent clause──────┐              ↑
the sea became much rougher.          incorrect (use ,)
```

NOT BETWEEN A CLAUSE AND A PHRASE

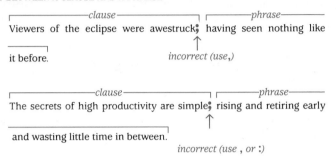

—clause—
Viewers of the eclipse were awestruck; having seen nothing like
it before.   *incorrect (use,)*

—clause—   —phrase—
The secrets of high productivity are simple; rising and retiring early
and wasting little time in between.
                              incorrect (use , or :)

■ **Exercise 11**

*Insert semicolons and change commas to semicolons where needed.
Write* C *by any correct sentence.*

1. Covered bridges once spanned many streams of New England ;
they are rare now.

2. It was a warm, humid evening in, as I remember, mid-August ;
and just outside the battered screen door, mosquitoes, thou-
sands of them, gathered as crickets chattered madly.

3. The assignment was to seek out successful, experienced exec-
utives, to interview them, asking particular questions about educational training, and to determine just how important they
themselves, looking back, considered their college training.

C   4. An advanced civilization is guided by enlightened self-interest; however, it is also marked by unselfish good will.

C   5. The Pawnees, who lived at one time in the valley of the Platte River in Nebraska, were once a numerous people; but their numbers diminished when the group, part of a confederacy of North American Plains Indians, moved from their ancestral homes to northern Oklahoma.

6. Irving was careful ; his friends said that he was indecisive.

7. The storm knocked down power lines, leaving the town dark ; uprooted trees, leaving the streets blocked ; and forced water over the levee, leaving the neighborhoods near the river flooded.

8. The gloomy hallway was narrow, long, and dark ; and at the end of it hung a dim, obscure painting of a lean, haggard beggar in eighteenth-century London.

9. The soybean plant is now widely cultivated in America ; it is native, however, to China and Japan.

10. Fortunetelling still appeals to many people ; they continue to patronize charlatans like palm readers.

27 Colons :

Use a colon as a formal mark of introduction.

Think of the colon as an arrow pointing to what follows it.

27a Use a colon after a formal introduction of a quotation.

> The editor of *Familiar Quotations* named his "foremost" purpose: "a salvage of those words which users of the English tongue have shown evidence not willingly to let die."

27b Use a colon after a formal introduction of a series of items.

BEFORE A SERIES

> An excellent physician exhibits four broad characteristics: [→] knowledge, skill, compassion, and integrity.

27c Use a colon after a formal introduction of an appositive.

An **appositive** is a word, phrase, or clause used as a noun and placed beside another word to explain, identify, or rename it.

> One factor is often missing from modern labor: pleasure in work. [Pleasure in work *is* the factor.]
>
> The author made a difficult decision: he would abandon the script. [To abandon the script *is* the decision.]

Frequently appositives are preceded by expressions like *namely* and
that is.

> The new law calls for a big change: namely, truth in advertising. [Note
> that the colon comes **before** *namely,* not after.]

27d Use a colon between two independent clauses when one explains the other.

> Music communicates: it is an expression of deep feeling.

27e Use a colon after the salutation of a formal letter, between figures indicating hours and minutes, and in bibliographical entries.

Dear Dr. Tyndale:	*PMLA* 99 (1984): 75
12:15 P.M.	Boston: Houghton, 1929

27f Do not use a colon after a linking verb or after a preposition.

NOT AFTER LINKING VERB

> *no colon*
> ↓
> Some chief noisemakers **are** automobiles and airplanes.

NOT AFTER PREPOSITION

> *no colon*
> ↓
> His friend accused him **of** wiggling in his seat, talking during the lec-
> ture, and not remembering what was said.

■ Exercise 12

Circle unnecessary colons, substituting other marks of punctuation when appropriate; add or substitute colons as necessary. Write C by sentences that are correct.

1. According to historians, the first ascent of Mount Everest was made by: Edmund Hillary and Tenzing Norgay.

2. Hillary and Norgay reached the top of Everest on May 29: 1953, at 6:50 in the morning.

3. Some climbers, however, dispute this historical account: they believe the first ascent was accomplished by George Mallory.

4. In 1924: Mallory disappeared while attempting an ascent of that same Himalayan giant, Mount Everest.

C   5. A few years ago another climbing party high on the mountain made an amazing discovery: a frozen body clad in climbing clothes of the 1920s.

6. Mallory's explanation of why he was trying to climb Everest has become famous: "Because it is there."

7. One of the greatest dangers in mountaineering is pulmonary edema: namely, the leakage of blood into the lungs.

8. Physicians on expeditions typically use two techniques to fight the symptoms: constant administration of oxygen and immediate evacuation to lower altitudes.

9. The route up the north face of Everest is steep, unprotected, and subject to avalanches.

C 10. A successful climbing expedition depends on three crucial elements: physical skill, psychological strength, and an element of luck.

28 Dashes --

Use dashes to indicate sudden interruptions, to provide emphasis, and to introduce summary statements after a series.

NOTE: In typing, a dash is shown by two hyphens--like this--usually with no space before, after, or between.

FOR SUDDEN INTERRUPTIONS (USUALLY IN SPEECH)
      That September--no, it was late August--the rain fell unceasingly.

TO PROVIDE EMPHASIS
      George--that unabashed extrovert--screamed encouragement to the timid candidate.

FOR SUMMARY (AFTER A SERIES)
      Hand fans, window fans, attic fans--all were ineffective that torrid summer.

29 Parentheses   ( )

Use parentheses to enclose a loosely related comment or explanation, figures that number items in a series, and references in documentation.

FOR A COMMENT

The frisky colt (it was not a thoroughbred) brought a good price at the auction.

A parenthetical sentence within another sentence has no period or capital, as in the previous example. A freestanding parenthetical sentence requires parentheses, a capital, and a period.

$$\underset{capital}{\downarrow} \qquad\qquad\qquad \underset{period\ here}{\downarrow}$$

On that day all flights were on time. (The weather was clear.)

FOR FIGURES IN A SERIES

The investor refused to buy the land because (1) it was too remote, (2) it was too expensive, and (3) the owner did not have a clear title.

FOR DATES OF BIRTH, DEATH, AND PUBLICATION

Ludwig van Beethoven (1770–1827) was a German composer.

The Old Red House (1860) was popular with young people in the nineteenth century.

FOR PAGE NUMBERS AND OTHER DOCUMENTATION

The Old Red House begins, "I have been sitting in my vine-clad arbor" (3).

Link does not agree (432).

One critic disagrees (Link 432).

FOR CROSS-FEFERENCES

(See pp. 381–382 for further information on the use of parentheses in documentation.)

30 Brackets   **[ ]**

Use brackets to enclose interpolations within quotations.

> In the opinion of Arthur Miller, "There is no more reason for falling down in a faint before his [Aristotle's] *Poetics* than before Euclid's geometry."

Parenthetical elements within parentheses are indicated by brackets ([ ]). Try to avoid constructions that call for this intricate punctuation.

> London truly is an international city (with a sizable population from Africa [Ethiopia], Asia [Pakistan, India] South America [Colombia], and other continents); some predict that thirty percent of its population may be ethnic minorities by 2010.

■ Exercise 13

Supply dashes, parentheses, and brackets where needed.

1. Malcolm Cowley commented in *The View from 80* (1980) that "old people —I wonder why— have written comparatively little about the problems of aging."

2. Malcolm Cowley (1898–1989) was surprised that old people did not write much about the difficulties of aging.

3. Malcolm Cowley has written that "old people [Cowley means the very old] have written comparatively little about the problems of aging."

( )

4.   Malcolm Cowley points out 1 that many old people are still alert,
     ∧∧
     ( )   ( )
     2 that they are highly sensitive to the difficulties of aging, and 3
     ∧∧   ∧∧

     that they do not write much about these problems.

5.   Malcolm Cowley points out that many old people are still alert,

     that they are highly sensitive to the difficulties of aging, and that

     they possess an unusual degree of wisdom all factors that make
                                                —
                                                ∧

     them capable of writing about the phenomenon of growing old.

31 Quotation Marks   " "

Use quotation marks to enclose the exact words of a speaker
and to set off some titles.

Most American writers and publishers use double quotation marks
(". . .") except for internal quotations, which are set off by single quotation marks (" '. . .' "). (See **31b**.)

31a Use quotation marks to enclose direct quotations and dialogue.

DIRECT QUOTATION

At a high point in *King Lear,* the Duke of Gloucester says, "As flies to
wanton boys are we to the gods."

NOTE: Do *not* use quotation marks to enclose indirect quotations.

> He said that the gods regard us as flies.

In dialogue a new paragraph signals each change of speaker.

DIALOGUE

> "What is fool's gold?" asked the traveler who had never before been prospecting.
>
> "Well," the geologist told him, "it's pyrite."

31b Use single quotation marks to enclose a quotation within a quotation.

> According to one critic, "Dorothy Parker is merely pretending sentimentality when she swoons over 'One perfect rose.'"

31c Use quotation marks to enclose the titles of essays, articles, short stories, short poems, chapters (and other subdivisions of books or periodicals), dissertations, professional Web sites (see pp. 374, 416), episodes of television programs, and short musical compositions.

> Kate Chopin's short work "The Story of an Hour" is about a woman's yearning for liberation.
>
> One chapter of *Walden* is titled "The Beanfield." [For titles of books, see **34a**.]

31d On your paper, do not use quotation marks around the title.

"Kate Chopin's Disappointed Woman"

31e Do not use quotation marks to emphasize or change the usual meanings of words or to justify slang, irony, or attempts at humor.

no

The beggar considered himself a "rich" man.

no

The old politician's enemies hoped that he would "croak."

Quotation marks do not give specialized or unusual definitions to words. They do not effectively add new meanings.

31f Do not enclose a block (set-off) quotation in quotation marks.

Do not use quotation marks to enclose prose quotations that are longer than four lines. Instead, indicate the quotation by blocking—indenting ten spaces from your left margin and single-spacing or double-spacing according to the preference of your instructor.

Unless your instructor specifies otherwise, poetry of four lines or more should be double-spaced and indented ten spaces. Retain the original divisions of the lines.

```
If you would keep your soul

From spotted sight or sound,

Live like the velvet mole;

Go burrow underground.
```

Quotations of three lines of poetry or less may be written like the regular text—not set off. Use a slash (/) with a space before and after it to separate lines:

Elinor Wylie satirically advises, "Live like the velvet mole; / Go burrow underground."

31g Follow established conventions in placing other marks of punctuation inside or outside closing quotation marks.

Periods and **commas** in American usage are placed *inside* closing quotation marks.

> All the students had read "Lycidas."
> "Amazing," the professor remarked.

Semicolons and **colons** are placed *outside* closing quotation marks.

> The customer wrote that she was "not yet ready to buy the first edition"; it was too expensive.

A **question mark** or an **exclamation point** is placed *inside* closing quotation marks when the quotation itself is a direct question or an exclamation. Otherwise, these marks are placed *outside*.

> He asked, "Who is she?" [Only the quotation is a question.]
> "Who is she?" he asked. [Only the quotation is a question.]
> Did he ask, "Who is she?" [A quoted question within a question takes only one question mark—inside the quotation marks.]
> Did he say, "I know her"? [The entire sentence asks a question; the quotation makes a statement.]
> She screamed, "Run!" [Only the quotation is an exclamation.]
> Curse the man who whispers, "No"! [The entire statement is an exclamation; the quotation is not.]

After quotations, do not use a period or a comma together with an exclamation point or a question mark.

> NOT   BUT
> "When?", I asked.   "When?" I asked.

■ **Exercise 14**

Insert double or single quotation marks where needed. Delete unnecessary quotation marks. Mark C by any correct sentence.

1. A "tall" person can reach the higher shelves, but a "short" person cannot.

2. Eugene McCarthy made the following statement: "An efficient bureaucracy is the greatest threat to liberty."

3. "The greater the number of laws and enactments," in the words of the Chinese philosopher Lao-tsu, "the more thieves and robbers there will be."

4. Robert Herrick's lyric poem "Upon Julia's Clothes" tells more about Julia than about her apparel.

5. "Only in America," said the owner of the restaurant, "could I have become wealthy in less than five years after immigrating." "Yes," replied the customer, "this country still offers opportunity for those who are willing to work hard."

6. An article in *Newsweek* titled "Re-Roofing the White House" deals with the changes that always accompany new administrations.

C   7. To paraphrase what Robert Frost wrote, he took the road that had fewer travelers.

8. Do you believe Mark Twain was right when he said, "Don't part with your illusions; when they are gone, you may still exist, but you have ceased to live?"

9. The new homeowner said that "she could hardly believe how low the taxes were on her new house."

10. The newspaper article with the heading "Bible Scholar Claims Discovery of Lost City" reads as follows: "Vendyle Jones said Thursday that the site lies at the center of a lost city. This city was, to quote Jones, 'greater than Troy, greater than Pompeii.' "

■ Exercise 15

Supply quotation marks as needed in the following passage and insert the sign ¶ where new paragraphs are necessary.

There was a pause. Then I knocked again. And almost immediately a light sprang up above and an upper window opened. ¶"Wer ist da?" cried a man's voice. ¶ I felt the shock of disappointment and consternation to my fingers. ¶"I want help; I have had an accident," I replied.

¶

Some muttering followed. Then I heard steps descending the stairs, the
∧

bolt of the door was drawn, the lock was turned. It was opened

abruptly, and in the darkness of the passage a tall man hastily attired,
                                                          ¶"
with a pale face and dark moustache, stood before me. What do you
            "   ¶   ∧
want? he said, this time in English. I had now to think of something to
      ∧   ∧
say. I wanted above all to get into parley with this man, to get matters

in such a state that instead of raising an alarm and summoning others
                              ¶"   "   "
he would discuss things quietly. I am a burgher, I began. I have had an
                              ∧   ∧   ∧
accident. I was going to join my commando at Komati Poort. I have

fallen off the train. We were skylarking. I have been unconscious for
                                                        "¶
hours. I think I have dislocated my shoulder. It is astonishing how one
                                                  ∧
thinks of these things. This story leapt out as if I had learnt it by heart.

Yet I had not the slightest idea what I was going to say or what the next
                        ¶"
sentence would be. . . . I think I'd like to know a little more about
                  ∧   "   ¶"
this railway accident of yours, he said, after a considerable pause. I
      "   "   ∧   "¶"   " ∧
think, I replied, I had better tell you the truth. I think you had, he
    ∧   ¶ ∧   ∧   ∧
said, slowly. So I took the plunge and threw all I had upon the board.
¶"   ∧
I am Winston Churchill, War Correspondent of the *Morning Post*. I es-
∧

caped last night from Pretoria. I am making my way to the frontier. I
„¶

have plenty of money. Will you help me? There was another long
∧

pause. My companion rose from the table slowly and locked the door.

After this act, which struck me as unpromising, and was certainly am-
¶"

biguous, he advanced upon me and suddenly held out his hand. Thank
∧

God you have come here! It is the only house for twenty miles where

you would not have been handed over. But we are all British here, and
"

we will see you through.
∧

WINSTON S. CHURCHILL
My Early Life: A Roving Commission

■ Exercise 16

Add quotation marks where needed; circle unnecessary ones.

1. "Failure is often necessary for humanity," the speaker said.
   "   "   "
   Without failure, he continued, how can we retain our humil-
   ∧   ∧   ∧
   ity and know the full sweetness of success? For, as Emily Dick-
   '
   inson said, Success is counted sweetest / By those who
   ∧, „
   ne'er succeed.
          ∧

2. Madam, said the talent scout, I know that you think your daugh-
   "   "   "
   ∧   ∧   ∧
   ter can sing, but, believe me, her voice makes the strangest

sounds I have ever heard. Mrs. Audubon took her daughter "Birdie" by the hand and haughtily left the room, wondering "how she could ever have been so stupid as to expose her daughter to such a "common" person."

3. Grandmother said, "I'm going to teach you a short poem that I learned when I was a little girl. It's called 'The Wind,' and it begins like this: 'I saw you toss the kites on high / And blow the birds about the sky.'"

4. The boy and his great-uncle were "real" friends, and the youngster would listen intently when the old man spoke. "Son," he would say, "I remember my father's words: 'You can't do better than to follow the advice of Ben Franklin, who said, "One To-day is worth Two To-morrows."'"

5. To demonstrate that the English language is always "changing," our teacher said that we should all come up with a list of new expressions.

6. A recent report states the following: "The marked increase in common stocks indicated a new sense of national security;"

however, the report seems to imply ⊙that this is only one of many gauges of the country's economic situation.⊙

7. Chapters in modern novels rarely have any titles at all, especially ⊙wordy⊙ ones like the title of Chapter 51 in *Vanity Fair* (1848): "In Which a Charade Is Acted Which May or May Not Puzzle the Reader."

8. On a hotel postcard sent to her ⊙former⊙ boyfriend, the young girl marked an *X* on the picture of the building by the room where she was spending her ⊙honeymoon⊙ with her new husband.

9. "This is where we are staying," she wrote. "Wish you were here."

10. It was not at all ⊙unusual⊙ for the wanderer to stop busy passers-by on the street and ask them ⊙why they were hurrying when life is so short.⊙

32 End Punctuation   .?!

Use periods, question marks, or exclamation points to end sentences and to serve special functions.

32a Use a period after a sentence that makes a statement or expresses a command.

> Some modern people claim to practice witchcraft.
>
> Water the flowers.
>
> The gardener asked whether the plant should be taken indoors. [This sentence is a statement even though it expresses an indirect question.]

32b Use periods after most abbreviations.

Periods follow such abbreviations as Mr., Dr., Pvt., Ave., B.C., A.M., Ph.D., e.g., and many others. In British usage, periods are often omitted after titles (Mr).

Abbreviations of government and international agencies often are written without periods (FCC, TVA, UNESCO, NATO, and so forth). Usage varies. Consult your dictionary.

A comma or another mark of punctuation may follow the period after an abbreviation, but at the end of a sentence only one period is used.

> After she earned her M.A., she began study for her Ph.D.

But if the sentence is a question or an exclamation, the end punctuation mark follows the period after the abbreviation.

> When does she expect to get her Ph.D.?

32c Use three spaced periods (ellipsis points) to show an omission in a quotation.

Note how the following quotation can be shortened with ellipsis points:

> The drab, severe costumes of the Puritan settlers of New England, and their suspicion of color and ornaments as snares of the devil, have left their mark on the present-day clothes of New Englanders. At any large

meeting, people from this part of the country will be dressed in darker hues—notably black, gray, and navy—often with touches of white that recall the starched collars and cuffs of Puritan costume. Fabrics will be plainer (though heavier and sometimes more expensive) and styles simpler, with less waste of material. Skirts and lapels and trimmings will be narrower.

ALISON LURIE
The Language of Clothes

ELLIPSIS POINTS TO INDICATE OMISSIONS

ellipsis points not necessary here
↓

Clothing "of the Puritan settlers of New England, and their suspicion of color and ornament **. . .**, have left their mark on the present-day clothes of New Englanders. At any large meeting, people from this part of the country will be dressed in darker hues **. . .** often with touches of white that recall the starched collars and cuffs of Puritan costume. Fabrics will be plainer **. . .** and styles simpler **. . . .**"

↑   ↑
Use three ellipsis points for omissions within sentences.
Use period plus three ellipsis points for omission at end of sentence.

NOTE: Although the comma after the ellipsis points in the first sentence could be omitted, it is permissible to include it, since it completes a parenthetical element of the sentence.

32d A title does not end with a period even when it is a complete sentence, but some titles include a question mark or an exclamation point.

Nobody Knows My Name   *Who Is Angelina* **?**
Absalom, Absalom **!**   *Ah* **!** *Wilderness*

32e Use a question mark after a direct question.

Do teachers file attendance reports **?**
Teachers do file attendance reports **?** [a question in declarative form]

Question marks may follow separate questions within an interrogative sentence.

Do you recall the time of the accident? the license numbers of the cars involved? the names of the drivers?

NOTE: A question mark within parentheses shows that a date or a figure is historically doubtful.

Pythagoras, who died in 497 B.C. (?), was a philosopher.

32f Do not use a parenthetical question mark or exclamation point to indicate humor or sarcasm.

NOT

The comedy (?) was a miserable failure.

32g Use an exclamation point after a word, a phrase, or a sentence to indicate strong exclamatory feeling.

Wait! I forgot my lunch!
What a ridiculous idea!
Stop the bus!

Use exclamation points sparingly. After mild exclamations, use commas or periods.

NOT

Well! I was somewhat discouraged!

BUT

Well, I was somewhat discouraged.

■ Exercise 17

Read the following passage carefully. Then follow the instructions that appear after it.

> American Indians picked good places to pitch their towns. They didn't tote water very far, partly because they didn't have anything but a clay pot to carry it in. All the towns were close to streams, often within the bend of a river for protection or where one stream ran into another. Even now you can look at a topographical map and guess where the Indians lived. Often the sites of modern towns and cemeteries and roads have been selected for the same reasons the Indians chose to live there.
>
> "An Alcovy River Indian Village"

Quote the previous passage in a blocked quotation and omit the following: "They didn't tote water very far, partly because they didn't have anything but a clay pot to carry it in" and "look at a topographical map." Indicate the omissions with ellipsis points.

Answers to Exercise 17 (Ellipses)

American Indians picked good places to pitch their towns. . . . All the towns were close to streams, often within the bend of a river for protection or where one stream ran into another. Even now you can . . . guess where the Indians lived. Often the sites of modern towns and cemeteries and roads have been selected for the same reasons the Indians chose to live there.

Mechanics

33   Manuscript Forms, Business Letters, and Résumés   *MS*

A manuscript or a letter can be so dirty, wrinkled, or torn that it is immediately self-defeating: an employer, a friend, or a lover may be repelled by the very device intended to attract and persuade. Because of such lack of care, you could jeopardize a chance for a job, a friendship, or affection. Neatness and attention to matters of form, on the other hand, may impress an employer, a friend, or a lover. So every time you write, you are inviting either a pleasant response or a rejection.

33a   Follow standard practices in preparing the final copy of a paper.

Most college papers are produced on word processors. Check with your instructor about requirements for paper and script or print.

Printouts

Present clean, dark copies with no smears. Avoid dot-matrix printers if possible. Tear off hole-punched edges and separate the pages if the computer uses continuous-feed paper. Double-space throughout. Use sturdy white paper, 8½ by 11 inches. Avoid unusual-sized or colored paper.

Handwritten papers

Write legibly with dark blue or black ink. Write across the page in straight lines or use good ruled white paper (8½ by 11 inches). Skip every other line and write on only one side. Do not submit any paper torn from a spiral-bound notebook.

Margins

Use one-inch margins on each side and margins of approximately an inch and a half at the top and bottom of the paper. Indent the first word of a paragraph five spaces. Indent every line of set-off (blocked) quotations ten spaces.

Spacing

Space twice after end punctuation (period, question mark, exclamation point). Space once after commas, closing parentheses, colons, and brackets. Do not space before or after a hyphen or a dash.

Title and name

If your paper has no separate title page, type your name, the name of the instructor, the course number, and the date on separate lines flush with the left margin. Then space again and center the title. Space twice between the title and the text. See pp. 385 and 421 for examples of separate title pages.

Page numbers

Use Arabic numbers (*4,* not *IV*) in the upper right corner of the page. Numbering the first page is optional. Write your last name before the page number in case pages are lost.

Example of correct manuscript form

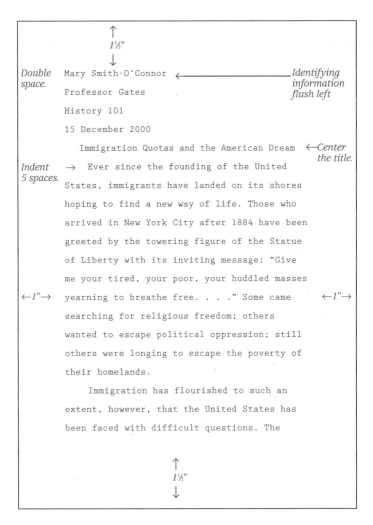

↑
1½"
↓

Double space.   Mary Smith-O'Connor ←——————— *Identifying information flush left*

Professor Gates

History 101

15 December 2000

     Immigration Quotas and the American Dream ←*Center the title.*

Indent 5 spaces. →   Ever since the founding of the United

States, immigrants have landed on its shores

hoping to find a new way of life. Those who

arrived in New York City after 1884 have been

greeted by the towering figure of the Statue

of Liberty with its inviting message: "Give

me your tired, your poor, your huddled masses

←*1"*→   yearning to breathe free. . . ." Some came   ←*1"*→

searching for religious freedom; others

wanted to escape political oppression; still

others were longing to escape the poverty of

their homelands.

     Immigration has flourished to such an

extent, however, that the United States has

been faced with difficult questions. The

↑
1½"
↓

↑
1½"
↓

name and page ↓ ½" ↑
flush right → Smith-O'Connor 2

notion of providing opportunity for the
dispossessed is an integral part of the
country's political identity. Yet should the
United States allow unlimited numbers of
people to immigrate given today's increasingly limited land, resources, and jobs?
          2 hyphens, no spaces for dash↓
     The first massive wave of immigration--
occurring in the nineteenth century—brought
in primarily Europeans: Irish, Scandina-
vians, Germans, Italians, and Poles. By the
1920s, the United States had enacted its
first comprehensive immigration legislation
and established specific geographical
quotas. Those decisions were significantly
revised in 1965.

33b Follow standard practices in preparing business letters and applications.

Business letters should be short, direct, and specific. Typed or printed letters should be single-spaced with double spaces between paragraphs. Business letters are usually written on printed letterheads. The **indented form** or **semiblock form** of a letter is shown on the next page. The **block form** is exactly like the indented except that every line (address, complimentary closing, and so forth) begins at the left margin.

A letter without the name of the addressee does not have much impact. Address men as *Mr.* and women as *Ms.* unless you know of a preference for *Miss* or *Mrs.*

When you do not know and cannot determine the name or the sex of the addressee, you must resort to *Dear Sir, Dear Madam,* or *Dear* with a title like *Director* or *Professor.* Or use no salutation at all. Include at your discretion and for the convenience of the addressee your email address, your telephone number, and your social security number.

33c Follow standard practices in preparing a résumé.

A résumé—a brief factual outline—presents an applicant's qualifications for employment. It should preferably be no longer than one page. Résumés are usually arranged topically under headings (such as "Education," "Work Experience," or "Extracurricular Activities"), then chronologically within each of these categories.

All résumés should include your name, address, phone number, and email address; employment objectives; education; past work experience; pertinent extracurricular activities; skills and interests (including languages and computer abilities); and a list of references or the address of the placement office of your college, which will provide your transcript and recommendations on request.

A sample résumé appears on p. 263.

Indented or semiblock form

```
                              Street address
                              City or Town, State  zip code
                              email address
                              Month, Day, and year

Ms. Carol Alvarez
Dean of Admissions
Name of Building or Department
Institution
Town or City, State zip code

Dear Dean Alvarez:

I am a senior at [name of your high school].

I wish to have a statement of your requirements for admission.

Please send me the necessary information and the forms that I
will need when I mail you my application.

May I also ask for a description of the scholarships available
to first-year students?

I wish to major in modern languages and later to find some
position in diplomacy at the State Department. If you have
information that might be helpful in my planning, please send
it to me.

I have long admired [name of institution], and I would be
pleased to be a student there.

                              Sincerely yours,

                              [Your signature]

                              Your name
                              Social security number
```

Folding the letter

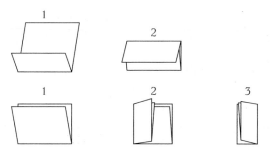

Place your return address, the address, and a stamp correctly on the envelope. Be careful. The stamp goes in the upper right corner.

```
Your name                                         Place
Street address  Apartment number                  stamp
City, State  zip code                             here.




                        Ms. Name, Title
                        Department
                        Organization
                        P. O. Box XXX
                        City, State  zip code
```

Résumé

George M. Levine
2244 Leigh Avenue, Apt. B
Seattle, WA 98119
(206) 555-2121
glevine@aol.com

OBJECTIVE
   To secure employment in the field of public relations.

EDUCATION
   University of Washington, B.A. degree in English, June
   1999.

WORK EXPERIENCE
   Student intern, the City of Seattle: worked as an
   assistant to Susan Miller, Director of Public Relations.
   Duties included writing press releases, editing copy,
   answering phones, coordinating publicity and site arrange-
   ments for the neighborhood festival program. (June
   1998-December 1998)

   Library assistant, Bellingham Public Library: checked out
   books, shelved books, processed new books. (Summers 1995,
   1996, 1997).

EXTRACURRICULAR ACTIVITIES
   Assistant Editor, The Lake Union Review (1998-1999)
   Publicity coordinator, Young Life Club (1996-1997)

SKILLS AND INTERESTS
   Computers: Word, Excel, PowerPoint, WordPerfect
   Language: Spanish
   Hobbies: Reading mysteries, kayaking, sailing

REFERENCES
   Available from the University of Washington Placement
   Office

34 Italics *ital*

Use italics for titles of separate publications (books, magazines, newspapers) and *occasionally* for emphasis.

Most books and magazines use mainly roman type: society. Type that slants to the right is called italic type: *society.* Many word-processing programs include italic type; in papers that are handwritten or typed, indicate italics by underlining: society.

34a Italicize or underline titles of books (except the Bible and other sacred books and their divisions), periodicals, newspapers, long poems published separately, films, paintings, sculptures, musical compositions, television and radio programs, plays, and other long works published separately.

Be precise: underline initial articles (*A, An,* and *The*) and any punctuation in a title.

BOOKS

    Adventures of Huckleberry Finn (*not* The Adventures . . .)

    An American Tragedy (*not* The American Tragedy)

    Not underlined: the Bible, John 3:16, the Koran

PERIODICALS

    The Atlantic and the American Quarterly

NEWSPAPERS

    The New York Times or the New York Times or the New York Times

LONG POEMS

    the Odyssey

FILMS

American Beauty

MUSICAL COMPOSITIONS, RECORD ALBUMS, COMPACT DISCS

Beethoven's Mount of Olives (*but not* Beethoven's Symphony No. 5)

The Best of Fleetwood Mac

PLAYS AND MUSICALS

The Cherry Orchard

Phantom of the Opera

RADIO AND TELEVISION SERIES

All Things Considered

Masterpiece Theatre

34b   Italicize or underline names of ships and trains.

the Queen Elizabeth II   the U.S.S. Hornet   the Zephyr

34c   Italicize or underline foreign words used in the English language, except those that are considered part of the English language in modern usage.

When in doubt, consult a dictionary to determine whether a word is foreign or has become part of the English language.

The governor claimed extravagantly to have been au courant since birth.

The dandelion, of the genus Taraxacum, is a common weed.

BUT

Use roman type for words that have become common in English.

faux pas, amigo, karate

34d Italicize or underline words, letters, and figures being named.

> Remember to cross your ts.
>
> Glee rhymes with flea.

NOTE: Occasionally quotation marks are used instead of underlining.

34e Avoid frequent italicizing or underlining for emphasis.

Numerous underlinings, dashes, and exclamation points on a page are distracting. Do not attempt to create excitement by overusing these marks.

34f Do not italicize or underline the title of your own paper.

■ Exercise 1

Underline words as necessary. Place an X over words unnecessarily underlined. Place a C over words correctly underlined.

1. The popular Broadway musical Cats is based on a book by T. S. Eliot called Old Possum's Book of Practical Cats.

2. The New Yorker reviewed the production last week along with the recent biographical study Eliot's New Life.

             X   X

3. The reviewer insisted that Eliot be considered an American poet

             X

   rather than a British one.

                                         X

4. In many of Eliot's poems, he draws on material from the Bible.

5. His poem "Ash Wednesday" is included in the anthology The

                           C

   New Oxford Book of Christian Verse, edited by Donald Davie.

                          C

6. Director Terry Gilliam's film Brazil might be considered a cine-

                                            C

   matic rendition of Eliot's most famous long poem, The Waste

   Land.

            X   C   C

7. The words burn and dry appear throughout the poem.

                                  X

8. The professor read the short poem Journey of the Magi to the

   class while playing selections from Handel's most famous ora-

                  C

   torio, the Messiah.

9. Eliot may have traveled from the United States to England

                                C

   aboard the grand ocean liner the Queen Mary.

                     X   C

10. One painting in the National Gallery is titled Eliot and Pound in

   London.

35 Spelling *sp*

Spell correctly. Proofread carefully. Check words in a dictionary or with a spell-checker.

Spelling is troublesome in English because many words are not spelled as they sound (*laughter, slaughter*) and because some pairs and triplets sound the same (*capital, capitol; their, they're, their; to, too, two*). Many words are pronounced with the vowel sound "uh," which gives no clue to the spelling (*sensible, capable, defiant*). A short word (*of, have*) may be sounded as "uh" and changed in writing: "some-a," "woulda," "coulda," "mighta," "musta" (*some of, would have, could have, might have, must have*).

Many misspellings result from the omission of syllables in habitual or careless mispronunciations (*accident-ly* for *acciden-tal-ly*); the addition of syllables (*disas-ter-ous* for *disas-trous*); or the changing of syllables or letters (*prespiration* for *perspiration, revelant* for *relevant, than* for *then* or vice versa). Spellings can sound correct but be wrong in writing (*alright* for *all right*). Spell the unemphasized parts of words carefully. Put the *d* on a word like *use (used)* for the past tense. Be careful when forming the plurals of words like *phenomenon (-mena)* and *criterion (-ria)*.

35a Spell-checking

Most word-processing programs include a spell-checker that will compare all the words in your paper against a dictionary that has been programmed into the computer. Such programs are good ways to do an initial check for spelling and proofreading errors, but they will not catch all of the errors.

In most programs, the computer will scroll through your manuscript and highlight words that do not match anything in the dictionary (names and unusual terms, even if properly spelled, will often be chosen). A spell-checker may also offer you several alternative spellings or words. You will have to make the final decision regarding each.

Spell-checkers do not determine whether a word is the right word for a particular sentence. You may, for example, accidentally type *the* for *they,* and the program will not catch the error. Similarly, if you confuse *its* and *it's, trail* and *trial,* or *to* and *two,* the program will not catch the error. Spell-checking must always be followed by proofreading.

35b Proofreading

Many misspellings are simple typographical errors that can be caught by proofreading. Always read a manuscript through at least once just for proofreading.

Normally, when most people read, they take in several words at a time and jump from one word cluster to another. If you are proofreading, slow down your reading and try to focus on individual letters. Reading aloud can help you slow down. Other proofreading techniques include placing a ruler or a straight edge under each line so that you focus on only one line. Read each paragraph or line word by word, forward or backward.

35c Distinguishing homonyms

Homonyms are words that sound exactly like other words but have different spellings (*morning* and *mourning; there, their,* and *they're*). Different words that sound similar (*except* and *accept; loose* and *lose*) are **near homonyms.** Many spelling problems occur because of homonyms and near homonyms.

The Glossary of Usage (pp. 445–457) identifies and distinguishes between many common homonyms and near homonyms. Keep a list of words that frequently give you trouble and remind yourself to consult the glossary.

35d Spelling strategies

English has no infallible guides to spelling, but the following suggestions are helpful.

ie *or* ei?

> Use *i* before *e*
> Except after *c*
> Or when sounded as *a*
> As in *neighbor* and *weigh*.

WORDS WITH *IE*
> believe, chief, field, grief, piece

WORDS WITH *EI* AFTER *C*
> receive, receipt, ceiling, deceit, conceive

WORDS WITH *EI* SOUNDED AS *A*
> freight, vein, reign

EXCEPTIONS TO MEMORIZE
> either, neither, leisure, seize, weird, height

Drop final silent e?

DROP *When suffix begins with a vowel*		KEEP *When suffix begins with a consonant*	
curse	cursing	live	lively
come	coming	nine	ninety
pursue	pursuing	hope	hopeful
arrange	arranging	love	loveless
dine	dining	arrange	arrangement

TYPICAL EXCEPTIONS	TYPICAL EXCEPTIONS
courageous	awful
noticeable	ninth
dyeing (compare *dying*)	truly
singeing (compare *singing*)	argument

Change y *to* i?

CHANGE		DO NOT CHANGE	
When y *is preceded by a consonant*		*When* y *is preceded by a vowel*	
gully	gullies	valley	valleys
try	tried	attorney	attorneys
fly	flies	convey	conveyed
apply	applied	pay	pays
party	parties	deploy	deploying

When adding -ing

try	trying
fly	flying
apply	applying

Double final consonant?

If the suffix begins with a consonant, do not double the final consonant of the base word (*man, manly*).

If the suffix begins with a vowel:

DOUBLE		DO NOT DOUBLE	
When final consonant is preceded by single vowel		*When final consonant is preceded by two vowels*	
		despair	despairing
		leer	leering
Monosyllables			
pen	penned	*Words ending with two or more consonants preceded by single vowel*	
blot	blotted		
hop	hopper	jump	jumping
sit	sitting	work	working

DOUBLE		DO NOT DOUBLE	
Polysyllables accented on last syllable		*Polysyllables not accented on last syllable after addition of suffix*	
defér	deferring		
begín	beginning	defér	déference
		prefér	préference

DOUBLE		DO NOT DOUBLE	
omít	omitting	devélop	devéloping
occúr	occurring	lábor	lábored

Add s *or* es?

ADD *S*		ADD *ES*	
		When the plural is pronounced as another syllable	
For plurals of most nouns			
girl	girls	church	churches
book	books	fox	foxes

For nouns ending in o *preceded by a vowel*		*Usually for nouns ending in* o *preceded by a consonant (consult your dictionary)*	
radio	radios	potatoes	
cameo	cameos	heroes	

BUT
flamingos *or* flamingoes
egos

NOTE: The plurals of proper names are generally formed by adding *s* or *es* (*Darby,* the *Darbys; Jones,* the *Joneses*). Do not use an apostrophe to make a name plural.

	FLURAL	NOT
Ann	three Anns	three Ann's

Words frequently misspelled

The following is a list of over two hundred of the most commonly misspelled words in the English language.

absence
accessible
accidentally
accommodate
accumulate
accuracy
acquaintance
acquitted
advice
advise
all right
altar
amateur
among
analysis
analyze
annual
apartment
apparatus
apparent
appearance
arctic
argument
arithmetic
ascend
athletic
attendance
balance
beginning
believe
benefited
boundaries
Britain
business
calendar
candidate
category
cemetery
changeable
changing
choose
chose
coming

commission
committee
comparative
compelled
conceivable
conferred
congratulations
conscience
conscientious
control
convenient
criticize
deceive
deferred
definite
democracy
description
desperate
dictionary
dining
disappearance
disappoint
disastrous
discipline
dissatisfied
dormitory
ecstatic
eighth
eligible
eliminate
embarrass
eminent
encouraging
environment
equipped
especially
exaggerate
excellence
exhilarate
existence
experience
explanation
familiar

fascinate
February
fiery
foreign
foreword
formerly
forty
fourth
frantically
fulfill or fulfil
generally
government
grammar
grandeur
grievous
guaranteed
gullible
harass
height
heroes
hindrance
hoping
humorous
hypocrisy
immediately
incidentally
incredible
independence
inevitable
intellectual
intelligence
interesting
irresistible
knowledge
knowledgeable
laboratory
laid
led
leisure
lightning
loneliness
maintenance
management

maneuver	precedence	separate
manual	preference	sergeant
manufacture	preferred	severely
marriage	prejudice	shining
mathematics	preparation	siege
miniature	prescribe	similar
mischievous	prevalent	sincerely
mysterious	privilege	sophomore
necessary	probably	specifically
ninety	professor	specimen
noticeable	pronunciation	stationary
occasionally	prophecy	stationery
occurred	prophesy	statue
omitted	quantity	studying
opportunity	quiet	subtly
optimistic	quite	succeed
parallel	quizzes	successful
paralyze	recede	summary
pastime	receive	supersede
perceive	recognize	suppose
performance	recommend	surprise
permanent	reference	temperamental
permissible	referred	tendency
perseverance	repetition	their
personnel	restaurant	thorough
perspiration	rhythm	through
pervert	ridiculous	vegetable
physical	roommate	vengeance
picnicking	sacrifice	villain
playwright	salary	weird
possibility	schedule	writing
practically	secretary	yield
precede	seize	

■ Exercise 2

Proofread the following passage; identify and correct all fifteen spelling or typing errors. Indicate with SC those errors that a spell-checker would not have identified.

women SC
One of the especially accomplished woman of the twentieth cen-
excellent
tury was the British author Dorothy L. Sayers. An excallant scholar of
medieval   **translator**
medeival literature and a respected translater of Dante, Sayers today is

perhaps best known as the author of a series of detective novels fea-

turing the suave and distinguished Lord Peter Wimsey. After taking a
degree
degre at Oxford, Sayers worked as a copywriter in an advertising
                    campaigns
agency, inventing some of the most famous British ad campaignes of

the 1920s. But eventually the success of her detective novels provided
            independance
her with financial independance.

Assisted   **manservant**   **variety**
Asisted by his able manservent, Bunter, Lord Peter solves a vareity of
                           occurring
intriguing mysteries—ranging from a mysterious death occuring at an
advertising   **fiancé SC**
advertiseing agency to the murder of his sister's finance. Lord Peter's most

famous case, however, introduces him to Harriet Vane, a brilliant and
passionate
passionete mystery writer who has been accused of poisoning the man

with whom she lives. Peter solves the case, but falls in love with Harriet in
                 Finally
a subplot that continues through several novels. Finaly, Harriet and Peter

are engaged at the conclusion of *Gaudy Night;* during their honeymoon,

recorded in *Busman's Honeymoon,* what should they discover but a corpse?

36 Hyphenation and Syllabication   -

Use a hyphen in certain compound words and in words divided at the end of a line.

Two related words not listed as an entry in a dictionary are usually written separately (*campaign promise*).

36a Consult a dictionary to determine whether a compound is hyphenated or written as one or two words (see **41a**).

HYPHENATED	ONE WORD	TWO WORDS
drop-off (noun)	droplight	drop leaf (noun)
white-hot	whitewash	white heat
water-cool	watermelon	water system

36b Hyphenate a compound of two or more words used as a single modifier before a noun.

HYPHEN	NO HYPHEN AFTER NOUN
She is a *well-known* executive.	The executive is *well known*.
Poe was a *nineteenth-century* writer.	Poe lived in the *nineteenth century*.

A hyphen is not used when the first word of such a group is an adverb ending in *-ly*.

HYPHEN	NO HYPHEN
a *half-finished* task	a *partly finished* task

36c Hyphenate spelled-out compound numbers from *twenty-one* through *ninety-nine*.

36d   Divide a word at the end of a line according to conventions.

Monosyllables

Do not divide.

> thought   strength   cheese

Single letters

Do not put a one-letter syllable on a separate line.

NOT
> a-bout   might-y

Prefixes and suffixes

May be divided.

> separ-able   pre-fix

Avoid carrying over a two-letter suffix.

NOT
> bound-ed   careful-ly

Compounds with hyphen

Avoid dividing and adding another hyphen.

> self-satisfied

NOT
> self-satis-fied

■ **Exercise 3**

Underline the correct form for the words indicated. Use a dictionary when needed.

1. Many (<u>summertime</u>, summer-time, summer time) pleasures build (<u>year-round</u>, year round) memories.
2. The (<u>thunderstorm</u>, thunder-storm, thunder storm) drove many people off the (golfcourse, golf-course, <u>golf course</u>) into the (justopened, <u>just-opened</u>, just opened) (<u>clubhouse</u>, club-house, club house).
3. The (<u>foxhound</u>, fox-hound, fox hound) was (welltrained, <u>well-trained</u>, well trained) not to chase rabbits.
4. The (twentyone, <u>twenty-one</u>, twenty one) dancers did not know how to (foxtrot, <u>fox-trot</u>, fox trot).
5. Several words in the paper were hyphenated at the end of lines: a-round, almight-y, <u>al-most</u>, self-in-flicted, marb-le.

37 Apostrophes ,

Use the apostrophe for the possessive case of many nouns, for contractions, for omissions, and for some plurals.

37a Use *'s* for the possessive of nouns not ending in *s*.

SINGULAR
child's, man's, deer's, lady's

PLURAL
children's, men's

37b Use *'s* for the possessive of singular nouns ending in *s*.

Charles's, Watts's, Dickens's, waitress's, actress's

NOTE: When a singular noun ending in *s* is followed by a word beginning with *s*, use only the apostrophe, not *'s*.

the actress' success, Dickens' stories

37c Use *'* without *s* to form the possessive of plural nouns ending in *s*.

the Joneses' car, the Dickenses' home, waitresses' tips

37d Use *'s* to form the possessive of indefinite pronouns.

anybody's, everyone's, somebody else's, neither's

NOTE: Use no apostrophe with personal pronouns like *his, hers, theirs, ours, its* (meaning "of it"). *It's* means "it is."

37e Use *'s* with only the last noun for joint possession in a pair or a series.

the architect and the builder's plan [The two jointly have one plan.]
the architect's and the builder's plans [They have different plans.]

37f Use *'* to show omissions or to form contractions.

o'clock, jack-o'lantern
we'll, don't, can't, it's [meaning "it is"]

NOTE: Be sure to distinguish between the following homonyms: *it's—its, you're—your, they're—their,* and *who's—whose.*

37g   Use *'s* to form the plural of acronyms and words being named.

> three IRA*'s*
>
> six *and's*

NOTE: The plurals for numerals, letters, and years may be written with or without apostrophes as long as no confusion results (*u's,* not us; *i's,* not is). Be consistent.

> three *7's* or three 7s, four *c's* or four cs, the 1960*'s* or the 1960s, the Roaring '20*'s* or the Roaring '20s

■ Exercise 4

Underline the words that contain correctly used apostrophes.

1. geese's honks, calves' hooves, ten dogs' yaps, a dogs' yap

2. his', her's, it's (for *it is*), its'

3. Charles' SAT's, Les's ACTs, her father's IRA's

4. The childrens' service, the men's club, the man's hair

5. Susan and Sam's patent (together they own one patent) Susan's and Sam's cars (each owns a car)

6. four oclock, four o'clock, four'o'clock

7. two *c's,* two *ds',* three *is*

8. can't, couldnt, wouldn't

9. the Beatles's songs, the <u>Beatles'</u> album, the Beatles's fame

10. a childs' blocks, the two <u>boys'</u> toys, a girls' building block's

38 Capital Letters　*cap*

Use a capital letter to begin a sentence and to designate a proper noun (the name of a particular person, place, or thing).

38a　Capitalize the first word of every sentence.

The bat was made from the wood of an ash tree.

38b　Capitalize first, last, and important words in titles, including the second part of hyphenated words.

Across the River and into the Trees
"The Man Against the Sky"
"After Apple-Picking"
"What You See Is the Real You"

NOTE:　Articles (*a, an,* and *the*), short prepositions, and conjunctions are not capitalized unless they begin or end a title.

38c　Capitalize the first word of a direct quotation introduced with a comma or a colon.

Bruno Bettelheim states, "The essential theme of 'Cinderella' is sibling rivalry."

NOTE: Do not capitalize the first word of a quotation if you are in-cluding that word in the structure of your own sentence.

> Bruno Bettleheim claims that "the essential theme of 'Cinderella' is sibling rivalry."

38d Capitalize titles preceding a name, following a name, or being used specifically as a substitute for a particular name.

> Professor Manoya
> Sandra Day O'Connor, Associate Justice of the Supreme Court
> Dean Wilson approved the petition; the Dean is often lenient.

NOTE: Do not capitalize a title that names an office if the title is not followed by a name (with the exception noted in **38e**).

> The professor gave the student the examination.
> A college president has more duties than privileges.
> A lieutenant usually leads a platoon.

38e Capitalize the title of the head of a nation.

> the President of the United States
> the Prime Minister of Great Britain

38f Capitalize proper nouns but not general terms.

PROPER NOUNS	GENERAL TERMS
Plato, Platonic, Platonism	pasteurize
Venice, Venetian blind	a set of china
the West, a Westerner	west of the river
the Republican Party	a republican government

PROPER NOUNS	GENERAL TERMS
the Senior Class of Ivy College	a member of the senior class
Clifton Street	my street, the street
the Mississippi River	the Mississippi and Ohio rivers
the Romantic Movement	the twentieth century

38g Capitalize words of family relationship that precede a name or that stand alone to represent a name.

After Father died, Mother and Aunt Alice carried on the business.

NOTE: Do not capitalize words of family relationship that are preceded by a possessive pronoun or the word *the*.

After my father died, my mother and my aunt carried on the business.

38h Capitalize the pronoun *I* and the interjection *O*.

My dear Romeo, O my dear Romeo, how I love you!

NOTE: Do not capitalize the interjection *oh* unless it begins a sentence.

Oh, I like that film.

38i Capitalize months, days of the week, and holidays.

April, Friday, the Fourth of July, Labor Day

NOTE: Do not capitalize seasons and numbered days of the month unless they name holidays.

spring, the third of July

38j Capitalize B.C. (used after numerals: 31 B.C.), A.D. (used before numerals: A.D. 33), words designating a deity, religious denominations, and sacred books.

> in 273 B.C.
>
> the Messiah, the Creator, Yahweh, Allah, Catholic, Protestant, Presbyterian, Muslim, Hindu, Jewish, the Bible, the Koran

NOTE: Pronouns referring to God are usually capitalized.

> Praise God from Whom all blessings flow.

38k Capitalize names of specific courses.

> Joseph registered for Biology 101 and Philosophy 200.

NOTE: Do not capitalize subjects (other than languages) that do not name specific courses.

> Joseph is taking French, biology, and philosophy.

■ Exercise 5

Supply capitals as needed. Change capital letters to lowercase as necessary.

1. Dr. Outback, an australian expert in Animal Behavior, lectures
      occasionally on Marsupial psychoses.

2. The Hostess, my aunt Zora, cried, "help yourself to the fried

      chicken," in a voice so shrill and strange that the dinner guests

      suddenly lost their appetites.

3. Captain Kaplan, united States army, arrived on wednesday to
                U   **A**   **W**

   find that he was late for the tour of buddhist temples.
            B

4. When she registered for Chemistry, amaryllis was told that she
          c   **A**

   would need to take Algebra 101.

5. Susan Curall, ~~m.d.~~, attended the meeting of the American Med-
         M.D.

   ical association and returned home before thanksgiving day.
     A   **T**   **D**

6. In the Twentieth Century, many of the qualities associated with
         t   **c**

   people of the American south disappeared.
             S

7. Augustus Caesar, who was born in 63 ~~b.c.~~ and died in ~~a.d.~~ 14, is
             B.C.   **A.D.**

   a character in Shakespeare's Tragedy *Antony and Cleopatra*.
          t

8. Though the printer lived for a while on Magoni avenue, he
                  A

   moved to detroit last August.
       D

9. The Salk vaccine has all but eliminated polio, according to an
        v   **p**

   article in a Medical Journal.
       m   **j**

10. She wanted to become a lawyer, she explained, because she
                   l

    saw a direct connection between the Law and Morals.
                  l   **m**

39 Abbreviations and Symbols *ab*

Avoid most abbreviations in formal writing.

39a Spell out names of days, months, units of measurement, and (except in addresses) states and countries.

> Friday (*not* Fri.)   pounds (*not* lbs.)
> February (*not* Feb.)   Sauk Centre, Minnesota (*not* Minn.)

Do not use note-taking or shortcut signs such as *w/* for *with* or & for *and* in formal writing.

39b Use only acceptable abbreviations.

BEFORE NAMES
> Mr., Mrs., Ms., Messrs., Mmes., Dr., St. *or* Ste. (for *Saint,* not *Street*), Mt., Rev. (but only with a first name: *the Rev. Ernest Jones,* not *Rev. Jones*)

AFTER NAMES
> M.D. (and other degrees), Jr., Sr., Esq.

FOR THE DISTRICT OF COLUMBIA
> Washington, D.C.

FOR WELL-KNOWN ORGANIZATIONS (WITHOUT PERIODS)

CIA, NAACP, FBI, IRS, NBC

NOTE: Initially, identify less familiar organizations in parentheses; subsequently, use the acronym.

The African National Congress (ANC) was banned as a political organization in South Africa for over fifty years. The ANC gained official recognition in 1992.

WITH DATES AND TIME

B.C. and A.D. (with dates expressed in numerals, as *500 B.C.*), A.M. and P.M. or a.m. and p.m. (with hours expressed in numerals, as *4:00 A.M.* or *4:00 a.m.*)

39c Use only acceptable symbols

PERCENT: %

Write out the word *percent* in formal writing unless it appears in a table or graph. In technical, scientific, and business writing, the percent sign after a percentage is acceptable: *5%*.

DOLLAR SIGN: $

Use a dollar sign only with specific dollar amounts: *$45.78* (but *several million dollars*).

CENT SIGN: ¢

In formal writing, do not use a cent sign except in a table or a graph. Write *five cents*.

40 Numbers   *num*

Spell out numbers or use numerals where appropriate.

40a Spell out numbers that can be written in one or two words. Use numerals for other numbers.

twenty-three, one thousand

123      $1^{13}/_{16}$ $1,001.00

NOTE: In technical, scientific, and journalistic writing, writers often use numerals for all numbers above ten.

EXCEPTION

Never use numerals at the beginning of a sentence. Spell out the number or rewrite the sentence.

40b Be consistent with numbers in a sequence.

NOT

One polar bear weighed 426 pounds; another, 538 pounds; and the third, two hundred pounds.

BUT

One polar bear weighed 426 pounds; another, 538 pounds; and the third, 200 pounds.

40c Use numerals for complete dates, street numbers, page and chapter references, percentages, and hours of the day used with A.M. or P.M.

USE NUMERALS	SPELL OUT
July 3, 1776 (*not* 3rd)	the third of July
1010 State Street	Fifth Avenue
See page 50.	The book has fifty pages.
He paid 15 percent interest.	
The concert begins at 6 P.M. (or 6:00 P.M.)	The concert begins at six o'clock.

■ Exercise 6

Place X *by the following that are not acceptable in formal writing and correct them. Place* C *by those that are acceptable.*

                            California

X 1. On 25 December 1962, in Los Angeles, ~~Calif~~.

          Dr.
X 2. Mr. Brown and ~~Doctor~~ Freidman

C 3. October twenty-third

C 4. four cents

         75
X 5. ~~Seventy-five~~ Jones Avenue

            Avenue
X 6. Devon ~~Ave.~~

        8
X 7. ~~eight~~ a.m.

            Department
X 8. Eng. 100 in the ~~Dept.~~ of English

           ounces
X 9. 8 pounds, 5 ~~oz.~~

        2,045
X 10. ~~two thousand and forty-five~~ signatures

        14,
X 11. June ~~14th,~~ 1994

C 12. $6.88 a pound

        and
X 13. Peter ~~&~~ Paul

C 14. three little pigs

        Thursday
X 15. ~~Thurs.,~~ February 14

C 16. page 24 in Chapter 12

        Jr.
X 17. Ken Griffey, ~~Junior~~

C 18. 500 B.C.

C 19. the IRS

        percent
X 20. The jacket cost ten ~~%~~ less.

Diction and
Style

41 Diction *d*

In speech and writing, use Standard English appropriate for the occasion.

Diction refers to choice and use of words. **Standard English** is the generally accepted language (written or spoken) of educated people in English-speaking countries. Though it varies in usage and pronunciation from one country or region to another (indicated in dictionaries by such labels as *U.S.* or *Brit.*), it is the standard form of the language taught in schools and colleges.

Informal or **colloquial English** reflects spoken language and is therefore more casual than is usually appropriate for college papers. For example, contractions—*don't, isn't,* and so on—are informal. Colloquial English does not refer to **dialect** or local language.

Nonstandard English consists of usages, spellings, and pronunciations not usually found in the speech or writing of educated people. For example, possibly use *am not, are not, is not, has not,* or *have not* for the nonstandard *ain't.* Usage labels in a dictionary indicate which words are nonstandard.

It is possible, of course, to choose correct words and still produce writing that is lifeless and dull. Diction is not only the choice of the most exact and effective words for the subject. It also consists of not using incorrect and inexact words and of avoiding language that is ineffective or in bad taste. Choosing good words and using them so that your language has life, flair, and exactness is the secret of good writing.

The first three sections of this part (**41a, 41b,** and **41c**) can help you to choose good words. The next five sections (**41d** through **41h**) should help you to keep from using either inexact language or words that are in bad taste. These sections' discussion of diction and the following sections' discussion of style should help with exactness, correctness, and grace.

41a Consult a good dictionary frequently. *dic*

Dictionaries are excellent sources of information about language. They record past and current usage. Make a good dictionary your constant companion. Particularly useful at the college level are the following desk dictionaries:

The American Heritage College Dictionary. Boston: Houghton Mifflin.
The American Heritage Dictionary of the English Language. Boston: Houghton Mifflin.
The Concise Oxford Dictionary. Oxford: Oxford University Press.
Merriam Webster's Collegiate Dictionary. Springfield: Merriam.
Random House Webster's College Dictionary. New York: Random House.
Webster's New World Dictionary of American English. New York: Prentice-Hall.
Webster's II New College Dictionary. Boston: Houghton Mifflin.

Become familiar with the various kinds of information offered in your particular dictionary. Read the front matter carefully and study its explanations. A typical entry from *Webster's II New College Dictionary* (1999) is represented on pages 294–295.

Dictionary entry

Every dictionary is unique in the ways in which it provides information in an entry. Know the ways used in your dictionary. The entry for the word *double* here tells many things about the word. Other entries may include synonyms, variants, capitalization, and other things.

■ Exercise 1

Read the preliminary pages in your dictionary and study the usage labels (such as Mus., Math., Nonstandard, Informal, Slang, Vulgar, Regional, Chiefly Brit., and so forth) that apply to particular words. Usage labels vary from one dictionary to another. Without using a

(1)————————

(8)————————

(9)————————

(10)————————

(1) Boldface entry   (2) Dot indicating division
between syllables   (3) Phonetic spelling, for
pronunciation (See key at the bottom of dictionary
page.)   (4) Accented syllable   (5) Abbreviation
for part of speech   (6) Etymologies   (7) First
of six definitions of the word used as an adjective
(8) Illustrative example   (9) Words or abbreviations
in red blocks indicate terms that label specialized or
technical meanings   (10) Part of speech—noun.
Note that the numbering of word meanings starts over
when the part of speech changes.   (11) Part of
speech—verb. Forms of the verb—past tense, present
participle, third-person singular   (12) Kind of verb—
transitive   (13) Kind of verb—intransitive
(14) Verb-adverb combination   (15) Part of
speech—adverb   (16) Idioms   (17) Usage
label   (18) A noun derived from the main entry

(11)————————
(12)————————

(13)————————

(14)————————
(15)————————
(16)————————
(17)————————
(18)————————

dou•ble (dŭb′əl) *adj.* [ME < OFr. < Lat. *duplus.*] **1.** Twice as much in size, strength, number, or amount <*double* trouble> **2.** Having two like parts <*double* windows> **3.** Having two unlike parts : DUAL <a *double* standard> **4.** Designed for or accommodating two <a *double* hotel room> **5. a.** Acting two parts. **b.** Marked by duplicity : DECEITFUL. **6.** *Bot.* Having many more than the usual number of petals, usu. in a crowded or overlapping arrangement. *–n.* **1.** Something increased twofold. **2. a.** A duplicate of another : COUNTERPART. **b.** An apparition. **3.** An understudy. **4. a.** A sharp turn in running : REVERSAL. **b.** An evasive shift in argument. **5. doubles.** A game, as tennis or handball, having two players on each side. **6.** *Baseball.* A two-base hit. **7. a.** A request for a bid in bridge indicating strength to one's partner. **b.** A bid doubling one's opponent's bid in bridge, thus increasing the penalty for failure to fulfill the contract. **c.** A hand justifying such a bid. *–v.* **-bled, -bling, -bles.** *–vt.* **1.** To make twice as great. **2.** To be twice as much as. **3.** To fold in two. **4.** To repeat : duplicate. **5.** *Baseball.* **a.** To cause the scoring of (a run) by hitting a double. **b.** To advance or score (a runner) by hitting a double. **6.** *Baseball.* To put out (a runner) as the second part of a double play. **7.** To challenge (an opponent's bid) with a double in bridge. **8.** *Mus.* To duplicate (another part or voice) an octave higher or lower or in unison. **9.** *Naut.* To sail around <*doubled* the cape> *–vi.* **1.** To be increased twofold. **2.** To turn sharply backward : REVERSE. **3.** To serve in an additional capacity <a math teacher who *doubles* as a coach> **4.** To replace an actor in the performance of a given action or in the actor's absence. **5.** *Baseball.* To hit a double. **6.** To announce a double in bridge. **–double up. 1.** To bend suddenly, as in laughter or pain. **2.** To share accommodations meant for one person. *–adv.* **1.** To twice the extent or amount : DOUBLY. **2.** Two together. **–on** (*or* **at**) **the double.** *Informal.* **1.** In double time. **2.** Immediately. **–see double.** To see two images of a single object, usu. as a result of visual impairment. **–dou′ble•ness** *n.*

dictionary, put by ten of the following words the labels, if any, that you believe they should have. Then look up each word and determine which label it has. If a word is not labeled, it is considered formal.

1. flat out (at top speed) **no label**
2. deck (data-processing cards) **no label**
3. gussy **no label**
4. be on to **informal**
5. flick (a movie) **informal**
6. flop (a failure) **informal**
7. cram (to gorge with food) **no label**
8. down the tube **slang**
9. tube (subway) **no label**
10. tube (television) **informal**
11. phony **informal**
12. bash (party) **slang**
13. enthused **informal**
14. pigeon (dupe) **slang**
15. drippy (very sentimental) **slang**
16. freak (an enthusiast) **slang**
17. squeal (to betray) **slang**
18. deck (a tape deck) **no label**
19. wimp **slang**
20. be on to **informal**

These labels are from *Webster's II New College Dictionary* (1999).

41b Use words in their exact meanings. *den*

Denotations of words are their precise meanings, the definitions as given in dictionaries. Know exactly what a word means when you use it. Look up all words about which you have a slight doubt. Misuse of a word so that it does not convey the intended meaning may cause confusion, misunderstanding, and even embarrassment.

The italicized words in the following sentences are misused.

MISUSED WORDS

The new rocket was *literally* as fast as lightning. [*Figuratively* may be the word intended.]

The captain of the team was *overtaken* by the heat. [Here *overcome* would be exact.]

Because of past problems, the young candidate is *venerable*. [*Venerable,* meaning "old and respected," is apparently not what the writer means. *Vulnerable,* meaning "open to attack," would be more like it.]

After a wrongful act, a good person is usually troubled by a guilty *conscious*. [*conscience*]

■ Exercise 2

Underline words used inexactly or inappropriately in the following sentences. Then suggest substitutions.

     lush
1. A <u>luscious</u> carpet covered the floor of the restaurant.

              delicious   impeccable
2. The meal was simply <u>fabulous</u> and the service <u>unbelievable</u>—

    all in all, fantastic.

       elegy
3. Gray's "<u>allergy</u>," a truly moving poem, was written during a time

               mourning
    of great change and <u>morning</u> for the past.

4. On the outskirts of the small town, a sign was erected that
  announced
    <u>renounced</u> that this was the home of Marvin Fish.

                 baffling
5. Far out in space are many <u>babbling</u> questions to be answered.

6. People who are not born in America may become citizens by

      naturalized
    being <u>nationalized</u>.
  Recounting
7. <u>Accounting</u> all the events that led to the fall of any great civi-

    lization is impossible in a single essay.

           keynote
8. The keystone speaker at the convention tonight is noted for

    youth and political liberalism.

                                                               moot
9. The attorney vehemently shouted objections: "That is a mute
                      irrelevant
    point. Besides, it is irreverent and immaterial."

10. At the retirement dinner, the president of the bank said that the
               presence   **sorely**
    teller's daily presents would be soarly missed.

41c Select words with desired connotations.   *con*

Many words carry **connotations:** associations or emotional overtones that go beyond denotations. Effective writers carefully select
words with connotations that will evoke particular emotional reactions. To suggest sophistication, the writer may mention a *lap dog;*
to evoke the amusing or the rural, *hound dog.* To make a social or
moral judgment, the writer may call someone a *cur.* Consider the
associations aroused by *canine, pooch, mutt, mongrel, puppy,* and
watchdog. Even the names of some breeds arouse different responses: *bloodhound, shepherd, St. Bernard, poodle.*

     Words that are denotative synonyms may have very different
connotative overtones. Consider the following:

     ambulance chaser—lawyer—attorney
     skinny—thin—slender

Be sure that your words give the suggestions you wish to convey. A
single word with the wrong connotation can easily spoil a passage.
President Lincoln once said in a speech:

> Human nature will not change. In any future great national trial, compared with the men of this, we shall have as weak and as strong, as silly and as wise, as bad and as good.

Next, notice how substituting only two words ruins the consistent high tone of the passage, even though the meanings of the substitutes are close to those of the original.

> **Folks** will not change. In any future great national trial, compared with the men of this, we shall have as weak and as strong, as silly and as wise, as **crooked** and as good.

■ Exercise 3

Advertisers in particular are sensitive to the power of connotations. In class, explain the differences in the connotations of each word or phrase in parentheses in the following advertising claims.

1. We have just received an unusually beautiful assortment of silk (lifelike, fake, artificial) flowers.
2. Our (boutique, store) has the largest selection in town of styles for (full-bodied, fat, stout) women.
3. (False teeth, Dentures) will sparkle after just one (scrubbing, brushing) with BriteUp.
4. For a (fun-filled, pleasurable) but (cheap, inexpensive, economical) tour of Europe, see Euro-Travel first.
5. If you (are a drunk, have a drinking problem), talk with a Curative Hospital (doctor, physician) today.
6. See Garden of Eden Florists for both potted plants and (severed, cut) flowers.
7. The Corner Shop carries (gifts, presents) for every occasion and specializes in (serving, waiting on) you promptly and courteously.
8. All (previously owned, used) automobiles at Olde Imports have been thoroughly (repaired, reconditioned).

9 The Empire Restaurant offers carefully (cooked, prepared) (food, meals, dishes) at reasonable prices.

10. We (guarantee, assure you) that our (toilets, restrooms, bathrooms) are the cleanest of any national chain of service stations.

■ **Exercise 4**

The ten words or phrases in the left column name a subject. The right column gives a word referring to that subject. For each word in the right column, list a close synonym that is much more favorable in connotation and another that is less favorable.

1. weight	stout
2. intelligence	sense
3. writing style	intelligible
4. food	edible
5. degree of value	economical
6. personality	fairly agreeable
7. physical skill	coordinated
8. exactness of measurement	close enough
9. efficiency	competent
10. beauty	attractive

41d Generally, avoid colloquialisms and contractions in formal writing.

A **colloquialism** is a word or expression suitable in everyday conversation and in some informal composition but inappropriate in college writing.

COLLOQUIAL
> *Fussing at kids* in public is a *no-no.*

FORMAL WRITING
> *Correcting children* in public is impolite.

A **contraction** is a word formed from two words by the omission of one or more letters. An apostrophe indicates the omission. Contractions are **informal.**

INFORMAL

     That *clerk* who said *she'd* wait on me *didn't.*

APPROPRIATE IN FORMAL WRITING

     That *clerk* said *she would* wait on me, but she *did not.*

■ **Exercise 5**

In class, discuss usage in the following sentences.

1. Teachers often get a bum rap even when they do a jam-up job.
2. The dispatcher reckoned that the semi would arrive soon, but he could not raise the driver on the radio.
3. If someone is putting you down, remain calm and simply tell him or her to chill out.
4. Why get bent out of shape over nothing? Play it cool.
5. That green stuff we had for dinner was really gross.
6. When the young stockbroker discovered the potential earning power of the mining company, he freaked out.
7. He couldn't do nothing without the supervisor's eyeballing him and giving him a hard time.
8. The truckers heard on their ears that smokey was only three miles away on the blacktop.
9. The teller of the bank was instructed to tote the money back to the vault and to follow the boss to his office.
10. What cleared him was that the feds found out who really had done the robbery.

41e   Generally, avoid slang.   *sl*

Slang expressions in student papers are usually out of place. They are particularly inappropriate in a context that is otherwise dignified.

In the opinion of many students, the dean's commencement address *stunk.*

When Macbeth recoiled at the thought of murder, Lady Macbeth urged him not to *chicken out.*

Often slang is not as precise or widely known as terms in Standard English. Some **slang** words are so localized or recent that many people do not know their meaning. As slang ages and acquires particular and precise meanings, it sometimes becomes Standard English. *Date* and *dropout,* for example, began as slang but came to be regarded as Standard English when no other words were found to convey the same exact social meanings.

Avoid slang in Standard English, or use it carefully and deliberately, knowing that it may be colorful, even lurid, and sometimes incomprehensible to some readers.

41f Avoid dialect. *dial*

Regional, occupational, or ethnic words and usages should be avoided in formal writing except when they are consciously used to give a special flavor to language.

There is no reason to erase all dialectal characteristics from talk and writing. They are a cultural heritage and a source of richness and variety.

41g Do not use a word as a particular part of speech when it does not properly serve that function.

The forms of nouns and adjectives, nouns and verbs, and adjectives and adverbs (see **4a,** p. 83; **4c,** p. 86; **4d,** p. 89; **4e,** p. 89) are not interchangeable.

> Do not use *reference* as a verb. Use *refer.*
> As a verb, *suspicion* is nonstandard. Use *suspect.*

Do not use *good* as an adverb. Use *well.* "She reads *well*" (not "She reads *good*").

Do not use *because* to introduce a noun clause. Use *that.*

The reason is *that* . . .

NOT

The reason is *because* . . .

Adverb clauses should not follow a linking verb.

NOT

is when or *is where.* Use *is that.*

Quote is a verb. As a noun meaning *quotation* or *quotation mark,* it is informal.

Many avoid *like* as a conjunction and instead use *as.*

I swam *as* (not *like*) he did.

41h Use correct idioms.

An idiom is an accepted expression with its own distinct form and meaning. Language is rich in idiomatic expressions, some of which do not seem to make much sense literally but nevertheless have taken on specific meanings with time.

An onyx ring in the jewelry store *caught her eye.*

Though the gale was fierce, there was nothing else to do but *ride it out.*

The travel agent indicated that the ship would sail *Friday week.*

Many expressions demand specific prepositions. One preposition used with a word idiomatically has one meaning; another preposition used with the same word has a different meaning. *Agree to* a thing (a plan or a proposal); *agree with* a person. The plural or singular may be determined by idiom. The plural *regards,* for example, is used in *as regards,* meaning "concerning"; the singular *regard* is the idiom in *with* (or *in*) *regard to.* The sign of an infinitive, *to,* rather than the conjunction *and* follows *sure* and precedes a verb: *sure to succeed,* not *sure and succeed; try to find,* not *try and find.*

Idioms such as those in the following list need to be memorized until their use becomes a habit.

UNIDIOMATIC	IDIOMATIC
according with	according to
capable to	capable of
capable to do	capable of doing
center around	center in [*or* on]
conform in	conform to
die from	die of
ever now and then	every now and then
excepting for	except for
identical to	identical with
in accordance to	in accordance with
in search for	in search of
intend on doing	intend to do
in the year of 2000	in the year 2000
kind of a	kind of
lavish with gifts	lavish gifts on
off of	off
on a whole	on the whole
outlook of life	outlook on life
plan on	plan to
prior than	prior to
similar with	similar to
superior than	superior to
sure and	sure to
try and	try to
type of a	type of

Dictionaries list many idiomatic combinations and give their exact meanings—usually in boldface type at the end of a definition.

■ Exercise 6

Select a verb that is the common denominator in several idioms, such as carry *(carry out, carry over, carry through, and so forth). Look it up in a dictionary. Make a list, study the idioms, and be prepared to discuss them in class. Does the change of a preposition result in a different meaning? A slight change in meaning? No change?*

■ Exercise 7

Underline the incorrect prepositions and supply the correct ones. Write C by correct sentences.

1. After studying with a tutor, the student who was behind in al-
   with
   gebra was able to catch up <u>to</u> the rest of the class.
   of
2. The jury acquitted him <u>for</u> the charge of assault and battery.
   to
3. The aging baritone reacted favorably <u>with</u> the suggestion that

   he retire and surprised all members of the opera company.
   of
4. The hiker said that he was incapable <u>to</u> going on.

5. The professor stated that his good students would conform
   to
   <u>with</u> any requirement.
   to
6. The employees complained <u>with</u> the manager because of their

   long hours.
   in
7. Many vitamins are helpful <u>to</u> preventing diseases.

C 8. Fourteen new people were named to posts in the university ad-

   ministration.

On
9. Upon the whole, matters could be much worse.

in
10. Let us rejoice for the knowledge that we are free.

41i Avoid specialized vocabulary in writing for the general reader. *tech*

All specialists, whether engineers, chefs, or philosophers, have their own vocabularies. Some technical words find their way into general use; most do not. The plant red clover is well known but not by its botanical name, *Trifolium pratense*.

Specialists should use the language of nonspecialists when they hope to communicate with general readers. The following passage, for instance, would not be comprehensible to a wide audience.

> The neonate's environment consists in primitively contrasted perceptual fields weak and strong: loud noises, bright lights, smooth surfaces, compared with silence, darkness and roughness. The behavior of the neonate has to be accounted for chiefly by inherited motor connections between receptors and effectors. There is at this stage, in addition to the autonomic nervous system, only the sensorimotor system to call on. And so the ability of the infant to discriminate is exceedingly low. But by receiving and sorting random data through the identification of recurrent regularity, he does begin to improve reception. Hence he can surrender the more easily to single motivations, ego-involvement in satisfactions.
>
> JAMES K. FEIBLEMAN
> *The Stages of Human Life: A Biography of Entire Man*

Contrast the previous passage with the following, which is on the same general subject but which is written so that the general reader—not just a specialized few—can understand it.

> Research clearly indicates that an infant's senses are functional at birth. He experiences the whack from the doctor. He is sensitive to pressure, to changes in temperature, and to pain, and he responds specifically to these stimuli. . . . How about sight? Research on infants 4–8 weeks of age shows that they can see about as well as adults. . . . The difference is that the in-

fant cannot make sense out of what he sees. Nevertheless, what he sees
does register, and he begins to take in visual information at birth. . . . In
summary, the neonate (an infant less than a month old) is sensitive not
only to internal but also to external stimuli. Although he cannot respond
adequately, he does take in and process information.

IRA J. GORDON
Human Development: From Birth Through Adolescence

The only technical term in the passage is *neonate;* unlike the writer
of the first passage, who also uses the word, the second author de-
fines it for the general reader.

Special vocabularies may obscure meaning. Moreover, they
tempt the writer to use inflated words instead of plain ones—a style
sometimes known as *gobbledygook* or *governmentese* because it
flourishes in bureaucratic writing. Harry S. Truman made a famous
statement about the presidency: "The buck stops here." This
straightforward assertion might be written by some bureaucrats as
follows: "It is incumbent upon the President of the United States of
America to uphold the responsibility placed upon him by his con-
stituents to exercise the final decision-making power."

41j Add new words to your vocabulary.   *vocab*

Good writers know many words, and they can select the precise
ones they need to express their meanings. A good vocabulary dis-
plays your intelligence, your education, and your talents as a writer.

In reading, pay careful attention to words you have not seen before. Look them up in a dictionary. Remember them. Recognize
them the next time you see them. Learn to use them.

■ Exercise 8

Underline the best definition.

1. *colossal:*   (a) colorful   (b) enormous   (c) terrible   (d) silent

2. *nominate:* (a) agree (b) calculate (c) think (d) <u>propose</u>

3. *liaison:* (a) <u>communication</u> (b) happy (c) descendant (d) loss

4. *armistice:* (a) seasoning (b) musical composition (c) hope (d) <u>truce</u>

5. *toxin:* (a) shoe (b) wagon (c) <u>poison</u> (d) champion

6. *charlatan:* (a) <u>fraud</u> (b) chef (c) North Carolinian (d) specialist

7. *mediator:* (a) meat cutter (b) <u>reconciler</u> (c) mechanic (d) test

8. *cryptic:* (a) mineral (b) <u>obscure</u> (c) tomb (d) orderly

9. *lassitude:* (a) <u>fatigue</u> (b) rope (c) collie dog (d) lecture

10. *gyration:* (a) fountain (b) speech (c) evasion (d) <u>revolving movement</u>

11. *kindle:* (a) <u>catch fire</u> (b) unearth (c) taper (d) hide

12. *harmonious:* (a) musical instrument (b) <u>in accord</u> (c) ugly (d) decent

13. *perennial:* (a) relating to parents (b) speedy (c) pretty (d) <u>recurrent</u>

14. *aspiration:* (a) medicine (b) <u>ambition</u> (c) drawing (d) enlightenment

15. *theology:* (a) system (b) theory (c) <u>study of religion</u>

 (d) political party

16. *quirk:* (a) fake (b) store employee (c) noise (d) <u>peculiarity</u>

17. *fathom:* (a) sailor (b) feather (c) animal magnetism (d) <u>understand</u>

18. *incorrigible:* (a) crated (b) <u>not reformable</u> (c) optimistic

 (d) encouraging

19. *somber:* (a) lovely (b) disputed (c) <u>gloomy</u> (d) Mexican hat

20. *referendum:* (a) <u>vote</u> (b) reference work (c) feast (d) operation

42 Style   *st*

Express yourself with economy, clarity, and freshness.

Style refers to the way writers express their thoughts in language, the way they put words together. The modes in which similar ideas are expressed can have different effects, and many of the distinctions are a matter of style. Acquire the habit of noticing the personality of what you read and write, and work to develop your own style.

42a Do not be wordy.   *w*

Conciseness increases the force of writing. A verbose style is flabby and ineffectual. Do not pad your paper merely to obtain a desired length.

USE ONE WORD FOR SEVERAL

> The love letter was written by somebody who did not sign a name. [13 words]

> The love letter was anonymous [*or* not signed]. [5 or 6 words]

USE THE ACTIVE VOICE FOR CONCISENESS (SEE **9**)

> The truck was overloaded by the workmen. [7 words]

> The workmen overloaded the truck. [5 words]

DELETE UNNEEDED WORDS; REVISE SENTENCES

> Another element that adds to the effectiveness of a speech is its emotional appeal. [14 words]

> Emotional appeal also makes a speech more effective. [8 words]

AVOID CONSTRUCTIONS WITH *IT IS* . . . AND *THERE ARE* . . .

> *It is* truth *that* will prevail. [6 words]

> Truth will prevail. [3 words]

> *There are* some conditions *that* are unsatisfactory. [7 words]

> Some conditions are unsatisfactory. [4 words]

DO NOT USE TWO WORDS WITH THE SAME MEANING (TAUTOLOGY)

> basic and fundamental principles [4 words]

> basic principles [2 words]

AVOID BUREAUCRATIC PHRASES

BUREAUCRATIC	USE
at that point in time	at that point *or* then
basic and fundamental	basic *or* fundamental [not both]
consensus of opinion	consensus
each and every	each *or* every [not both]
early on	early
equally as good	equal *or* as good [not both]

Make your sentences concise by using all the preceding methods. Do not, however, sacrifice concreteness and vividness for conciseness and brevity.

CONCRETE AND VIVID

     At each end of the sunken garden, worn granite steps, flanked by large magnolia trees, lead to formal paths.

EXCESSIVELY CONCISE

     The garden has steps at both ends.

■ Exercise 9

Express the following sentences succinctly but do not omit important ideas.

1. The kudzu plant is a plant that was introduced into America from Japan in order to prevent erosion and the washing away of the land and that has become a nuisance and a pest in some areas because it chokes out trees and other vegetation.
   Kudzu, which was introduced into America from Japan to prevent erosion, has become a nuisance in some areas because it chokes out other plants.

2. The cry of a peacock is audible to the ear for miles.
   The cry of a peacock is audible for miles.

3. The custom that once was so popular of speaking to fellow students while passing by them on the campus has almost disappeared from college manners and habits.
   The once-popular custom of speaking to fellow students on the campus has almost disappeared.

4. There are several reasons why officers of the law ought to be trained in the law of the land, and two of these are as follows. The first of these reasons is that police officers can enforce the

law better if they are familiar with it. And second, they will be less likely to violate the rights of private citizens if they know exactly and accurately what these rights are.

Officers should know the law so that they can enforce it better and avoid violating the rights of citizens.

5. Although the Constitution gives American citizens the right

legally to bear arms, ~~it is thought by~~ many modern lawmakers
                                         believe this law to be

to be useless and harmful ~~law that is no longer needed in this~~
   ∧

~~day and time.~~

6. Some television programs, especially public television programs, assume a high level of public intelligence and present their shows to the public in an intelligent way.

Some public television programs assume an intelligent audience and present their shows accordingly.

                       Trees on

7. ~~It is not likely that~~ land where forests have been clear-cut will
 not   ∧   as

   grow again quickly ~~enough with~~ a large, ~~number of different~~
∧   forest.   ∧

  ~~and~~ diverse ~~species.~~

8. The plane was flown by a cautious pilot who was careful.

A cautious pilot flew the plane.

9. It is a pleasure for some to indulge in eating large quantities of food at meals, but medical doctors of medicine tell us that such pleasures can only bring with them unpleasant results in the long run of things.

The joys of overeating, doctors say, can have unpleasant results.

10. The essay consists of facts that describe vividly many aspects of the work of a typical stockbroker. In this description the author uses a vocabulary that is easy to understand. This vocabulary is on neither too high a level nor too low a level, but on one that can be understood by any high school graduate.

    In simple language the essay describes vividly many aspects of the work of a typical stockbroker.

42b Avoid repeating ideas, words, or sounds. *rep*

Unintentional repetition is a mark of bad style. Avoid it by omitting words and by using synonyms and pronouns.

REPETITIOUS

The history of human flight is full of histories of failures on the part of those who have tried flight and were failures.

IMPROVED

The history of human flight recounts many failures.

Do not revise by substituting synonyms for repeated words too often.

WORDY SYNONYMS

The history of human flight is full of stories of failures on the part of those who have tried to glide through the air and met with no success.

Do not needlessly repeat sounds.

REPEATED SOUNDS

The biologist again *checked* the *charts* to determine the *effect* of the poison on the *insect*.

IMPROVED

The biologist again studied the charts to determine the effect of the poison on the moth.

NOTE: Effective repetition of a word or a phrase may unify, clarify, or create emphasis, especially in aphorisms or poetry.

Searching without knowledge is like *searching* in the dark.
"Beauty is truth, truth beauty." [John Keats]

■ Exercise 10

Rewrite the following passage. Avoid wordiness and undesirable repetition.

 P   and ages
One of the pleasing things that all peoples of all lands have

always enjoyed since the earliest dawning of civilizations is the

                                                    , which,
pleasure of listening to the melodious strands of music, Music,
some famous poet has said,
wrote some famous poet, can soothe a savage breast and make
     Some younger people, however, may be listening
him or her calm. A question may arise in the minds of many,
too frequently to their favorite music.
however, as to whether some of our members of the younger

generation may not be exposing themselves too frequently to

music they like and listen to almost constantly.

     Nearly every day, for example, one meets a young person who
          To me, the answer to the previous question is just possibly in
listens to music
the affirmative, and the evidence that I would give would be in

the form of a figure that we see nearly every day. This is the

figure, usually a young person but not always, of a person with a radio or stereo headset who is listening to music while doing an

should   **her full**   .   **At**

activity that used to occupy all of one's attention and time. In the

times a person in the library looks through books while   ∧

library of a college such a figure is now at times to be seen looking

wearing a headset.

through books with a headset on his or her head. Some of these

of this sort   **and enjoying**

music lovers seem incapable of even taking a walk to enjoy the
    ∧   ∧

beauty of nature without their headsets.

If we enjoy good music,

If music is good and if we enjoy it, the reader may now ask,
    ∧

                                  it as   **as modern**

what is wrong with listening to music more frequently than we

electronics enables us to do? It is not old-fashioned to believe

used to be able to listen to music thanks to the present modern

that those who spend much of their time with headsets on

improvements and developments in the electronic medium? It

are missing other important and pleasurable sensory

may seem old-fashioned and out-of-date to object to headsets just

experiences—the sounds of birds and even the quiet of

because we did not once have them and they are relatively new

morning. Further, it is hard to think while the ear is piped full

on the scene. What is important, here, however, is the point that

of music. Time that should be used for thinking is also lost—

those who spend so much of their time with headsets on are

time when we develop and mature intellectually. All kinds of

missing something. They may be getting a lot of music, but they

music, even rock, have an important place, but music should not

are missing something. What they are missing can be classified

be allowed to exclude too many other valuable experiences.

under the general heading of other important and pleasurable sensory

experiences that they could be experiencing, such as hearing the

~~sounds that birds make and just enjoying the quiet that morning some-~~

~~times brings. In addition to this, it is hard for the listener to think while~~

~~music is being piped into the ear of the listener. We lose time, therefore,~~

~~that should by all rights be reserved for thinking and contemplation,~~

~~which is to say, that time when we all develop and mature intellectu-~~

~~ally. Music, all kinds of music, even rock music, has an important place~~

~~in the lives of humankind, but let us not so fall in love with its seduc-~~

~~tive appeal that beckons us that we let it intrude upon the territory of~~

~~other valuable and essential experiences.~~

42c Avoid flowery language. *fl*

Flowery language is wordy, overwrought, and artificial. Often falsely elegant, it calls attention to itself. Do not attempt to substitute sophisticated words for naturalness, simplicity, and substance.

PLAIN LANGUAGE	FLOWERY LANGUAGE
the year 2000	the year of 2000
now	at this point in time
lawn	verdant sward
shovel	simple instrument for delving into Mother Earth
a teacher	a dedicated toiler in the arduous labors of pedagogy
reading a textbook	following the lamp of knowledge in a textual tome
eating	partaking of the dietary sustenance of life
going overseas	traversing the ever-palpitating deep

42d Be clear. *cl*

A hard-to-read style annoys and alienates. Do not take for granted that others will be patient or understanding enough to pore over your writing to determine your meaning. If you have any doubt that a sentence or a passage conveys the precise meaning you intend, revise and clarify. Nothing in writing is more important than making sense.

Write specifically.

Abstract writing may communicate little information or may even cause misunderstanding. Specific words say what you think. Their meaning is not ambiguous.

NOT SPECIFIC
> There was always a certain something in her personality that created a kind of positive effect.

SPECIFIC
> Her optimism always conveyed a sense of hope and joy.

Give concrete examples.

Concrete examples often pierce to the heart of meaning, whereas vague and abstract writing ineffectually ranges around the periphery.

CONCRETE
> Her bright, quick smile and her musical way of saying, "Good morning!" conveyed a sense of hope and joy.

■ Exercise 11

The following ten words or phrases are general. For any five of them, substitute four specific and concrete words. Do not let your substitutions be synonymous with each other.

EXAMPLE

       tools   claw hammer, screwdriver, monkey wrench, saw

1. associations
   labor union, Medal of Honor Winners' Association, credit union, Airline Pilots' Association

2. rural or (urban) buildings
   barn, stable, city hall, post office

3. officers of court
   judge, attorneys, court reporter, bailiff

4. works of art
   watercolor, oil painting, sculpture, fresco

5. terrain
   dune, piedmont, coastal plain, wetland

6. nuts (or vegetables or meats or breads)
   pecan, carrot, roast, pita

7. missives
   first-class letter, overnight letter, email letter, memo

8. mammals
   black bear, Bengal tiger, howler monkey, German shepherd

9. foot races
   hundred-yard dash, twenty-five–yard dash, two-hundred-meter relay, cross-country race

10. ways to walk
    strolling, ambling, fast gait, marching

■ Exercise 12

Write your personal definition of one of the following abstract terms in a paragraph of about two hundred words. Write specifically from your own experience.

1. education
2. family
3. maturity
4. pride
5. prejudice

42e Avoid triteness and clichés. Strive for fresh and original expressions. *trite*

Clichés are phrases and figures of speech that were once fresh and original but have been used so much that they have lost their effectiveness. A stale phrase leaves the impression of a stale mind and a lazy imagination. Develop a sensitivity to clichés and reject them for fresher writing.

Study the following twenty phrases as examples of triteness. Avoid pat expressions like these:

words cannot express	method in their madness
each and every	straight from the shoulder
Mother Nature	first and foremost
sober as a judge	hard as a rock
other side of the coin	in the final analysis
slowly but surely	felt like an eternity
in this day and age	the bottom line
few and far between	all walks of life
last but not least	easier said than done
interesting to note	better late than never

■ Exercise 13

Underline the clichés in the following sentences.

1. Once in a blue moon, Professor Alhambra tells a joke that is funny, but then he spoils it by laughing like a hyena.

2. Small Internet companies have become a dime a dozen on the stock market. Many dyed-in-the-wool old-school analysts believe that they are dangerously overrated.

3. It goes without saying that the value of a college education cannot be measured in money, but tuition is as high as a kite.

4. As he looked back, the farmer thought of those mornings as cold as ice when the ground was as hard as a rock and when he shook like a leaf as he rose at the crack of dawn.

5. The survivor was weak as a kitten after eight days on the ocean, but in a few days he was fit as a fiddle.

6. The brothers were as different as night and day, but each drank like a fish.

7. The heiress claimed that she wanted to marry a strong, silent type, but she tied the knot with her hairdresser.

8. It was raining cats and dogs, but still she managed to look as pretty as a picture.

9. Surely it is possible to keep abreast of the times without giving up the tried and true values of the past.

10. If you pinch pennies now, you can enjoy the golden years with more peace of mind.

42f   Use fresh and effective figures of speech. Avoid mixed and inappropriate figures.   *fig*

Figures of speech compare one thing (usually abstract) with another (usually literal or concrete). Mixed figures associate things that are not logically consistent.

MIXED

> The humidity is 93 percent, and that is going to add fuel to the fire tomorrow. [Humidity or water increases dampness or rainfall. It does not add fuel to fire.]

Inappropriate figures of speech compare one thing with another in a way that violates the writing's mood or intention.

INAPPROPRIATE

> Shakespeare is the most famous brave in the tribe of English writers. [It is inappropriate and puzzling to compare Shakespeare to an Indian brave and a group of writers to an Indian tribe.]

Use figurative comparisons (of things not literally similar) for vivid explanation and for originality. Using a simile, a metaphor, or a personification gives you a chance to compare or to explain what you are saying in a different way from the sometimes prosaic method of pure statement, argument, or logic.

METAPHORS (IMPLIED COMPARISONS)

> Though calm without, the young senator was a volcano within.
>
> Old courthouse records are rotting leaves of the past.

SIMILES (COMPARISONS STATED WITH *LIKE* OR *AS*)

> Though calm without, the young senator was *like* a volcano within.
>
> Old courthouse records are *like* rotting leaves of the past.

■ Exercise 14

Explain the flaws in these figures of speech.

1. The new race car flew once around the track and then limped into the pit like a sick horse into its stable.
   Comparing a machine first to a bird and then to a horse is a flawed mixture.

2. The speaker's flamboyant oration began with all the beauty of the song of a canary.
   The volume, pitch, and rhythm of an oration are not embodied well in a sound like the song of a canary.

3. Crickets chirped with the steadiness of the tread of a marching army.
   The pounding of a marching army does not describe the sounds of crickets well.

4. The warm greetings of the students sounded like a horde of apes rushing through a jungle.
   Mannerly human responses are not well expressed in the simile of rushing apes.

5. He nipped the plan in the bud by pouring cold water on all suggestions.
   Nipping (cutting) is not similar to pouring a cold liquid.

■ Exercise 15

Compose and bring to class two fresh and appropriate figures of speech.

■ Exercise 16

Find two figures of speech in your reading and show how they are mixed or especially appropriate or inappropriate.

Literature

43 Writing About Literature

Novels, short stories, plays, and poems are works of art. They convey meaning, and they also seek to reveal form and beauty, to amuse and entertain as well as to provide information. Expository writing, nonfiction prose, and essays primarily attempt to explain and to inform. Criticism of literature also deals with ideas—but not exclusively.

The broadest critics concentrate not only on what an author is saying but also on the art itself, *how* it is said. In the best literature, the craft is as important as what is said. Critics seek to identify artistic devices in literature: setting, characters, structure, imagery, and style are just a few of the myriads of devices that literary artists use to achieve effects.

This section will help you to think about short stories and poems, to discuss them, and to write papers of interpretation and appreciation. State your opinions, but avoid excessive subjectivity, quick and personal reactions that are not corroborated by solid evidence. Delve into the work of art, describe what you find, and offer analysis and proof.

43a Choose a literary work that interests you. Write about the feature of the work that interests you most.

Your instructor may assign you a particular work for a paper, or you may be allowed to choose for yourself. If you have any freedom of choice, select carefully. An unwise selection will make success difficult even if you write well.

Give thought to your choice. You are likely to write a better paper if you choose a **work new to you,** a work that no one has ever taught to you and that you have never written about before. Search for the kind of topic you like. Look at familiar authors, famous authors, works recommended to you by people who have tastes somewhat like yours. Look at shelves of books and lists of authors you have heard about but not read, new stories and poems, anthologies, collections. You are unlikely to write a good paper about a work that you regard as dull or mediocre. If a literary work contains no mystery for you at first, you are unlikely to explain it in an original or interesting way to others.

Avoid shallow and obvious literature. If you read something that makes you think, "That is exactly what I have always known," you should doubt the originality of the author. If you think, "True, but I never thought of anything like that before," you may have a good selection on your hands. A work that interprets or explains itself will not leave much for you to write about. Good papers are often derived from literature that is somewhat puzzling and obscure during and immediately after the first reading. Additional readings and careful thought can produce surprises to write about.

Do not decide to write on a particular subject before you read the work. What you think will be a good subject may not be there at all. Find your subjects as you read and as you think. Let good subjects grow and develop; bad ones will disappear or fade away. The most surprising and significant topics may come to you when you least expect them—as you slowly wake in the morning, for example, or as you engage in some kind of physical activity.

The basic methods for planning and writing a paper about literature are the same as those you would use for writing any other kind of paper (see p. 18, 19, 20). List topics and subtopics; group them; arrange them; rearrange them; write whatever comes into your mind, whether it seems good or bad at the moment; write to keep the words going, even when what you are writing seems unimportant. Cross out. Put check marks by important points; photocopy parts of works; make notations of lines, passages, images, sentences. Write quickly for a time. Think and write slowly and carefully about crucial subjects. Stop writing and walk about. Use every physical and mental device you can think of to tease good thoughts out of your mind.

Be willing to give up ideas that are inferior. Expect surprises and twists and turns during the process of writing. Few papers are written like bullets speeding toward a single idea with a calculated aim; most of the time they act more like floods, gathering valuables and debris at the same time. After the first draft, you can begin separating bad from good ideas.

Kinds of Literary Papers

Writings about literature fall into several categories. A few of the more significant ones are explained next.

Interpretation

Many papers are interpretations derived mainly from close study of the literary work. An interpretive paper identifies methods and ideas. Through analysis, the writer presents specific evidence to support the argument.

Distinguish carefully between the thinking of a character and that of the author. Unless an author speaks in her own voice, you can deduce what the author thinks only from the work as a whole, from effects of events in the plot, and from attitudes that develop from good or bad characters. Some works of literature depict a character whose whole way of life is opposite to the author's views. To confuse the character with the author is to make a crucial mistake. Sometimes it is clear immediately what an author thinks about the characters, but not always.

Review

A good review of a book or an article

1. identifies the author, the title, and the subject.
2 summarizes accurately the information presented and the author's argument.
3. describes and perhaps categorizes the author's methods.

4. provides support (with evidence and argument) for the good points and explains the author's mistakes, errors, misjudgments, or misinterpretations.
5. evaluates the work's accomplishments and failures.

Character analysis

A character sketch is a tempting kind of paper to write, but a good analysis of a character or an explanation of an author's methods of characterization is truly a difficult task. This kind of paper easily turns into a superficial summary when it fails to consider motivations, development, change, and interrelationships of characters. Meaningful interpretation of a character may define something that the character does not know about himself or herself, traits that the author reveals only by hints and implications. For example, if you can show that a character clearly lacks self-understanding, you may be on the way to writing a good paper.

Of course, an analysis may *not* deal at all with *what the character is* but consider instead the *methods* the author uses to reveal the character. Body language and modes of speech, facial expressions or changes in mood, excessive talking or silence, and appearance are some of these methods. Remember that the author characterizes; the critic discusses the methods of characterization.

Analysis of setting

Often the time and place in which a work is set reveal important moods and meanings. Setting may help to indicate the manners and emotions of characters by showing how they interact with their environments. When you write about setting, you accomplish very little by merely describing it. Show what its functions are in the literary work.

Technical analysis

The analysis of technical elements in literature—imagery, symbolism, point of view, structure, prosody, and so on—requires special study of the technical term or concept as well as of the literary work itself. Begin by looking up the term in a good basic reference book such as *A Handbook to Literature*. However, you should never be concerned with vocabulary and technical terms for their own sake. If you discover in a work an aspect that you wish to examine, find the exact term for it by discussing it with your teacher, looking it up in a dictionary, and studying it in a handbook or an encyclopedia. Then determine what the technique does in the work you are writing about.

Combined approaches

Many papers combine different approaches. A thoughtful paper on imagery, for example, does more than merely point out the images, or even the kinds of images, in the literary work; it uses the imagery to interpret, analyze, or clarify something else as well—theme, structure, characterization, mood, relationship, recurrent patterns, and so on. Depending on the subject and the work you are writing about, many aspects can mingle to accomplish a single objective.

43b Give the paper a precise title.

Do not search for a fancy title at the expense of meaning. Authors of literary works often use figurative titles like *Death in the Afternoon* and *The Grapes of Wrath,* but you would be wise to designate your subject more literally. Be precise; state your subject in the title.

Do not use the title of the work as your own title, as in "Robert Frost's 'Directive.' " Do not merely announce that you are writing about a work by calling your paper "An Analysis of Frost's 'Directive' " or "An Interpretation of . . ." or "A Criticism of. . . ." The fact that you are writing the paper indicates that you are writing an analysis, a criticism, or something of the sort.

Stick to the topic named in the title. The topic sentence of every paragraph should point back to the title, the introduction, and the thesis statement.

43c Do not begin with broad philosophical statements.

You do not have to create for your paper an introduction composed of sage observations about history or human nature as a prelude to your focus upon more specific matters. In fact, such opening statements and the comments that follow them usually tend toward the trite and commonplace (see **42e**); therefore, get immediately to your subject without philosophical fanfare, which often comes across as mere padding. Avoid openings like the following:

> "In today's complex world . . ."
> "Human beings have always . . ."
> "From the beginning of time . . ."
> "In the annals of . . ."
> "Throughout the past . . ."
> "From the dawn of civilization . . ."

43d Organize and develop the paper according to significant ideas.

Do not automatically organize your paper by following the sequence of the literary work. Sometimes the result of this order can be poor topic sentences, summary rather than analysis, mechanical organization, and repetitive transitional phrases.

Usually it is better to break up your overall argument into several aspects and to move from one of these to the next.

First sentences that provide mechanical and dull information do not encourage further reading. Avoid generality, as in the following sentence:

> T. S. Eliot, in his famous poem written in 1922, *The Waste Land,* expressed a theme that has been a frequent subject of works of literature.

Instead, you might try something like this:

> The relationship between the physical, mental, and spiritual health of a ruler of a nation and the condition of the people is a subject of T. S. Eliot's poem *The Waste Land*.

The first sentence states nothing of true significance; the second announces a particular topic to be explored.

Just as a paper should not begin mechanically, the parts should not contain mechanical first sentences and dull transitions. Your paragraphs will not create interest if they use beginnings like these:

"In the first stanza . . ."
"In the following part . . ."
"At the conclusion . . ."

43e Avoid extensive paraphrasing and plot summary.

Keep summarizing to a minimum, just enough to furnish context and to be clear. Mere plot-summary of fiction or paraphrase of poetry is inadequate. Summary should make your argument clear and concrete; it should not be an end in itself. Extensive plot-summary and paraphrase are often the sure marks of writers who have not thought enough about a work of literature to do more than retell the story or slide along the surface of the poem. When you paraphrase, distinguish clearly between the author's thinking and your own.

NOTE: When you do summarize, use the historical present tense (see **8a**). Tell what *happens,* not what *happened.*

43f Think for yourself.

Thinking—hard, concentrated thinking—is probably the most important single preparation for writing an effective essay. Start early enough on your assignment so that you can devote time to this essential step in the process.

You do not have to come up with an idea that no one else has ever thought of, as long as you do come up with an idea, one that is original in the sense that you thought of it yourself. It may not be profound or unusual, but it is *yours,* and that is the important factor. You are developing the eye of a critic when you can read a work of literature and (after a period of brainstorming and germination) can think up your own angle (even if your instructor has assigned you a specific topic).

43g Write about the literature, not about yourself or "the reader."

The process by which you discovered what you are writing about is usually a dull subject to other people. Give the results of your explorations, not details of the various steps.

Your teacher will know that what you write is your opinion unless you indicate otherwise; therefore, you should not repeat expressions like "In my opinion" or "I believe that." Extensive use of first-person pronouns (*I, my*) takes the emphasis away from what you are writing about.

In an effort to avoid the pronoun *I,* do not develop the annoying habit of repeating the phrase "the reader." Writing about "the reader" is logically erroneous because the expression implies readers in general, and you cannot speak for this vast, varied, and complex group. Once you begin using "the reader," it is difficult to stop, and your style will be greatly weakened by the resulting wordiness. Though you may not realize it, when you make extensive use of first-person pronouns and "the reader," you are creating an impression of self-consciousness that can annoy or even alienate.

43h Provide evidence to support your ideas.

Generalizations without illustrations are seldom convincing. Make a specific point. Then back it up with evidence. Paraphrase, quote, and select details to support your argument.

Usually it is not good to begin with a quotation. Say what you think and then quote to illustrate or to provide proof.

43i Quote sparingly and effectively.

Appropriate quotations from the work of literature you are writing about are indispensable. Many times they make the best evidence, even though they may be brief. You can weave them into your argument in a number of ways, one of the most effective of which is to work them into a sentence of your own.

BRIEF QUOTATION AT THE BEGINNING OF A SENTENCE
"A devilish thing" is what Captain Loft calls chocolate in Steinbeck's *The Moon Is Down* (158).

BRIEF QUOTATION IN THE MIDDLE OF A SENTENCE
Captain Loft's reference to chocolate as "a devilish thing" in Steinbeck's *The Moon Is Down* comes near the end of the novel (158).

BRIEF QUOTATION AT THE END OF A SENTENCE
In Steinbeck's *The Moon Is Down,* Captain Loft calls chocolate "a devilish thing" (158).

Prefer brief but telling quotations over long ones. Long quotations can become boring, and they often leave the impression of haste in composition. Paraphrase is sometimes more effective than long quotations. Quote enough to make your case convincing; do not quote too often or too lengthily.

43j Do not moralize.

Good criticism does not preach. Do not use your paper as a platform from which to state your views on the rights and wrongs and conditions of the world. A literary paper can be spoiled by an attempt to teach a moral lesson.

Begin your paper by introducing the work and your ideas about it as literature. If the author discusses morals, religion, or social causes, her literary treatment of these subjects is a proper topic. Do not begin your paper with your own ideas about the world and then attempt to fit the literature to them or merge your ideas with the author's. Think for yourself, but *think about the author's writing*.

43k Acknowledge your sources.

Define the difference between what other critics have written and what you think. State your contribution. Do not begin papers or paragraphs with the names of critics and their views before you have presented your own ideas.

Develop your own thesis. Stress your views, not those of others. Use sources to show that other critics have interpreted the literature correctly, to correct errors in criticism that is otherwise excellent, to show that a critic is right but that something needs to be added, or to show that no one has previously written about your subject.

It is not a problem if no critic has written about the work or the point you are making unless your instructor requires you to have a number of sources. However, it is a serious error to state incorrectly that nothing has been written about your subject. Be thorough in your investigation.

For bibliographies of writings about literature, see **44d**. For information about plagiarism and documentation, see **44g** and **44i**.

43l Writing about a story

Read Alice Walker's short short story "The Flowers," which follows. As you read the story for the first time, think about the character of the girl, the time in her life, the place where she lives, what happens in the story, and what it all means to her. Take notes and ask questions.

The Flowers

Alice Walker

It seemed to Myop as she skipped lightly from hen house to pigpen to smokehouse that the days had never been as beautiful as these. The air held a keenness that made her nose twitch. The harvesting of the corn and cotton, peanuts and squash, made each day a golden surprise that caused excited little tremors to run up her jaws.

Myop carried a short, knobby stick. She struck out at random at chickens she liked, and worked out the beat of a song on the fence around the pigpen. She felt light and good in the warm sun. She was ten, and nothing existed for her but her song, the stick clutched in her dark brown hand, and the tat-de-ta-ta-ta of accompaniment.

Turning her back on the rusty boards of her family's share-cropper cabin, Myop walked along the fence until it ran into the stream made by the spring. Around the spring, where the family got drinking water, silver ferns and wildflowers grew. Along the shallow banks pigs rooted. Myop watched the tiny white bubbles disrupt the thin black scale of soil and the water that silently rose and slid away down the stream.

She had explored the woods behind the house many times. Often, in late autumn, her mother took her to gather nuts among the fallen leaves. Today she made her own path, bouncing this way and that, vaguely keeping an eye out for snakes. She found, in addition to various common but pretty ferns and leaves, an armful of strange blue flowers with velvety ridges and a sweetsuds bush full of the brown, fragrant buds.

By twelve o'clock, her arms laden with sprigs of her findings, she was a mile or more from home. She had often been as far before, but the strangeness of the land made it not as pleasant as her usual haunts. It seemed gloomy in the little cove in which she found herself. The air was damp, the silence close and deep.

Myop began to circle back to the house, back to the peacefulness of the morning. It was then she stepped smack into his eyes. Her heel became lodged in the broken ridge between brow and nose, and she reached down quickly, unafraid, to free herself. It was only when she saw his naked grin that she gave a little yelp of surprise.

He had been a tall man. From feet to neck covered a long space. His head lay beside him. When she pushed back the leaves and layers of earth and debris, Myop saw that he'd had large white teeth, all of them cracked or broken, long fingers, and very big bones. All his clothes had rotted away except some threads of blue denim from his overalls. The buckles of the overalls had turned green.

Myop gazed around the spot with interest. Very near where she had stepped into the head was a wild pink rose. As she picked it to add to her bundle, she noticed a raised mound, a ring, around the rose's root. It was the rotted remains of a noose, a bit of shredded plowline, now blending benignly into the soil. Around an overhanging limb of a great spreading oak clung another piece. Frayed, rotted, bleached, and frazzled—barely there—but spinning restlessly in the breeze. Myop laid down her flowers.

And the summer was over.

Before you discuss the story with anyone, ponder the following questions.

1. How old is Myop, and what is the importance of her age?
2. Where does she live? At what time in history?
3. What is the season? What is the importance of the seasons and weather? What do they suggest about mood and meaning?
4. What is the significance of the last sentence in the story?
5. What do you find that is especially beautiful, and what is its importance? What is ugly? How?

Consider these points and take notes on anything else you think is important in the story.

■ Exercise 1

Be prepared to discuss in class the points you have raised about the short story. Take notes. What other topics about the story do you find significant?

Your instructor may require that you write a paper about the story. Decide on a topic and compose a title whether or not a paper is required.

43m   Writing about a poem.

A writer of good fiction is a highly specialized artist. Even so, poems have different characteristics from fiction and may be in some ways more technical than prose. The following poem by Denise Levertov, for example, has two-line stanzas but no rhymes, which are usually found with couplets. The last five words are a striking conclusion (a single line) that resembles the stark last line of the previously discussed story, "Flowers." Make plans to write a paper about this poem, just as you did while reading the story. What would your title be? Write down three or four major points that you would make.

In Mind

There's in my mind a woman
of innocence, unadorned but

fair-featured, and smelling of
apples or grass. She wears

a utopian smock or shift, her hair
is light brown and smooth, and she

is kind and very clean without
ostentation—
                   but she has
no imagination.
                     And there's a
turbulent moon-ridden girl

or old woman, or both,
dressed in opals and rags, feathers

and torn taffeta,
who knows strange songs—

but she is not kind.

DENISE LEVERTOV

Consider the subject of the following model paper. Do the points resemble those in your plan? How are they different? Several readers of the poem might produce a wide variety of papers.

Actually, the model paper does not treat any topics that are uniquely poetic. Criticism of a work of literature does not have to be highly specialized. A careful interpreter of poetry needs at first to find a subject that is meaningful but not extremely technical.

43n Model paper

Innocence and Imagination: Contrasts in

Denise Levertov's "In Mind"

Two very different women appear in the poem "In Mind" by Denise Levertov. Both are attractive in some ways, but both also have shortcomings. As the speaker of the poem describes the two women who are "in my mind" (1), she may be talking about two actual people she knows. It is more likely, however, that she is describing two halves of herself: two kinds of people that she could be or has been at different stages in her life. Through

these two women, Levertov examines the contrasts
between innocence and imagination.

The first part of herself the speaker considers
is the "woman / of innocence" (1-2), who is characterized in simple and natural terms. She is
described as "unadorned" and lacking "ostentation"
(2, 8). Practicality governs this woman, who wears
"a utopian smock or shift" (5) rather than any
elaborate costume. Levertov notes that this woman
is "fair-featured," but the only specific visual
detail of her appearance given is that her hair "is
light brown and smooth" (3, 6). This description
suggests a simple attractiveness but little
glamour. The woman's innocence may call to mind the
Biblical Eve, a resemblance that is further
developed by the fact that she smells of apples or
grass rather than of an artificial perfume.

The generally positive description of the woman
of innocence comes to an abrupt halt, however, with
a dash and the transitional word <u>but</u>. Levertov
concludes the first half of the poem by noting that
this woman

> is kind and very clean without
>
> ostentation--
>
>   but she has
>
> no imagination. (7-10)

Such simplicity and practicality do not encourage
the unpredictable imagination.

The second woman in the poem is neither simple
nor natural. She is a "turbulent moon-ridden girl /
or old woman, or both" (12-13). Levertov's initial
account is also turbulent or even contradictory:
she cannot even decide this woman's age. The
unusual description of her as "ridden" by the moon
implies that she is haunted by or obsessed with it--
perhaps by its beauty or association with romantic
love. Her physical appearance is also unusual.
Instead of a neat, clean smock, the second woman
wears an exotic but ragged costume: she is "dressed
in opals and rags, feathers / and torn taffeta"
(14-15).

Her uncertain age, association with the moon,
and bizarre clothing contrast sharply with the
character of the woman of innocence. Levertov never

word <u>imagination</u> to refer to the second woman, but these descriptions demonstrate that she has a great deal of imagination, which is further revealed by the fact that she "knows strange songs--" (16). These songs could refer to the creative ability to compose poems. Yet the dash again signals that Levertov is moving to this woman's shortcomings. The poem concludes with the isolated line "but she is not kind" (17).

With the portraits of these two women, Levertov explores the paradoxical contrasts between innocence and imagination. The imagination is exotic, beautiful, and unpredictable, but it is also turbulent, strange, and rude. The woman of imagination, however, is the one who writes poems. The practical woman lacks imagination, but she is clean and fair, with her own simple beauty. She may also practice kindness and consideration for others.

The speaker of the poem seems to have found both of these women within herself at different times. Their differing ages suggest that imaginative

```
stages of life—during youth or old age—may be
complemented by the innocence and kindness of
middle age. Levertov thus affirms both innocence
and imagination in her brief but thoughtful poem
"In Mind."
```

■ Exercise 2

From a recommended list, an anthology, a magazine of verse, or a collection by a well-known poet, carefully select a poem one or two pages long to write about, one that appeals to your heart and that makes you think about it with originality.

Your instructor may wish you to select two or three poems and may then help you to choose the final one. Before making your selection or when submitting your paper, you may need to submit one or more photocopies.

Read the poem several times. What are its parts? What does it say about beauty or ugliness, human sorrow or joy? What is the center of the poem? After a day or two, you will probably know a great deal more about the poem. Sometimes it is wise to write at least two pages more than the required paper length. Then cut out the less important points. If the paper is still longer than the requirement, something may be wrong with your subject or your writing.

Research

44 Writing a Research Paper

You do research so that you can speak and write knowledgeably about a subject. Know what has already been written. Learn what you can from fact itself and from the raw data of life.

While researching a topic, you discover many facts and encounter many opinions. Your task is not to present them all. You must select only those that are most clearly related to your purpose. You must also include your own ideas, your experience, your judgments, and your perspective. A successful research paper must do much more than present a series of paraphrases and quotations. It must achieve a unique blending of your personality and your reading.

44a Choose a subject area that interests you and write on a specific aspect of that subject.

Research always takes longer than you think it will. Start early. First, find a suitable topic. Thumb through magazines or encyclopedias, surf the Internet, or browse through indexes like the *New York Times Index*. Do not waste time. Instead, develop the instincts of a canny journalist or a skilled photographer. Learn to find the unique angle, the untold story, the significant issues hidden in the commonplace topics of the day. What will pique your curiosity, hold your interest, and stimulate your thoughts? Whatever will do so will probably have the same effect on your peers and your instructor.

Choose a general subject area.

If your instructor does not assign a general area for your research, then you must discover one yourself. Free your imagination and let it roam. If nothing comes to mind and if paying close attention to the media, to your other classes, or to your reading produces no promising leads, you should consult a general list of subject areas like the following one.

advertising	ecology	marketing
religion	science	psychology
acting	law	television
literature	art	sports
ethics	history	government
anthropology	economics	medicine
computers	sociology	archaeology
folklore	agriculture	education

Get more specific.

Almost always, your first idea will be too broad. You will have a subject area to investigate but not a researchable topic. Suppose you have chosen computers as your general area. How can you reduce this immense subject to a manageable size?

One way is to use a list like the following one. Circle your area of primary interest—perhaps *computers*. Then draw arrows to two or three other subjects that you also find interesting, such as *economics* and *law*.

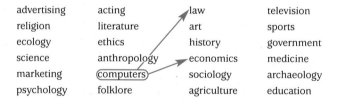

advertising	acting	law	television
religion	literature	art	sports
ecology	ethics	history	government
science	anthropology	economics	medicine
marketing	(computers)	sociology	archaeology
psychology	folklore	agriculture	education

Instead of expanding your topic, as you might expect, this process will help you to narrow it. Rather than considering the subject as a whole, you will now be looking at points where this subject intersects with your other areas of interest. In addition to helping you narrow your topic, making these connections will help you to identify some of the new or unresolved issues worth considering. After marking the list, for example, you might consider how the Internet is changing

America. You might also wonder what challenges this new medium presents to existing laws governing privacy or freedom of speech.

Phrase a research question.

Your next step is to phrase your research interest as a question. Doing so will help you to discover your purpose. It will also help you to evaluate your topic, and it can suggest the kinds of information that will enable you to write in an engaging way on that topic.

Suppose you are reading about efforts to regulate the Internet. If you stopped thinking at this point, your research question would be something like "What efforts are being made to regulate content on the Internet?" This narrower topic has possibilities, but it lacks a unique twist. All you can do with it is paraphrase and summarize the work of the various authorities who have written on the topic.

If you apply the previously explained process and consider economics as well as computers and law, you may be led to a richer research question. You might, for example, ask, "Do efforts to regulate the Internet violate constitutional rights to free speech?" You will also have a topic that will let you use some personal observation. (For instance, you may have encountered questionable or inflammatory material while surfing the Internet.)

With an entirely different set of interests, you might circle, say, *science* and then draw arrows to *archaeology* and *ecology*. Many possibilities for a good topic exist in such a combination, but this procedure brings to light a pattern of interest that gets you closer to your final topic, which might be, in this instance, "Can cloning ever be used to revive extinct species?" The author of the model paper on pages 385–421 circled *education* and then drew arrows to *sociology* and *psychology*. Some hard thinking then resulted in a good subject, "Heroism in a Time of School Violence."

Avoid inappropriate subjects.

After you have tentatively selected a subject, refined it into a researchable topic, phrased it as a research question, and polished it into a definite title, you should ask yourself the following six questions.

1. *Is it too broad?* If you set out to write a research paper of two thousand words on "How Computers Have Been Changing the World," your final product would be broad, general, and uninteresting. If you tried to address all of the issues implied by your topic in this relatively short space, you could say little that everyone wouldn't already know.

2. *Is it too technical?* You may know a great deal about "Fusiform Rust in Old Growth Forests," but general readers will not have the academic background or the vocabulary to understand what you plan to say. Try to reconstitute your subject into one that is more understandable, like "Should Commercial Pine Forests Be Burned Annually?"

3. *Is it too intricate or too mechanical?* You may know quite a bit about a topic like "Rebuilding a V-8 Engine" or "Repairing a Pocket Watch," but these will be difficult and unwieldy topics for both writer and reader.

4. *Does it promise more than it can deliver?* Examine your title carefully to ensure that your paper can meet the expectations it raises. No research paper could satisfactorily answer all the questions arising out of a title like "Immortality Is a State of Mind: Using Aroma Therapy to Live Forever." Even a topic that seems sufficiently limited and unspecialized can be inappropriate because its claims are too ambitious.

5. *Is it too controversial?* Topics such as "Abortion: Another Word for Murder" or "Racism and American Schools" are quite volatile and emotional.

6. *Is it dull?* You may be fascinated by a topic like "Four Types of Bathroom Tubs," but few other people will be. To enliven the subject of bathtubs and to make it appealing to general readers, try connecting it to your other areas of interest. You might try linking bathtubs with art ("The Bathtub in Contemporary Photography") or with sociology (" 'Cleanliness Is Next to Godliness': The Evolution of the American Bathroom").

44b   Become familiar with major research tools.

After you have narrowed your subject to a manageable topic, your next step is to compile a working bibliography, a list of works you want to read about this topic. At this point, your entries need to include only the author's name, the title, and the information you need to locate the source. You will find useful information in many places and forms, including paper and electronic formats.

Print sources—including books, newspapers, magazines, and academic journals—can be found in a library. Reference librarians are eager to help you locate these sources by using a library catalog and perhaps also an appropriate index.

Some electronic sources may be accessed through CD-ROMs, which are available in most libraries. Reference librarians will usually be on hand to help you use them. Other electronic sources are accessed through the World Wide Web. To find these, you will need to use an Internet browser such as Netscape Navigator or Microsoft's Internet Explorer to conduct key word searches and directory searches.

Using the library catalog

The library catalog is the basic tool for finding books in a library. Some libraries still use traditional card catalogs—drawers of three-by-five-inch cards filed alphabetically by author, by title, and by subject—to record their holdings. Other libraries use computerized or online catalogs that you can access through computer terminals located within the library. With a proper modem connection, you can also access many of these catalogs from computers outside the library. Online catalogs vary considerably from library to library. All of them are easy to use, providing prompts to guide novice users.

Searching online catalogs

A subject search for books on school violence may produce a list of works like the following one.

| Your search: S = SCHOOL VIOLENCE |

Line

\#---------Author---------------------------------------Title------------------------Date

1 Blauvelt, Peter D.   Effective strategies for school security /
                             1981

2 Gaustad, Joan.   Schools respond to gangs and violence / Jo
                             1991

3 Goldstein Arnold P.   Student aggression : prevention, manageme
                             1994

4 Gottfredson, Gary D.   Victimization in schools / Gary D. Gottfre
                             1985

5 Health and Administrat   Stopping school violence : an essential gu
                             1999

6   Programing for aggressive and violent stu
                             1991

7 Quarles, Chester L.   School violence : a survival guide for sch
                             1989

8   Risks to students in school.
                             1995

9 Rubel, Robert J.   The unruly school : disorders, disruptions
                             1977

10 Vestermark, Seymour D.   Controlling crime in the school : a comple
                             1978

Enter: Line #   (1,2,3, etc.) to see more information.

          N   to see Next screen.

          P   to see Previous screen.

          ST   to start over.

Use the online catalog's full-record option to view comprehensive information about your source. A sample online catalog entry for one of these books follows.

(Record 5 of 10)

AUTHOR: Health and Administration Development Group (Aspen
            Publishers)

TITLE: Stopping school violence : an essential guide: special report

PUBLISHER: Aspen, ©1999.

SUBJECTS: School violence--United States.   Students--Crimes
            against--United States.   Schools--Risk management--United
            States

LIBRARY HOLDINGS:
  3rd FLOOR
  1. CALL NUMBER: LB3013.3 .H43 1999 -- Book - Available
  2.

Press (return) for more holdings.
Select a line number for detailed information about that line.
Enter: P   to see Previous screen.
          F   to see the Full Title record.
          REL   to see Related works.

Using Internet searches

An astonishing number of documents can be accessed through computer servers located throughout the world. Not all of these are reliable and informative, but many are, especially those managed by universities, government offices, and commercial information services. Most of these provide information free of charge, but some do charge fees. To access these online sources, you will need a computer that is connected to the Internet. You will also need to have an Internet browser like Netscape Navigator or Microsoft's Internet Explorer to search for these documents as well as to print them or download them to a disk to use later.

To begin your search of the Internet, you will need to activate a search engine through your browser's search button. GoTo.com, Lycos, Excite, Northern Light, Ask Jeeves, and Yahoo! are some of the more popular ones used to explore the World Wide Web, the largest and most easily accessed part of the Internet. One easy way to begin is by doing a keyword search. To conduct this kind of search, simply type one or more terms into the space provided and click the Search button. Use two or three terms linked by such words as *and* or *or* to narrow your search.

A keyword search of the Internet on the topic of school violence, for example, might resemble the following:

school AND violence AND prevention OR solutions

The more terms you include, the fewer "hits," or responses, you will receive. Add and remove key words until you discover a manageable number of hits. Most search engines offer advanced search options to help to narrow your inquiries. One search engine may refer to this option as Power Search or Advanced Search.

Another way to explore the World Wide Web is through a subject directory. Subject directories categorize information by topic and allow you to scroll through lists of topics and subtopics until you find the information you need. Some of the most useful subject directories include the following:

- Yahoo! (http://www.yahoo.com)
- The WWW Virtual Library (http://vlib.org/overview.html)
- The Michigan Electronic Library (http://mel.lib.mi.us/)

- The Argus Clearinghouse (http://www.clearinghouse.net/index.html)
- Galaxy (http://galaxy.einet.net/)

When you find useful information, whether through a keyword search or a directory search, be sure to save it, either on your hard drive or on a floppy disk. Click on the File button; then use the Save As button to specify where you want to save the information. Saving files will allow you to print and to use them later.

44c   Consult general reference aids.

Comprehensive encyclopedias

Consult general reference sources as you further narrow and refine your topic. Some of these, like comprehensive encyclopedias, can provide a useful overview of your topic. Although these sources provide essential background information and many interesting facts, you should not document from them unless your instructor tells you otherwise. More specialized sources are generally preferred for that purpose. A list of some of the better-known comprehensive encyclopedias follows.

> *Collier's Encyclopedia.* 1997.
> *Encyclopedia Americana.* 1997.
> *The New Encyclopedia Britannica.* 1987, 1990. (Available online at *http://search.eb.com*)
> *World Book Encyclopedia,* 1997.

Internet Reference Sites

The World Wide Web contains a number of reference sites not available in print. Some of the better-known ones are listed next.

> *StudyWeb: The Learning Portal* (http://studyweb.com)
> *Electric Library* (http://www.elibrary.com)
> *GovSpot* (http://www.govspot.com)
> *Refdesk.com* (http://www.refdesk.com)

General periodical indexes

Articles in magazines and newspapers are a rich source of information on almost every subject. Some general-interest periodical indexes are listed next. Specialized ones are listed in the following section (see **44d**). Many of these indexes are in book format, others are available on CD-ROM, and still others are in both formats. Usually the book formats cover more years than the computerized versions, especially on a topic that is not a current one. Your reference librarian can tell you which indexes are available in what format, how far back they go, and how you can use them.

> *Readers' Guide to Periodical Literature* (available online if your library has bought access)
> *Infotrac* (available on CD-ROM and online if your library has bought access)
> *Book Review Index* (available on CD-ROM)
> *National Newspaper Index* (available on CD-ROM and online if your library has bought access)
> *New York Times Index* (available on CD-ROM and online if your library has bought access)

44d Consult specialized reference aids.

Specialized reference materials exist in almost every field of inquiry. Your librarian can help you to identify the ones most suited to your research. Some helpful specialized dictionaries, encyclopedias, indexes, and Internet sites are listed next.

Arts and Humanities

PRINT

> *Art Index.* 1974–.
> *Articles on American Literature.* 1900–1950; 1950–1967; 1968–1975.
> *Cambridge Bibliography of English Literature.* 1941–1957. 5 vols.; *New Cambridge Bibliography of English Literature.* 1969–1977. 5 vols. 3rd ed., 1999–.
> *Contemporary Authors.* 1962–.

Contemporary Literary Criticism. 1973–.
Dictionary of Literary Biography. 1978–.
Encyclopedia of World Art. 1959–1968. 16 vols. 2 supplements, 1983–1987.
English Novel Explication. 1973. 6 supplements, 1976–1997.
Essay and General Literature Index. 1900–.
Facts on File: Bibliography of American Fiction. 1991–.
Halliwell's Filmgoer's and Video Viewer's Companion. 12th ed., 1997.
Humanities Index. 1974–.
Magill's Bibliography of Literary Criticism. 1979. 4 vols.
McGraw-Hill Encyclopedia of World Drama. 2nd ed., 1984. 5 vols.
MLA International Bibliography of Books and Articles on the Modern Languages and Literatures. 1919–.
New Grove Dictionary of Music and Musicians. 1980. 20 vols.
New Princeton Encyclopedia of Poetry and Poetics. 1993.
Oxford Classical Dictionary. 3rd ed. 1996.
Oxford Companion to American Literature. 6th ed., 1995.
Oxford Companion to English Literature. 5th ed., second revision, 1998.
Oxford History of English Literature. 1945–.

INTERNET
    Voice of the Shuttle [Literature and Literary Criticism].
      http://vos.ucsb.edu/
    World Wide Arts Resources Corporation.
      http://wwar.com/categories/Museums/index.html
    Music Resources on the Internet.
      http://www.music.indiana.edu/music_resources/

Biography

PRINT
    Cambridge Biographical Dictionary. 1996.
    Current Biography. 1940–.
    Dictionary of American Biography. 1928–1937. 20 vols. 10 supplements, 1941–1990.
    Dictionary of National Biography. 1885–1901. 22 vols. 10 supplements, 1901–1996.

INTERNET
    Internet Oracle: Online Biographies.
      http://www.searchgateway.com/biograph.htm

Social Sciences

PRINT

Cambridge Histories. Ancient, 12 vols. rev. ed. In progress. Medieval, 8
vols. Modern, 13 vols. *New Cambridge History.* 14 vols.
Chambers World Gazetteer. 1988.
Encyclopedia of World Cultures. 1996. 6 vols.
Facts on File: Weekly World News Digest with Cumulative Index. 1940–.
Harvard Encyclopedia of American Ethnic Groups. 1980.
Hutchinson Dictionary of World History. 1993.
International Encyclopedia of Social Sciences. 1968. 17 vols. *Biographical
Supplement.* 1979. *Social Science Quotations.* 1991.
Social Sciences Index. 1974–.
*Statesman's Yearbook: Statistical and Historical Annual of the States of
the World.* 1854–.
Statistical Abstract of the United States. 1878–.
World Almanac and Book of Facts. 1868–.

INTERNET

American Studies Web.
http://www.georgetown.edu/crossroads/asw/lit.html
Civnet.
http://civnet.org/
Fedworld.
http://www.fedworld.gov
Govspot.
http://www.govspot.com/
World History Archives.
http://www.hartford-hwp.com/archives/

Science, Technology, and Business

PRINT

Applied Science and Technology Index. 1958–.
Biological and Agricultural Index. 1916–.
Business Periodical Index. 1958–.
A Concise Dictionary of Business. 1990.
Concise Oxford Dictionary of Geography. 1992.
General Science Index. 1978–.
HarperCollins Dictionary of Environmental Science. 1992.
McGraw-Hill Encyclopedia of Science and Technology. 8th ed., 1997. 20 vols.
Supplemented by *McGraw-Hill Yearbook of Science and Technology.*
Merriam-Webster's Geographical Dictionary. 3rd ed. 1998.

INTERNET

American Association for the Advancement of Science.
   http://www.aaas.org
Michigan State University Center for International Business Education
   and Research.
   http://ciber.bus.msu.edu/busres.htm
United States Bureau of Labor Statistics.
   http://www.bls.gov
United States Environmental Protection Agency.
   http://www.epa.gov

44e Evaluate your sources.

Pause and take stock. What kinds of materials have you found? How much of this information will you need to document?

Some of your sources may be *primary.* A **primary source** is any material that other works are written about. If you are writing a research paper on Annie Proulx's *Postcards,* then that novel is a primary source. If you are writing about tourism and you interview a tourist, that material is also considered primary.

Consider using another primary source as well—your own observations. If you've seen an NBA game, deplored the pollution of a river near your home, or noted new security measures taken at your younger sister's school, then your observations are also valid primary material. Use them. They will make your paper more individual and more interesting.

Other sources you have found will be *secondary.* That is, they will have been written about primary works or events. A review of Proulx's novel, a magazine article on the state of professional basketball, a newspaper editorial on the pollution of a local river, or a Department of Education report on school security nationwide would all be **secondary sources.** Not all secondary sources are equally objective or reliable. Consider the author's credentials and the soundness of her arguments. Analyze conflicts and seek the truth. See page 3 (**1a**) on evaluating sources.

After identifying the kinds of sources you have found, you will need to determine which facts and ideas you will need to document.

Some of the information that your sources contain will be common knowledge. Although you may not have known that the Berlin Wall was built in 1961 or that Edgar Allan Poe was born in Boston, that information is undisputed, commonly known, and easily available. You can and should use such pieces of information, but you do not need to document them.

Other sources will contain less widely known or less well-established information, much of which will involve some estimation, calculation, or subjective judgment. Figures representing the number of Americans killed in handgun accidents in a given year or the projected world population in 2050 are only as credible as their source. To the best of your ability, be sure your source is authoritative; then use the information. Be sure to document it, since not everyone knows or accepts such information. Also, you must provide documentation every time you refer to another writer's theory, adapt her explanation, or borrow any idea or language. Words and ideas are their writer's possessions, and documentation is the coin with which you pay for borrowing them.

44f Take accurate, useful notes from your sources.

Accurate, specific, well-organized notes are critical to the success of your research paper. Do not let procrastination short-circuit this stage of the process. At the same time, remember that notes are merely a means to an end, not an end in themselves. They are valuable only if they lead to a lucid, balanced, and factual paper. **Note-taking** can be time-consuming and is sometimes tedious. For this reason, put your notes on cards, since they will withstand more handling.

Copy important sources.

The first step is to make accurate copies of your most promising sources. If you are using library materials, you will need to photocopy the pertinent articles, chapters, or sections. Be sure your copy includes essential information like page numbers. Also, photocopy both the title page and the copyright page; they contain the publication information you will need to compile your bibliography. If you are using material taken from the Internet, be sure to print the home page, which also lists information you will need for documentation. Once you have made copies, you can read your sources carefully, underlining pertinent sections, jotting topics in the margins, and cross-referencing other analyses you have read. As you take notes, you should do three things: make your note cards specific, record information needed to document each source, and provide subject headings for your cards.

Make your note cards specific.

Your first response may be to summarize the main idea of what you have read. However, several note cards repeating the same generalization will not be very useful. Instead, look for numbers, dates, statistics, names of experts, eyewitnesses, other relevant people, and places. These will make your topic vivid and give your discussion the flavor of life. Read the following passage and then compare the two sample note cards that summarize it.

Original passage

Incidents of multiple-victim homicides in schools are indeed on the rise. In 1994–95 there was one such shooting. In 1997–98 there were five, according to the Department of Education's 1999 Annual Report on School Safety.

Yet the number remains small enough so that the rise does not necessarily constitute a trend, statistically speaking. And overall school violence continues to decline. In 1993, there were about 155 school-related crimes for every 1,000 students age 12 to 18. In 1997, that figure fell to 102.

Perhaps more important, the report found a significant decrease in the number of students carrying weapons of all sorts into school. Some 3,930 children were expelled for carrying guns in 1997–98—down from 5,724 in the previous school year.

> PETER GRIER AND GAIL RUSSELL CHADDOCK
> "Schools Get Tough as Threats Continue,"
> *Christian Science Monitor Electronic Edition,* 5 November 1999

Poor note card

How common is school violence?

While the number of school shootings increased between 1994 and 1997, school violence as a whole dropped.

Fewer students were expelled in 1997-98 than in 1996-97.

Although this note card accurately summarizes the gist of the passage under consideration, it lacks specificity. It presents a conclusion but records none of the evidence that supports it. Compare this card's general content with that of a more specific card based on the same passage.

Stronger note card

> *How common is school violence?*
>
> *Between 1993 and 1997, the number of "school related" crimes committed by middle school and high school students dropped by 35%, from 155 incidents per thousand students to 102 per thousand. More importantly, the number of students caught bringing guns to school dropped by 35%, from 5,724 in 1996-97 to 3,930 in 1997-98—a total of about 1,800 incidents*
>
> *Grier and Chaddock*

Like the student who took these notes, you should also take time to digest the facts included in your sources. Of course, you might not use all or even any of these facts, but this card will make them available as you draft your paper.

Record the information you will need to document each source.

Once you have found a useful source, you will need to create a **bibliography card** for it, preferably on a three-by-five-inch filing card. This card will contain a full and exact record of the information you will need for compiling your list of Works Cited or References. A sample card is shown on page 361.

If the source is in print, this card should include the name of the author, the title of the work, the place and date of publication, and the name of the publisher. If the work has an editor or a translator, is in more than one volume, or is part of a series, include these facts as well. For later checking, record the library call number. If your source is a magazine or periodical, record the volume number, the issue number, and the page numbers.

If the source is electronic, record the author, the name of the source, the original place of publication (if it has been reprinted), the date, and the web address or URL **(uniform resource locator).**

Bibliography card for print source

Health and Administration Development Group

Stopping School Violence: an Essential Guide

Aspen: Aspen Publishers, 1999

LB3013.3H43.1999

Bibliography card for online source

Peter Grier and Gail Russell Chaddock
"Schools Get Tough as Threats Continue"

The Christian Science Monitor Electronic Edition,

5 November 1999.
http://www.csmonitor.com/durable/1999/11/05/f
p1s1-csm.shtml

Your note cards must also contain important bibliographic information, recording the exact page number where each piece of information appeared. If your note card happens to contain information from two pages, then use a slash to indicate where one page
ended and the other began.

Provide appropriate subject headings.

Finally, you should begin classifying the information you have
found by jotting subject headings at the top of each card. Have you
discovered several sources citing the causes of school violence?
Have other sources discussed the psychological effects of school
violence upon teachers and students? If so, then placing such headings as "Causes of school violence," "Effects of violence on teachers," or "Effects of violence on students" on your note cards is a
good idea.

Headings are valuable for several reasons. They help you to organize your information into manageable units. They also suggest specific kinds of information to look for while exploring other sources. They may even lead directly into paragraph divisions in your final paper. Write your card headings in pencil. They may change as your research project takes shape.

44g Take useful notes. Quote and paraphrase accurately. Avoid plagiarism.

Not all note cards have the same purpose. Some will *summarize* main ideas that you discover in your sources, including authors' conclusions, theories, predictions, and other significant generalizations. Other note cards will *paraphrase* important facts, definitions, explanations, anecdotes, or proposals. Still others will *quote* memorable statements, perhaps by an authority or an eyewitness. Consider your purpose; then prepare an appropriate card.

Use **direct quotation** when you want to reproduce information from a source exactly, word for word (usually because the original is very concisely or very strikingly worded). Enclose directly quoted material in quotation marks, even if the borrowing is only a phrase or a single distinctive word, and always identify the source.

Use **paraphrase** when you need to borrow all of the ideas from a source passage whose original wording would be too difficult for your audience to understand. To paraphrase, translate the source passage completely into clearer words and sentence patterns of your own. When completed, a paraphrase is usually about the same length as the source passage—sometimes slightly briefer, often slightly longer. Use introductory phrases or verbal tags to ensure that your reader can clearly distinguish between the paraphrased material and your own ideas, and always identify the source.

Use **summary,** by contrast, when you want to convey only the essence or "gist" of a source to your audience. To summarize, restate in your own words only the most relevant idea or ideas in the source passage; omit everything else. A completed summary should always be much briefer than its source. Use introductory phrases or verbal tags to ensure that your readers can clearly distinguish between the summarized material and your own ideas, and always identify the source.

Compare the following source with the passages that plagiarize them.

SOURCE

The infectious diseases that visit us as epidemics, rather than as a steady trickle of cases, share several characteristics. First, they spread quickly and efficiently from an infected person to normally healthy people, with the result that the whole population gets exposed within a short time. Second, they're "acute" illnesses: within a short time, you either die or recover completely. Third, the fortunate ones of us who do recover develop antibodies that leave us immune against a recurrence of the disease for a long time, possibly for the rest of our life. Finally, these diseases tend to be restricted to humans. All four of these traits apply to what Americans think of as the familiar acute epidemic diseases of childhood, including measles, rubella, mumps, pertussis, and smallpox.

JARED DIAMOND
Guns, Germs, and Steel: The Fates of Human Societies

STUDENT PASSAGE WITH PLAGIARISM

The diseases that cause epidemics share several characteristics. First, they spread quickly and efficiently from an infected person to a healthy person. Second, they are acute diseases that you either die or recover quickly from. Third, fortunate ones who recover develop antibodies that leave them immune. Finally, these diseases tend to be restricted to human beings. All four of these traits apply to the American diseases of measles, rubella, mumps, pertussis, and smallpox.

SOURCE

It is curious watching Harrison Ford grow older onscreen. His movies have been more successful, on the whole, than those of any other star, but they have had to be adventure movies, and he has had to be boyish, an action star of a new kind. He cares about everyone; clothes and haircut matter to him. He has a sort of rumpled face—rumpled like Jeanne Moreau's. In seven of Hollywood's twenty-one top-grossing movies, he is a messiah figure, successful in the story but—unlike, say, Eastwood—softly, reasonably so: not a killer.

HAROLD BRODKEY
"Elements of Film: Variations on Sex"

STUDENT PASSAGE WITH PLAGIARISM

It is interesting watching Harrison Ford grow old onscreen. His movies have been more successful than those of other stars because he is an action star of a new kind. He has a somewhat wrinkled face, and he has been in seven of Hollywood's twenty-one top-grossing movies as a messiah figure who succeeds but is not a killer.

Even though the student writers of these passages with plagiarism have changed some of the language of their sources, they also employ words and phrases lifted directly from their sources without surrounding them with quotation marks, and neither identifies the specific source of the borrowed words and ideas. Even if the student writers had acknowledged the sources of their ideas at the end of the passage, their failure to mark borrowed language with quotation marks still makes them guilty of **plagiarism.**

Furthermore, both students misrepresent their sources. By leaving out some of the original words in her source's last sentence, the student writing about epidemics has changed its meaning; the source says that measles, rubella, and so on are diseases that Americans *think of* as being childhood epidemics, not that they are *American* diseases. Likewise, the student writing about Harrison Ford has wrongly substituted the word *wrinkled* for *rumpled* without bothering to consider that those words are not always synonymous. *Rumpled* in the original passage clearly must mean something like "rough" or "unpolished" instead because Ford's face is not wrinkled. Such careless handling of his source thus makes this student an unworthy writer and insults his audience's intelligence.

Good and bad summary

A good summary expresses only the most essential ideas from a source (always acknowledging it) in fewer words, presenting the basic sense but not the form or language of the original. It does not merely delete some sentences or phrases from the original; it is a genuine and very concise restatement in new language of the key ideas in a source. The following examples of improper and proper summary are based on the passage about epidemic diseases by Jared Diamond quoted previously.

POOR SUMMARY

> The infectious diseases that visit us as epidemics share several characteristics. First, they spread quickly and efficiently. Second, they are acute. Third, the ones who recover develop antibodies. Finally, these diseases tend to be restricted to humans.

Although the previous passage is much shorter than its source, its words and sentence patterns are simply lifted from the source without acknowledgement—a clear case of plagiarism.

PROPER SUMMARY

> According to Jared Diamond, epidemic diseases possess four common characteristics: (1) they affect only humans, (2) they are highly contagious, (3) they are severe but short-lived, and (4) their survivors develop some measure of immunity.

This summary opens by acknowledging the source of the ideas. It borrows only the source's key ideas, restating them accurately and concisely in new words and sentence patterns.

Good and bad paraphrasing

A good paraphrase restates most or all of the ideas in the source passage (which it always acknowledges) but does so in clearer language, preserving the sense but not the form of the original. It does not simply retain the source's sentence patterns and merely substitute synonyms for the original words, nor does it retain the original words and merely rearrange the sentence patterns. Instead, it clarifies the ideas of the source by restating them in new words arranged in new sentence patterns. The following examples of improper and proper paraphrases are based on the previous passage about Harrison Ford by Harold Brodkey.

IMPROPER PARAPHRASE

It is interesting watching Harrison Ford mature on-screen. His films have been more profitable, on the whole, than those of any other star, but they have had to be adventure films, and he has had to be masculine, a new kind of action star. He cares about everyone; fashion and hairstyle matter to him. Of Hollywood's twenty-one top-earning movies, he has been in seven as a Jesus figure, successful in the story but not a killer, unlike Eastwood.

In the previous first three sentences, this paraphrase merely substitutes synonyms for a few words while leaving most of them—as well as the basic sentence patterns—unchanged, with no credit given to their source. Further, the substitutions distort the meaning of the original. Replacing *boyish* with *masculine,* for example, makes the second sentence a ridiculous statement (masculine actions are not new) that is practically contradicted by the rest of the passage. Although the last sentence follows a new pattern, the substitutions and omissions again misrepresent the ideas of the source.

PROPER PARAPHRASE

The aging of Harrison Ford over the course of his film career, says writer Harold Brodkey, is a curious phenomenon. Starring in some very successful action films, Ford established a new kind of action hero, one more youthful and more sensitive about others' feelings. Unlike Clint Eastwood, who exemplifies the more traditional action hero who can kill people without batting an eye, Ford is a much gentler kind of hero, more like a sacrificial victim than a ruthless avenger (Brodkey 63).

This paraphrase clearly acknowledges the source of its ideas and restates them in new language and in new sentence patterns that are more likely to be understood by an audience *unfamiliar* with older foreign films.

Frequently, using a combination of direct quotation and paraphrase can be effective.

PARAPHRASE WITH DIRECT QUOTATION

The career of Harrison Ford, however, illustrates the development of a new kind of film hero. Although he has starred in seven of Hollywood's most successful films, "they have had to be adventure movies, and he has had to be boyish, an action star of a new kind." With his "rumpled" good looks, his sensitivity to others' feelings, and his concern for personal appearance, Ford represents the kind of action hero who is more often a "messiah figure" than a "killer" (Brodkey 63).

44h Produce an effective outline.

Because a research paper addresses multiple subtopics, presents many facts, and evaluates diverse opinions, you will need a good outline to help to organize your ideas.

Begin by jotting down the various headings you made on your note cards. Which of these belong together in a single paragraph or, perhaps, in a cluster of paragraphs? Do you have enough information to write with some authority on this subtopic? Which headings now seem unrelated to the rest? They may represent dead ends, topics that you momentarily found interesting but now need to abandon. Set these cards aside. Which of your headings seem important but are not supported by enough note cards to be developed effectively? Use this opportunity to identify new directions for future research.

Throughout this process, keep the purpose of your research firmly in mind. Do you find yourself working from a problem to a solution? Are you trying to reconcile differing viewpoints? Is your goal to answer a riddle, discover the best course of action, explode a common misconception? Write down what you hope to accomplish at the top of your outline. The major headings—and their necessary sequence—should become clearer in light of this statement. Consult Section 2a about the various forms your outline may take.

Finally, study your tentative outline. Does it leave out anything you wanted to include? Do any headings repeat the same information? Does it have a logical and easy-to-follow order? See the model outline on page 387.

44i Follow an accepted system of documentation.

Different academic fields, periodicals, and publishers use different forms of documentation. Follow the documentation style suggested by your instructor or editor. Later, in more advanced courses and fields of learning, professors and editors will require you to use a standard reference system. The following three are the most common.

> *Chicago Manual of Style.* 14th ed. Chicago: U of Chicago P, 1993.
> Gibaldi, Joseph. *MLA Handbook for Writers of Research Papers.* 5th ed. New York: MLA, 1999.
> *Publication Manual of the American Psychological Association.* 4th ed. Washington: APA, 1994.

The model paper on pages 385–410 follows the description of documentation described in the *MLA Handbook for Writers.* This system is widely used in the humanities.

44j MLA style of documentation

List of works cited

A section called "Works Cited" appears after the body and the endnotes (if any) of your research paper. Here you list alphabetically the sources to which you refer in the text (see the list for the model paper, pp. 407–410). The following examples illustrate some of the various forms used in MLA documentation.

A BOOK BY A SINGLE AUTHOR

Kopka, Deborah L. <u>School Violence: A Reference Handbook</u>. Santa Barbara: ABC-CLIO, 1997.

A BOOK WITH TWO EDITORS OR AUTHORS

Canter, Andrea S., and Servio A. Carroll, eds. <u>Crisis Prevention and Response: A Collection of NASP Resources</u>. Bethesda: NASP, 1999.

A BOOK WITH THREE OR MORE EDITORS OR AUTHORS

Boatwright, Becki H., et al. <u>Getting Equipped to Stop Bullying: A Kid's Survival Kit for Under-standing and Coping with Violence in the Schools</u>. Minneapolis: Educational Media, 1998.

The phrase *et al.* is a Latin term that means "and others."

A TRANSLATED BOOK

Lorenz, Konrad. <u>On Aggression</u>. Trans. Marjorie Latzke. London: Routledge, 1966.

NOTE: The title page lists both London and New York as places of publication. In your entry, list only the first city named.

A MULTIVOLUME WORK

Hendrick, Burton J. <u>The Life and Letters of Walter H. Page, 1855-1918</u>. 2 vols. Garden City: Doubleday, 1927.

A REPUBLISHED BOOK

Langdon, William Chauncey. <u>Everyday Things in American Life, 1776-1876</u>. 1941. New York: Scribner's, 1969.

A SECOND OR LATER EDITION OF A BOOK

Cangelosi, James S. <u>Classroom Management Strategies: Getting and Maintaining Students' Cooperation</u>. 2nd ed. New York: Longman, 1993.

AN ESSAY IN A COLLECTION OF ESSAYS OR AN ANTHOLOGY

Hafen, Bruce C. "Education and Social Morality." <u>Moral Values and Higher Education: A Nation at Risk</u>. Ed. Dennis L. Thompson. Albany: State U of New York P, 1991. 65-75.

AN INTRODUCTION, FOREWORD, PREFACE, OR AFTERWORD IN A BOOK

Soltis, Jonas F. Foreword. <u>Responsive Teaching: An Ecological Approach to Classroom Patterns of Language, Culture, and Thought</u>. By C. A. Bowers and David J. Flinders. New York: Teacher's College P, 1990. vii-ix.

MORE THAN ONE WORK BY THE SAME AUTHOR

Powell, Marvin. <u>The Psychology of Adolescence</u>. 2nd ed. Indianapolis: Bobbs-Merrill, 1971.
---. <u>Youth: Critical Issues</u>. Columbus: Bobbs-Merrill. 1972.

SIGNED ARTICLE IN A REFERENCE WORK

De Anda, Diane. "Adolescents." <u>Encyclopedia of
    Social Work</u>. 18th ed. Ed. Anne Minahan et al. 2
    vols. Silver Spring: NASW, 1987.

UNSIGNED ARTICLE IN A REFERENCE WORK

"Ethics." <u>The New Encyclopedia Britannica: Macro-
    pedia</u>. 15th ed. 1987.

NOTE: One does not need full publication information when citing
familiar reference works.

GOVERNMENT PUBLICATION

United States. Bureau of the Census and Dept. of
    Justice. <u>School Crime Supplement to the National
    Crime Victimization Survey</u>. Washington: GPO, 1994.

NOTE: The entry for this document illustrates many of the difficulties
encountered when documenting government publications. Since no
individual author is named, the government agency issuing the document is listed as the author. Since this document was sponsored by
two agencies, the Census Bureau and the Department of Justice, both
appear as authors. Like almost all federal documents, it is published in
Washington by the Government Printing Office (GPO).

ARTICLE IN A MONTHLY PERIODICAL

Stephens, Ronald D. "Ten Steps to Safer Schools." <u>The
    American School Board Journal</u> Mar. 1998: 30-35.

ARTICLE IN A WEEKLY PERIODICAL

Quindlen, Anna. "The C Word in the Hallways."
    <u>Newsweek</u> 29 Nov. 1999: 112.

ARTICLE IN A JOURNAL WITH CONTINUOUS PAGINATION

Catterall, James S. "Risk and Resilience in Student
    Transitions to High School." <u>American Journal of
    Education</u> 106 (1997-98): 302-333.

ARTICLE IN A JOURNAL PAGINATED BY ISSUE

Hannabuss, Stuart. "Issues of Censorship for
    Students." <u>Education Today</u> 46.1 (1996): 45-53.

NOTE: When each issue of a journal is paginated separately, include the issue number (in this case, *1*) as well as the volume
number.

BOOK REVIEW IN A PERIODICAL

Cherlin, Andrew J. Rev. of <u>A Generation at Risk:
    Growing Up in an Era of Family Upheaval</u>, by Paul
    A. Amato and Alan Booth. <u>American Journal of
    Sociology</u> 104 (1999): 1230-32.

ARTICLE IN A DAILY NEWSPAPER

Butterfield, Fox. "Hole in Gun Control Law Lets
    Mentally Ill Through." <u>New York Times</u> 11 Apr.
    2000, natl. ed.: A1.

NOTE: *A* refers to the section of the paper; *1,* to the page within that
section. For newspaper sections designated by numbers instead of
letters, add *sec.:* sec. 4: 7. For newspapers not divided into sections,
simply give the page number after the date: 25 Nov. 2000. The edition should be specified when possible. If the article is not signed,
begin the entry with the title of the article.

A VIDEOTAPE

<u>Adolescent Cognition: Thinking in a New Key</u>.
　　Written and Narr. David Elkind. Dir. John M.
　　Davidson. Videorecording. Davidson Films, 1999.

A PERSONAL WEB SITE

Nash, Mike. <u>Some Thoughts about School Violence</u>.
　　n.d. 29 Mar. 2000 <http://www.wtp.net/~mpa/
　　pg000014.htm>.

NOTE:　The date on which the page was published should immediately follow the title of the page. The abbreviation *n.d.* (no date)
notes the absence of this information. The second date is the date
on which this page was accessed.

A PROFESSIONAL WEB SITE

Center for the Prevention of School Violence.
　　"Stats 1999: Selected School Violence Research
　　Findings." Winter 2000. North Carolina State
　　University. 8 Apr. 2001 <http://www.ncsu.
　　edu/cpsv/>.

AN ARTICLE IN AN ELECTRONIC MAGAZINE

Morris, Jim. "Study: School Violence Down, but
　　Still Too High." <u>CNN.com</u> 4 Aug. 1999. 28 Mar.
　　2001 <http://www.cnn.com/US/9908/04/school.
　　violence/>.

AN ARTICLE FROM THE ELECTRONIC EDITION OF A PRINT MAGAZINE OR NEWSPAPER

```
Morse, Jodie. "The Perception Gap: School
    Violence." Time 24 Apr. 2000. 28 Mar. 2001
    <http://www.time.com/time/magazine/articles/
    0.3266.43161.00.html>.
```

AN EDITORIAL FROM THE ELECTRONIC EDITION OF A NEWSPAPER

```
Cohen, Jonathan R. "Defining Rebellion Up."
    Editorial. New York Post Online Edition 26 Apr.
    1999. 4 Apr. 2001 <http://208.248.87.252/
    042699/8622.htm>.
```

AN ARTICLE RETRIEVED FROM LEXIS-NEXIS OR A SIMILAR ONLINE DATABASE

```
Campbell, Colin. "Classroom Slaying Is a Tragic
    Waste." Atlanta Journal and Constitution 29 Sep.
    1996: G1. Online. LEXIS-NEXIS Academic Universe.
    News/Majpap. 10 Apr. 2001.
```

NOTE: The URL is not listed because this article cannot be accessed directly. It is available only by subscription.

■ Exercise 1

Using the MLA style, make up a list of Works Cited from the following information. Place entries in the correct form and the correct order. Omit unnecessary information. Answers are on pages 377–378.

A work in three volumes titled *Mark Twain: A Biography* by Albert Bigelow Paine, published by Harper and Brothers in 1912 in New York City.

An editorial titled "Seizing the Day to Help Schools" by Thomas Birmingham, president of the Massachusetts Senate. It appeared on page E7 of the 3rd edition of the *Boston Globe* on Sunday, April 9, 2000. You found it on November 11, 2000, in the Lexis-Nexis Academic Universe database by looking in "News" and "Major Papers." The piece is 809 words long.

An essay in a collection of essays titled *The Arts and the American Home, 1890–1930,* published by the University of Tennessee Press in Knoxville, Tennessee, in 1994. The essay is titled "The Piano in the American Home" and is by Craig H. Roell. The volume is edited by Jessica H. Foy and Karal Ann Marling. The essay is on pages 85 through 110.

An article from volume 12 (March 1996) of the electronic version of the journal *British Archaeology.* Written by Mike Richards, it is titled " 'First Farmers' with No Taste for Grain." The URL is http://www.britarch.ac.uk/ba/ba12/ba12feat.html#richards. It was accessed on October 15, 2000.

An article in a scholarly journal issued quarterly, the *Journal of Social Philosophy,* published in 1993 on pages 233 through 242 of volume 24, issue number 3. The author is Victoria Davion. The title is "The Ethics of Self-Corruption."

A videotape titled *Forensic Science: The Crime Fighter's Weapon.* It was written and produced by Noah Morowitz and produced by Bruce Nash for the History Channel, a presentation of the A&E Television Networks. It is published by A&E Home Video and distributed in the United States by New Video Group, which is located in New York City. It is 50 minutes long and was copyrighted in 1997.

The second edition of a book titled *The Literature of Jazz: A Critical Guide* by Donald Kennington and Danny L. Read. The place of publication is Chicago, the date of the second edition is 1980, and the publisher is the American Library Association.

A book from the Oxford University Press of Oxford, England, by Luh Ketut Suryani and Gordon D. Jensen, published in 1993 and titled *Trance and Possession in Bali.*

An article in a weekly periodical titled *The Nation* with the title "Free Speech on the Internet" by Jon Wiener, appearing on pages 825 through 828 of this magazine on June 13, 1994.

No author is given for this newspaper article with the heading "Chinese Cooperation in U.N. Efforts Vowed" in the June 13 issue of the *Miami Herald* in 1994 and on page 6 of the *A* section.

■ Answers for Exercise 1, p. 376

Works Cited

Birmingham, Thomas. "Seizing the Day to Help

Schools." Editorial. <u>Boston Globe</u> 9 Apr. 2000,

3rd ed.: E7. Online. LEXIS-NEXIS Academic

Universe. News/Majpap. 11 Nov. 2000.

"Chinese Cooperation in U.N. Efforts Vowed." <u>Miami</u>

<u>Herald</u> 13 June 1994: A6.

Davion, Victoria. "The Ethics of Self-Corruption."

<u>Journal of Social Philosophy</u> 24 (1993): 233-42.

<u>Forensic Science: The Crime Fighter's Weapon</u>.

Written and Prod. Noah Morowitz and Prod. Bruce

Nash for the History Channel. Videorecording.
     A&E Home Video, 1997.

Kennington, Donald, and Danny L. Read. <u>The Litera-
     ture of Jazz: A Critical Guide</u>. 2nd ed. Chicago:
     American Library Assn., 1980.

Paine, Albert Bigelow. <u>Mark Twain: A Biography</u>. 3
     vols. New York: Harper, 1912.

Richards, Mike. "'First Farmers' with No Taste for
     Grain." <u>British Archaeology</u> 12 (Mar. 1996). 15
     Oct. 2000. <http://www.britarch.ac.uk/ba/ba12/
     ba12feat.html#richards>.

Roell, Craig H. "The Piano in the American Home."
     <u>The Arts and the American Home, 1890-1930</u>. Ed.
     Jessica H. Foy and Karal Ann Marling. Knoxville:
     U of Tennessee P, 1994. 85-110.

Suryani, Luh Ketut, and Gordon D. Jensen. <u>Trance
     and Possession in Bali</u>. Oxford: Oxford UP, 1993.

Weiner, Jon. "Free Speech on the Internet." <u>The
     Nation</u> 13 June 1994: 825-28.

■ **Exercise 2**

Follow the instructions for Exercise 1. Answers are on p. 380.

A book from Cambridge, Massachusetts, with the date 1994, with the publisher listed as Harvard University Press, and with the title *Darwin, Machines, and the Nature of Knowledge.* The author is Henry Plotkin.

An article by Ellen J. Langer titled "A Mindful Education" published on pages 42 through 50 of a quarterly periodical, the *Educational Psychologist,* in volume XXVIII, issue number 1, in the winter of 1993.

A travel book by Sargent F. Collier. It is titled *Down East: Maine, Prince Edward Island, Nova Scotia, and the Gaspé* and is published in Boston by Houghton Mifflin Company with the date of 1953.

An article from a United States Government monthly publication, the *Federal Reserve Bulletin,* titled "Recent Trends in the Mutual Fund Industry" by Phillip R. Mack. The date is November 1993, and the article appears on pages 1001 through 1012.

An article titled "The Fury of El Niño" by J. Madeleine Nash, which appeared in Time.com, an online version of a weekly magazine, on February 16, 1998. You accessed it on November 12, 2000. The URL for this article is http://www.time.com/time/magazine/1998/dom/980216/science.the_fury_of_el_n9.html.

A Simon and Schuster book by Louise Levathes with the title *When China Ruled the Seas* and the subtitle *The Treasure Fleet of the Dragon Throne, 1405–1433.* The book was published in 1994 in New York, New York.

An article in a monthly magazine, *The American Spectator,* by Kenneth S. Lynn, titled "Dwight Stuff," on pages 56 through 58 of the June issue in 1994.

■ **Answers for Exercise 2, p. 379**

Works Cited

Collier, Sargent F. <u>Down East: Maine, Prince Edward</u>
<u>Island, Nova Scotia, and the Gaspé</u>. Boston:
Houghton, 1953.

Langer, Ellen J. "A Mindful Education." <u>Educational</u>
<u>Psychologist</u> 28.1 (1993): 42-50.

Levathes, Louise. <u>When China Ruled the Seas: The</u>
<u>Treasure Fleet of the Dragon Throne, 1405-1433</u>.
New York: Simon, 1994.

Lynn, Kenneth S. "Dwight Stuff." <u>The American</u>
<u>Spectator</u> June 1994: 56-58.

Mack, Phillip R. "Recent Trends in the Mutual Fund
Industry." <u>Federal Reserve Bulletin</u> Nov. 1993:
1001-12.

Plotkin, Henry. <u>Darwin, Machines, and the Nature of</u>
<u>Knowledge</u>. Cambridge: Harvard UP, 1994.

Nash, J. Madeleine. "The Fury of El Nino." <u>Time.com</u>
16 February 1998. 12 Nov. 2000. <http://www.
time.com/time/magazine/1998/dom/980216/science.
the_fury _of_el_n9.html>.

Parenthetical references

The list of Works Cited indicates the sources you used, but precisely what you derived from each entry must also be revealed at particular places in the paper. Document each idea, paraphrase, or quotation by indicating the author (or the title if the work is anonymous) and the page reference at the appropriate place in your text.

> The extent of dissension that year in Parliament has been pointed out before (Levenson 127). [*Writer cites author and gives author's name and page number in parentheses, without a comma.*]

> Accordingly, no "parliamentary session was without severe dissension" (Levenson 127). [*Writer quotes author and gives author's name and page number in parentheses.*]

> Levenson points out that "no parliamentary session was without severe dissension" (127). [*Writer names author, places quotation marks at beginning of quotation and before parenthesis, and gives only page number in parentheses.*]

These references indicate that the quotation is to be found in the work by Levenson listed in Works Cited at the end of the text of the paper.

If two authors in your sources have the same last name, give first names in your references.

> It has been suggested that the general's brother did not arrive until the following year (Frederick Johnson 235).

> The authenticity of the document, however, has been questioned (Edwin Johnson 15).

If two or more works by the same author are listed in Works Cited, indicate which one you are referring to by giving a short title: (Levenson, *Battles* 131). The full title listed in Works Cited is *Battles in British Parliament, 1720–1721.*

If a work cited consists of more than one volume, give the volume number as well as the page: (Hoagland 2:173–74).

If your work appears in an electronic source and the paragraphs are numbered, place the paragraph number in the parenthetical citation: (Johnson para. 15).

If your work appears in an electronic source and the paragraphs are not numbered, the parenthetical citation will include only the author's name: (Phillips).

Some sources—the Bible and well-known plays, for example—are cited in the text of the paper but not listed as sources in Works Cited. Use the following forms:

> . . . the soliloquy (*Hamlet* 2.2). [The numbers designate act and scene. Some instructors prefer Roman numerals: *Hamlet* II.ii.]
>
> . . . the passage (1 Kings 4.3). [That is, chapter 4, verse 3.]

For further illustrations of parenthetical references to works cited, see the model research paper that follows the MLA method, beginning on p. 385.

Notes (endnotes, footnotes)

You will probably need few if any numbered notes (called *footnotes* when at the bottom of the page, *notes* or *endnotes* at the end of the paper) because sources are referred to in the text itself and listed after the body of the paper. Explanatory notes are used to give further information or to comment on something you have written. To include incidental information in the text itself would be to interrupt the flow of the argument or to assign undue importance to matters that add to the substance only tangentially. Make your decision as to where to place such information—in the text or in a note at the end—on the basis of its impact and direct relevance.

Explanatory notes are also useful in referring to sources other than those mentioned in the text or in commenting on sources. If you wish to list several books or articles in connection with a point you are making, it may prove awkward to include all of this information in parentheses. Therefore, a note is preferable.

The sign of a note is an Arabic numeral raised slightly above the line at the appropriate place in the text. The *MLA Handbook* recommends that notes be grouped at the end of the paper. Notes should be numbered consecutively throughout.

EXAMPLES

[1]See also Drummond, Stein, Van Patten, Southworth, and Langhorne.
[*Lists further sources. Full bibliographic information given in Works Cited at end of paper.*]
[2]After spending seventeen years in Europe, he returned to America with a new attitude toward slavery, which he had defended earlier.
[*Remark parenthetical to main argument but important enough to include in a note.*]
[3]This biography, once considered standard, is shown to be unreliable by recent discoveries.
[*Evaluates a source.*]
[4]Detailed census records are available only for the 1850–1880 period. Earlier censuses do not provide the exact names of inhabitants nor any financial or social information. Later census schedules that do have detailed information on individuals are not available to the public; one may obtain only summaries of the data gathered.
[*Provides background on a source.*]
[5]Andrews uses the term *koan* to mean any riddle. To prevent confusion, however, *koan* will be used in this paper to designate only riddles in the form of paradoxes employed in Zen Buddhism as aids to meditation.
[*Clarifies terminology.*]

44k Model research paper, MLA style

A model research paper using the MLA method of documentation is presented on the following pages along with an outline and explanatory notes.

PREPARATION OF MANUSCRIPT

Allow ample and even margins.

Indent five spaces to begin paragraphs.

Double-space throughout the entire manuscript.

MLA style requires neither a title page nor an outline. However, some instructors prefer them. Find out your teacher's preference. If you use a title page, balance the material on the page. Center the title and place it about one-third of the way down. Include your name, the name of the course (with section number), the instructor's name, and the date.

Copycat Killers and Unexpected Heroes

By Elaine Rodman

English 1102 C

Professor Jane Smith

22 April 2001

The outline should occupy a separate, unnumbered page following the title page and should follow the form illustrated on page 387.

Place the thesis statement between the title and the first line of the outline.

Copycat Killers and Unexpected Heroes

Thesis: Puzzling outbreaks of violence have become almost commonplace in today's schools, often leading to both despair and heroism.

   I.   Introduction: Violence in American schools

       A. A new war

       B. Epidemic violence

  II.   Reasons for school shootings

       A. Modern society

       B. Teasing

       C. Lost relationships

       D. Immaturity or mental illness

       E. Unexplained

 III. Responses to school shootings

       A. Altruistic attitudes

       B. Courageous actions

          1. Protecting others

          2. Preventing attacks

       C. Concerned compassion

          1. Offering help

          2. Offering apologies

  IV. Conclusion

Place the page numbers in the upper right-hand corner, two lines above the first line of text. Use Arabic numerals (1, 2, 3); do not place a period after the number. Add your last name before the number of each page. Center your title on the page. Double-space to the first line of the text.

MLA requires student's name, instructor's name, course number, and date of paper.

The author goes immediately to the subject by presenting the thesis of the paper as the first sentence. Avoid overly broad generalities or historical commonplaces in the opening.

The first two paragraphs, the introduction, explain and develop the thesis. The writer first establishes that some American schools have become dangerous. She then makes the essential point that this danger is hard to explain; it may not totally follow a pattern.

The parenthetical reference ("School Violence") toward the middle of the second paragraph illustrates the proper way to document a reference to an unsigned Internet article. The second parenthetical reference (*NBC Evening News*) demonstrates the correct way to document a televised electronic source. The third parenthetical reference (Health and Administration Development Group #6) shows the proper way to document textually an agency or formal group as a source.

Rodman 1

Elaine Rodman

Professor Jane Smith

ENGL 1102 C

22 April 2001

Copycat Killers and Unexpected Heroes

American schools became dangerous places at the end of the twentieth century. Children as young as twelve and thirteen came to school not to study but to shoot as many people as possible. Even as these students transformed schools into war zones, teachers and other students did what they could to restore order and to save lives. In doing so, they became unlikely heroes on America's latest battlefield.

Although violence in schools is nothing new, multiple shootings are. According to the 1999 Annual Report on School Violence, the number of such shootings increased from one in 1994-95 to five in 1997-98 ("School Violence"). Tragically, the epidemic of violence continued, and in December 1999, one television newscast called a shooting in Oklahoma the ninth nationwide since 1997 (NBC Evening News). The most serious incident occurred on April 20, 1999, when two teenagers in Littleton,

The parenthetical reference to Devine in the second sentence illustrates the proper way to document a print source with one author.

Prose quotations of five lines or more should be set off ten spaces as indicated here. Leave the right margin unchanged. MLA style calls for double-spacing of quotations that are set off. Do not further indent the first line unless more than one paragraph is being quoted.

The reference to McBrien at the end of the blocked quotation illustrates the most frequently used form of documentation: author's last name, no punctuation, page number. Note that after a blocked quotation, the period comes before the parenthetical documentation rather than after it.

After a quotation that has been set off, you do not necessarily have to begin a new paragraph. Here the same paragraph continues.

Colorado, killed fifteen of their classmates (Health and Administration Development Group 6).

Why so many children committed mass murder in so short a time is a mystery. In the past, some crimes were justified because they were committed "against an unjust system" (Devine), but these school shootings were not attached to any worthy causes. One writer has summarized many factors that may have played a part in these shootings. He mentions

> parental neglect, a breakdown of societal morality, the easy availability of assault weapons, the lack of metal detectors, [and] the perverse influence of violently graphic video games and films, of certain kinds of music and of material on the Internet. (McBrien 19)

To these general causes we may add a desire for celebrity. Many of the killers seemed to be copycats, merely imitating the violence they heard and saw in the news. However, a look at some individual cases reveals the presence of other motives as well.

Where appropriate, you always should add the section number as well as the page number when citing an article from a newspaper. See, for example, the parenthetical documentation of an article by Lore in the first paragraph.

Also in the first paragraph, note the use of a short title ("Jonesboro Dazed") in the parenthetical citation of an article by Bragg. When you cite more than one work by the same author or works by authors with the same last name, you should distinguish sources by adding a short title after an author's name.

The last two sentences in the first paragraph are not directly quoted; they are paraphrased. Document paraphrases or summaries with parenthetical citations—in this case, with the last name of Helmore. No page number is necessary here because the article comes from only one page.

Several killers named teasing as a reason for murdering their classmates. One such case occurred in Moses Lake, Washington, in February 1996 when Barry Loukaitis killed a "popular boy who had teased him" (Egan). But he also killed another student and a teacher. Asked why he shot the other two, Loukaitis was not able to give any reason. He said mysteriously, "I don't know. I guess reflex took over" (Egan). If revenge is sometimes a motive, it is clearly not the only one.

Failed romantic relationships also seem to motivate some shootings, although most romances seem too casual to explain this level of violence. According to some experts, teenagers--especially those who come from "fractured" families--"depend more on each other than [on] their parents" (Lore A1). As a result, they may feel the sting of rejection more deeply than they would otherwise. This emotional pain may lead to violence. One such case may have occurred in Jonesboro, Arkansas.

Mitchell Johnson listed the names of a teacher and four girls whom he planned to kill, including his ex-girlfriend (Bragg, "Jonesboro Dazed"). A student in Pearl, Mississippi, killed his mother with a butcher knife and shot nine students. Two died, and one of them was a former girlfriend (Helmore).

Sometimes, immaturity or mental illness played an undeniable role. Such was certainly the case at an alternative school in DeKalb County, Georgia, where a student gunned down Horace Pierpont ("Bucky") Morgan. Morgan--who taught reading, poetry, and creative writing--was popular and known as someone who "wanted to make a difference" (Cumming A1). However, the student, David Dubose, Jr., claimed that Morgan had threatened "to kill him" and that he had "to kill him first." Those who knew Morgan described him as gentle and "unlikely to have made such a threat." Later, Dubose was diagnosed as suffering from an "extreme case" of paranoid schizophrenia (Oglesby 1H).

When you have omitted words within a sentence in a direct quotation, use three ellipsis points (. . .), putting spaces after each one. When you omit words from the end of a sentence in a direct quotation, represent the omission by using a period and ellipsis points (four periods, no space before the first one). Ellipses go in brackets, according to the most recent edition of the *MLA Handbook*. Space before the opening bracket.

Use single quotation marks to indicate a quotation within a quotation, as illustrated in the last sentence of the first paragraph.

Even stranger are the shootings for which no one seems to know any reason. Police in Edinboro, Pennsylvania, said they did not know the motive of an eighth grader who killed John Gillette, a teacher for nearly thirty years ("Student Guns Down"). Another student killer, Kip Kinkel, when asked why he shot someone, replied, "I had no other choice," as if he were powerless. He called a boy who was choking on his own blood "a bastard that deserves to die" (Egan), but he did not give a reason. Instead, he said, "This sure beats algebra, doesn't it?" In Fort Gibson, Oklahoma, a seventh grader pulled out a gun and "blank-faced and calm . . . emptied a 9-millimeter semiautomatic into a crowd of school-mates [. . .]." Strangely, a deputy sheriff said, "He doesn't know who it was he shot [. . .]. This was not a hate thing. I asked him why. He said, 'I don't know' " (Kolker).

Fortunately, most students did not share these antisocial feelings. Before these multiple school shootings began, one expert wrote, "The majority of students in our schools [. . .] have a clear sense of justice [. . .]" (Besag xii). After the shootings started, most students expressed a desire to help others. In fact, nine out of ten students who were polled in one study reported that they "would be willing to take an active role in trying to do something about violence" (Farrington 6). When students began firing, no one was trained to be a hero or a martyr. However, many spontaneously rose to the occasion. Their courage and compassion proved to be the first line of defense against the madness around them.

At the first round of shots, many teachers and students acted with amazing courage. When a gunman aimed at twelve-year-old Emma Pittman in Jonesboro, Arkansas, a teacher, Ms. Shannon Wright, "acted instinctively [. . .] jumped into the line of fire," shielded the student, and was killed

Use one parenthetical citation when you paraphrase and directly quote from the same source in the same sentence, as demonstrated in the last sentence of the first paragraph on the opposite page.

(Ayres). After Jerry Safely was shot in the leg and in his left foot, he "lay over his girlfriend to protect her" ("Witnesses Recount Shooting").

Several heroes stopped shootings in brave and almost casual ways. After Kip Kinkel killed a student and shot twenty-three others, five critically, Jacob Ryker, "who was shot in the stomach and hands, [. . .] fought with Kinkel and got the gun, [. . .] then pulled him to the floor." His father explained that Jacob "did what he had to do" (Ritter). In another case, Benjamin Strong, a minister's son and a football player, talked Michael Carneal into giving up after he killed three students and wounded eight others in West Paducah, Kentucky. "Put down the gun," Strong is reported to have said. "Don't shoot anybody. What are you doing?" (Bragg, "Forgiveness").

Also acting spontaneously, other students showed amazing concern and compassion for their classmates. In a tiny closet in Columbine High

The conclusion of this paper—the last paragraph—avoids lurid appeal to emotion and melodrama, although such a topic could easily slip into this approach. The author also wisely avoids the temptation to become overtly judgmental and didactic here—and throughout the paper. Reasoning often is more effective than preaching.

School, two students lifted two asthmatic classmates toward the ceiling so that they could breathe (Barron). After the shooting in Kentucky, many of the victims forgave their attacker. Members of the prayer group into which he fired held up a sign that read, "We forgive you, Mike." Benjamin Strong, who talked Michael into putting down his gun, wanted to meet the assailant. His intent was not revenge, but healing. "I'd talk to him like a friend," he said. "I'd see why he did it and I would pray with him" (Bragg, "Forgiveness").

Mass school shootings have been a nightmare for many students, parents, and teachers. No doubt, the tragedy of this needless violence will not be restricted to the twentieth century. Psychologists and educators have looked for answers, but they have found few that really can help them anticipate and prevent random, apparently unmotivated acts of violence. Metal detectors, school evacuation plans, and improved counseling can reduce the likelihood

Rodman 9

of another tragic killing spree. However, if and
when violence erupts, the first line of defense
will remain heroic teachers and students who, in
times of crisis, act courageously and selflessly to
save others and to start the process of healing.

Begin a new page for the list of Works Cited, which comes at the very end of the paper. Center the title. Double-space throughout.

Do not indent the first line of an entry; indent succeeding lines five spaces.

List only those sources actually mentioned in your paper and referred to in the parenthetical documentation.

Authors are listed with last names first. If a work has more than one author, list names after the first in normal order.

List entries alphabetically by the authors' last names. If an author's name is not known, as in the last three entries (see pp. 409–410), arrange the entry according to the first word of the title (excluding *A, An,* and *The*).

Give the inclusive pages for articles.

Notice that the important divisions in each entry are separated by periods.

Many entries show the proper way to list online sources.

Rodman 10

Works Cited

Ayres, Drummond B., Jr. "Bloodshed in a School-
     yard." <u>New York Times</u> 26 Mar. 1998: A23.
     Online. LEXIS-NEXIS Academic Universe.
     News/Majpap. 28 Mar. 2000.

Barron, James, with Mindy Sink. "Terror in
     Littleton." <u>New York Times</u> 21 Apr. 1999, late
     ed.: A1. Online. LEXIS-NEXIS Academic
     Universe. News/Majpap. 23 Mar. 2000.

Besag, Valerie E. <u>Bullies and Victims in Schools: A
     Guide to Understanding and Management</u>.
     Philadelphia: Open UP, 1989.

Bragg, Rick. "Forgiveness, After 3 Die in Shootings
     in Kentucky." <u>New York Times</u> 3 Dec. 1997, late
     ed.: A16. Online. LEXIS-NEXIS Academic
     Universe. News/Majpap. 23 Mar. 2000.

---. "Jonesboro Dazed by Its Darkest Day." <u>New York
     Times</u> 14 Apr. 1998, late. ed.: sec. 1: 1.
     Online. LEXIS-NEXIS Academic Universe.
     News/Majpap. 23 Mar. 2000.

Cumming, Doug. "Slain Teacher: 'He Wanted to Make a
    Difference,' " <u>Atlanta Journal and Constitu-
    tion</u> 26 Sep. 1996: A1.

Devine, John. <u>Maximum Security: The Culture of
    Violence in Inner-City Schools</u>. Chicago: U of
    Chicago P, 1996.

Egan, Timothy. "Where Rampages Begin." <u>New York
    Times</u> 14 June 1998, late ed.: sec. 1:1+.
    Online. LEXIS-NEXIS Academic Universe.
    News/Majpap. 25 Mar. 2000.

Farrington, Jan. "When Violence Comes to School."
    <u>Current Health</u> 2.24 (1998): 6.

Health and Administration Development Group.
    <u>Stopping School Violence: An Essential Guide:
    Special Report</u>. Gaithersburg: Aspen, 1999.

Helmore, Edward. "Inside Story: Murder at Pearl High."
    <u>The Guardian</u> [London] 18 November 1997: 6.

Kolker, Claudia. "13-Year-Old Shoots Four School-
    mates." <u>Los Angeles Times</u> 7 Dec. 1999, home
    ed.: A16. Online. LEXIS-NEXIS Academic
    Universe. News/Majpap. 25 Mar. 2000.

Lore, Diane. "Failed Romances Helped Trigger School
    Violence." <u>Atlanta Journal and Constitution</u> 23
    May 1999, home ed.: A1+.

McBrien, Richard P. "It's Our Response to Evil That
    Matters." <u>National Catholic Reporter</u> 4 June
    1999: 19.

<u>NBC Evening News</u>. WXIA. 13 Dec 1999.

Oglesby, Christy. "Student in DeKalb Claims Self-
    Defense." <u>Atlanta Journal and Constitution</u> 11
    Oct. 1996: H1.

Ritter, John. " 'Nobody Took Him Seriously': Oregon
    Student 'Joked' He Would 'Get People.' " <u>USA
    Today</u> 22 May 1998, final ed.: A3+. Online.
    LEXIS-NEXIS Academic Universe. News/Majpap. 26
    March 2000.

"School Violence Continues to Decline; Multiple
    Homicides in Schools Rise." <u>Safe and Drug-Free
    Schools Program: Current Headlines</u> 19 Oct.
    2000. <http://www.ed.gov/PressReleases/10-
    1999/violence.htm>.

"Student Guns Down Science Teacher Chaperoning
     School Dance." <u>New York Times</u> 12 August 1998,
     late ed.: A1. Online. LEXIS-NEXIS Academic
     Universe. News/Majpap. 30 Mar. 2000.
"Witnesses Recount Shooting at Mississippi High
     School." <u>New York Times</u> 11 June 1998, late
     ed.: A28. Online. LEXIS-NEXIS Academic
     Universe. News/Majpap. 26 Mar. 2000.

441 The APA Style of Documentation

An alternate method of documentation—used widely in the sciences and the social sciences—is that explained in the *Publication Manual of the American Psychological Association* (APA), 1997.

Note that the list of works at the end of the paper is called not "Works Cited" but "References," that in the entries the date of publication comes immediately after the author's name, that initials are used instead of given names, that only the first word of a title is capitalized (except where there is a colon), that no quotation marks are used for titles, and that there are other differences from the method recommended by the Modern Language Association. Follow the preferences of your instructor as to which method you use. See the APA's website for updates on citations of electronic sources and for other answers to frequently asked questions about citations (http://www.apa.org/journals/fac.html).

List of references

Include a list titled "References" immediately after the body of the paper and before the footnotes (if any).

According to the APA *Manual,* all sources cited in the text must be cited in the reference list, and all sources cited in the reference list must also be cited in the text. Alphabetically arranged, the list furnishes publication information necessary for identifying and locating all the references cited in the body of the paper. See the list for the model paper, pp. 440–445, and study the following examples of forms used in APA documentation for various kinds of sources.

A BOOK BY A SINGLE AUTHOR

Kopka, D. L. (1997). <u>School violence: A reference
    handbook</u>. Santa Barbara: ABC-CLIO.

A BOOK WITH TWO EDITORS OR AUTHORS

Mack, A. S., & Carroll, S. A. (Eds.). (1998).
    <u>Crisis prevention and response: A collection of
    NASP resources</u>. Bethesda: NASP.

A BOOK WITH THREE, FOUR, OR FIVE EDITORS OR AUTHORS

Boatwright, B. H., Mathis, T. A., & Smith-Rex,
    S. J. (1998). <u>Getting equipped to stop bullying:
    A kid's survival kit for understanding and
    coping with violence in the schools</u>.
    Minneapolis: Educational Media.

A TRANSLATED BOOK

Lorenz, K. (1966). <u>On aggression</u>. (M. Latzke,
    Trans.). London: Routledge.

A MULTIVOLUME WORK

Pederson, L., McDaniel, S. L., Adams, C., & Liao,
    C. (Eds.). (1998). <u>Linguistic atlas of the Gulf
    States</u>. (Vol. 3). Athens: University of Georgia
    Press.

A REPUBLISHED BOOK

Langdon, W. C. (1969). <u>Everyday things in American
    life</u>. New York: Scribner's. (Original work
    published 1941)

A REVISED EDITION OF A BOOK

Zabel, M. D. (Ed.). (1951). <u>Literary opinion in
    America</u>. (Rev. ed.). New York: Harper.

A SECOND OR LATER EDITION OF A BOOK

Cangelosi, J. S. (1993). <u>Classroom management strategies: Getting and maintaining students' cooperation</u> (2nd ed.). New York: Longman.

AN ESSAY IN A COLLECTION OF ESSAYS OR AN ANTHOLOGY

Hafen, B. C. (1991). Education and social morality. In D. L. Thompson (Ed.), <u>Moral values and higher education: A notion at risk</u> (pp. 65-75). Albany: State University of New York Press.

AN INTRODUCTION, FOREWARD, PREFACE, OR AFTERWORD IN A BOOK

Bowers, C. A., & Flinders, D. J. (1990). Foreword. In J. F. Soltis, <u>Responsive teaching: An ecological approach to classroom patterns of language, culture, and thought</u> (pp. vii-ix). New York: Teacher's College Press.

MORE THAN ONE WORK BY THE SAME AUTHOR

Powell, M. (1971). <u>The psychology of adolescence</u> (2nd ed.). Indianapolis: Bobbs-Merrill.
Powell, M. (1972). <u>Youth: Critical issues</u>. Columbus: Bobbs-Merrill.

NOTE: Works by the same author are arranged according to dates of publication, earlier date first, as illustrated. If works appeared in the same year, arrange them alphabetically according to the first letter of the title (disregard *A* or *The*) and add distinguishing letters (*a, b, c,* etc.) to the dates in parentheses.

SIGNED ARTICLE IN A REFERENCE WORK

DeAnda, D. (1987). Adolescents. In <u>Encyclopedia of
    social work</u> (18th ed.). (Vol. 1, pp. 51-67).
    Silver Springs: National Association of Social
    Workers.

GOVERNMENT PUBLICATION

United States. Bureau of the Census and Department
    of Justice. (1994). <u>School crime supplement to
    the national crime victimization survey</u>. Wash-
    ington, DC: GPO.

NOTE: The sample entry for this document illustrates many of the
difficulties encountered when documenting government publications. In the absence of an identified author, cite the government
agency that issued the document.

ARTICLE IN A MONTHLY PERIODICAL

Stephens, R. D. (1998, March). Ten steps to safer
    schools. <u>The American School Board Journal, 185</u>,
    30-35.

ARTICLE IN A WEEKLY PERIODICAL

Quindlen, A. (1999, November 29). The c word in the
    hallways. <u>Newsweek</u>, 112.

ARTICLE IN A JOURNAL WITH CONTINUOUS PAGINATION

Catterall, J. S. (1997-98). Risk and resilience in
    student transitions to high school. <u>American
    Journal of Education, 106</u>, 302-33.

ARTICLE IN A JOURNAL PAGINATED BY ISSUE

Hannabuss, S. (1996). Issues of censorship for
    students. <u>Education Today, 46</u>(1), 45-53.

NOTE: When each issue of a journal is paginated separately, include
the issue number (in this case, *1*) as well as the volume number.

BOOK REVIEW IN A PERIODICAL

Cherlin, A. J. (1999). [Review of the book <u>A gener-
    ation at risk: Growing up in an era of family
    upheaval</u>]. <u>American Journal of Sociology, 104</u>,
    1230-32.

NOTE: If the review has a title, place it before the material in brackets.

ARTICLE IN A DAILY NEWSPAPER

Butterfield, F. (2000, April 11). Hole in gun
    control law lets mentally ill through. <u>New York
    Times</u>, p. A1.

NOTE: *A* refers to the section of the paper; *1,* to the page within that
section. For newspaper sections designated by numbers instead of
letters, add *sec.:* sec. 4: 7. For newspapers not divided into sections,
simply give the page number after the title of the newspaper. If the article is not signed, begin the entry with the title of the article. Note that
APA style uses *p.* or *pp.* before page numbers of newspaper articles.

A VIDEOTAPE

Elkind, D. (Writer and Narrator). Davidson, J. M.
    (Director). (1999). <u>Adolescent cognition:
    Thinking in a new key</u>. [videorecording]. San
    Luis Obispo, CA: Davidson Films.

A PERSONAL WEB SITE

Nash, Mike. (no date).<u>Some thoughts about school
    violence</u>. [Online] Retrieved March 29, 2000,
    from the World Wide Web: http://www.wtp.net/
    ~mpa/pg000014.htm

NOTE: The date the page was published should immediately follow
the title of the page. The notation (*no date*) documents the absence
of this information. Online entries in APA style differ markedly from
online entries in MLA style. In MLA style, URLs are underlined and
followed by a period. However, in APA style, URLs are not underlined and are not followed by a period.

A PROFESSIONAL WEB SITE

Center for the Prevention of School Violence.
    (2000, Winter). Stats 1999: Selected school
    violence research findings. [Online] North
    Carolina State University. Retrieved April 8,
    2000, from the World Wide Web: http://
    www.ncsu.edu/cpsv/

AN ARTICLE IN AN ELECTRONIC MAGAZINE

Morris, Jim. (1999, August 4). Study: School violence
    down, but still too high. <u>CNN.com</u>. [Online]
    Retrieved March 28, 2000, from the World Wide Web:
    http://www.cnn.com/US/9908/04/schoolviolence/

AN ARTICLE FROM THE ELECTRONIC EDITION OF A PRINT MAGAZINE OR
NEWSPAPER

Morse, Jodie. (2000, April 24). The perception gap:
    School violence. Survey: School violence. <u>Time</u>.
    [Online] Retrieved May 3, 2000, from the World
    Wide Web: http://www.time.com/time/magazine/
    articles/0.3266.43161,00.html

AN EDITORIAL FROM THE ELECTRONIC EDITION OF A NEWSPAPER

Cohen, Jonathan R. (2000, April 26). Defining
    rebellion up. [Commentary]. <u>New York Post Online
    Edition</u>. [Online] Retrieved April 4, 2001, from
    the World Wide Web: http://208.248.87.252/
    042699/8622.htm

AN ARTICLE RETRIEVED FROM LEXIS-NEXIS OR A SIMILAR ONLINE DATABASE

Campbell, Colin. (1996, September 29). Classroom
    slaying is a tragic waste. <u>Atlanta Journal and
    Constitution</u>, p. G1. [Online] Retrieved April
    10, 2001, from LEXIS-NEXIS Academic Universe
    database (News/major papers) on the World Wide
    Web: http://www.lexis-nexis.com/lncc/academic/
    AcademicAccess.htm

Reference citations in text

As you quote, summarize, or simply refer to sources in the body of your paper, identify these sources immediately in parentheses. Give the last name of the author (or last names if more than one author) and, after a comma, the date of publication: (Golightly & Walksoftly, 1973). If you are quoting or referring to a specific part of a work, furnish the page number: (Beamish, 1901, p. 34). You can work in this information in various ways, as illustrated next. By using all these formats for parenthetical citations, you will achieve greater flexibility and thus avoid monotony.

> In motion pictures of the silver-screen era, "character development and story were paramount"; in modern films, "those essentials tend to be neglected for the less basic attributes of special effects and 'realistic' language" (Brienza, 1990, p. 183).

> Brienza (1990) observes that in the current cinema important aspects, such as characterization and plot, tend to be neglected. Several other critics (Lamond & Greely, 1983; Secord, 1989; Seltzer, 1990) feel that the art of the motion picture is currently at its highest point.

> According to Brienza (1990), "character development and story were paramount" in motion pictures of the thirties and forties, a contrast to films of our time, in which "those essentials tend to be neglected for the less basic attributes of special effects and 'realistic' language" (p. 183).

For other examples, see the model paper, pp. 421–445. In the APA style, set off (block) quotations of forty words or more. From the left margin indent five spaces; do not use quotation marks; do not indent from the right margin; place the parenthetical reference after the period ending the quotation; do not use a period after the reference. Note the following example:

Many of our struggling young people like to complain about unfairness, about how difficult it is for those without the advantages of inheritances to make it in today's world. They are not the only ones faced with inequalities, however:

> Age has inequalities that are even greater than those of youth. In the matter of income, for example, most of the old are well below the national median, but others are far above it. Many of the great American fortunes are now controlled by aged men (or by their widows or lawyers). (Cowley, 1980, p. 39)

Footnotes

The APA *Manual* (p. 163) advises writers to use footnotes sparingly since all truly pertinent information should be included with parenthetical documentation in the body of the paper. Footnotes are allowed for certain purposes (most of which are not relevant to student writing assignments). You may wish, however, to include "content" footnotes, which add data or information.

44m Model research paper, APA style

A model research paper in the APA style of documentation with accompanying explanations is given on the following pages.

Beginning with the title page, place a shortened version of your title (or the entire title if it is brief) in the upper right corner of each page, with the page number in Arabic numerals. Note that in the APA style, the title page is numbered *1*. Use the same heading and number pages consecutively throughout the paper.

Center the title on the page. APA advises against using in titles "words that serve no useful purposes," such as "A Study of" or "An Experimental Investigation of" (p. 7).

After double-spacing, center your name under the title.

Follow your teacher's instructions in regard to any other information to be included on the title page. Student papers usually include, as here, the name of the course (with a section number, if pertinent), the name of the professor, and the date that the paper is submitted. Double-space between all lines.

Copycat Killers and Unexpected Heroes

Elaine Rodman

ENGL 1102 C, Professor Jane Smith

22 April 2001

The abstract, usually required when following the APA format, serves as a kind of outline and thesis statement combined. It should not be more than 120 words in length. It should be carefully prepared so that it gives an accurate account of the contents and the purpose of your paper. Do not include in the abstract materials that are not in the text itself. Note: The abstract is a *summary* of the paper, not a commentary on it.

The abstract should be a separate page. Place the title of the paper (or an abbreviated form of it) in the upper right corner of the page with the numeral 2. Double-space and center the word *Abstract*. Double-space and begin at the far left margin. Do not indent.

Copycat Killers   2

Abstract

School shootings have become almost commonplace in America. They are mysterious and puzzling. These shootings seem to come in waves, and no one is certain why--although routine teasing, social alienation, and problems with relationships contribute. Even during times of stressful violence, however, public schools often are places of significant kindness, charity, and selfless heroism.

Allow five spaces between the title (or abbreviated title) in the upper right-hand corner and the page number. Double-space between the title of the paper (centered) and the first line of text. Leave adequate margins on the right and left as well as at the top and bottom. Indent five spaces for paragraphs.

The first paragraph effectively introduces expressions of school violence as a recent and troubling phenomenon. The second paragraph moves with alacrity to concrete evidence and recent accounts. Notice that the author does not try to gloss over the seriousness of this violence, nor does she sensationalize. To be convincing, this author understands that she must convey the impression of objectivity.

The title rather than the author's name is given in the first reference ("School Violence") because the source—*1999 Annual Report on School Violence*—is given in the text of the sentence. Note that in the APA style, the date of publication is an essential part of most parenthetical references.

Copycat Killers and Unexpected Heroes

American schools became dangerous places at the end of the twentieth century. Children as young as 12 and 13 came to school not to study but to shoot as many people as possible. Even as these students transformed schools into war zones, teachers and other students did what they could to restore order and to save lives. In doing so, they became unlikely heroes on America's latest battlefield.

Although violence in schools is nothing new, multiple shootings are. According to the <u>1999 Annual Report on School Violence</u>, the number of such shootings increased from one in 1994-95 to five in 1997-98 ("School Violence"). Tragically, the epidemic of violence continued, and in December 1999, one television newscast called a shooting in Oklahoma the ninth nationwide since 1997 (<u>NBC Evening News</u>, 1999). The most serious incident occurred on April 20, 1999, when two teenagers in Littleton, Colorado, killed 15 of their classmates (Health and Administration Development Group, 1999, p. 6).

When the name of a source's author is given, the title is not necessary (see the citations for both Devine's and McBrien's sources on the facing page), but the date of publication is included together with the number of the page on which the material appears.

Note the effective transition to "other motives" in the sentence just before the beginning of the last paragraph. Clear transitions among and within paragraphs help to ensure a paper's coherence.

Why so many children committed mass murder in so short a time is a mystery. In the past, some crimes were justified because they were fought "against an unjust system" (Devine, 1996), but these school shootings were not attached to any worthy causes. One writer has summarized many factors that may have played a part in these shootings. He mentions

> parental neglect, a breakdown of societal
> morality, the easy availability of assault
> weapons, the lack of metal detectors, the
> perverse influence of violently graphic video
> games and films, of certain kinds of music
> and of material on the Internet. (McBrien,
> 1999, p. 19)

To these general causes we may add a desire for celebrity. Many of the killers seemed to be copycats, merely imitating the violence they heard and saw in the news. However, a look at some individual cases reveals the presence of other motives as well.

Several killers named teasing as a reason for murdering their classmates. One such case occurred

in Moses Lake, Washington, in February 1996 when Barry Loukaitis killed a "popular boy who had teased him" (Egan, 1998, p. 1). But he also killed another student and a teacher. Asked why he shot the other two, Loukaitis was not able to give any reason. He said mysteriously, "I don't know. I guess reflex took over" (Egan, 1998, p. 1). If revenge is sometimes a motive, it is clearly not the only one.

Failed romantic relationships also seem to motivate some shootings. Most romances seem too casual to explain this level of violence. According to some experts, teenagers--especially those who come from "fractured" families, "depend more on each other than [on] their parents" (Lore, 1999, p. A1). As a result, they may feel the sting of rejection more deeply than they would otherwise. This emotional pain may lead to violence. One such case may have occurred in Jonesboro, Arkansas. Mitchell Johnson listed the names of a teacher and four girls whom he planned to kill, including his

When you do not introduce the name of your source in either paraphrase or direct quotation, you must give the name, title (or short title), date, and page number of the source. See the citation for Bragg as a source for Mitchell Johnson's list, for instance.

Paraphrase or summarize when possible; however, note that the addition of the brief quotation ("extreme case") in the paraphrase of Oglesby effectively stresses the extreme nature of Dubose's behavior—implying, of course, that not all of those who suffer from emotional illness are violent.

Note the especially good transition at the beginning of the final paragraph on this page ("Even stranger are. . .").

ex-girlfriend (Bragg, "Jonesboro Dazed," 1998,
p. 1). A student in Pearl, Mississippi, killed his
mother with a butcher knife and shot nine students.
Two died, and one of them was a former girlfriend
(Helmore, 1997, p. 6).

Sometimes, immaturity or mental illness played
an undeniable role. Such was certainly the case at an
alternative school in DeKalb County, Georgia, where a
student gunned down Horace Pierpont ("Bucky") Morgan.
Morgan--who taught reading, poetry, and creative
writing--was popular and known as someone who "wanted
to make a difference" (Cumming, 1996, p. A1).
However, the student, David Dubose, Jr., claimed that
Morgan had threatened "to kill him" and that he had
"to kill him first." Those who knew Morgan described
him as gentle and "unlikely to have made such a
threat." Later, Dubose was diagnosed as suffering
from an "extreme case" of paranoid schizophrenia
(Oglesby, 1996, p. 1H).

Even stranger are the shootings for which no
one seems to know any reason. Police in Edinboro,

The Publication Manual of the American Psychological Association strongly advises against using such terms as *the investigator* and *the author* as awkward attempts to avoid using the first-person pronoun. This manual permits the use of the first person (*I, my*) but advises you to use it sparingly. Otherwise, the paper may become more about yourself than about your topic. The author of this sample paper chooses to avoid using the first person altogether, thus establishing a tone of objectivity.

The last paragraph on this page illustrates a major shift in direction from documented events of violence to documented instances of heroic selflessness. ("Fortunately, most students did not share these antisocial feelings.")

Pennsylvania, said they did not know the motive of an eighth grader who killed John Gillette, a teacher for nearly thirty years ("Student Guns Down," 1998). Another student killer, Kip Kinkel, when asked why he shot someone, replied, "I had no other choice," as if he were powerless. He called a boy who was choking on his own blood "a bastard that deserves to die" (Egan, 1998, p. 1), but he did not give a reason. Instead, he said, "This sure beats algebra, doesn't it?" In Fort Gibson, Oklahoma, a seventh grader pulled out a gun and "blank-faced and calm . . . emptied a 9-millimeter semiautomatic into a crowd of schoolmates. . . ." Strangely, a deputy sheriff said, "He doesn't know who it was he shot. . . . This was not a hate thing. I asked him why. He said, 'I don't know' " (Kolker, 1999, p. A16).

Fortunately, most students did not share these antisocial feelings. Before these multiple school shootings began, one expert wrote, "The majority of students in our schools . . . have a clear sense of

Be sure to include the section number for documentation of newspaper articles (see citation for Ayres).

justice . . ." (Besag, 1989, p. xii). After they started, most students expressed a desire to help others. In fact, nine out of ten students who were polled in one study reported that they "would be willing to take an active role in trying to do something about violence" (Farrington, 1998, p. 6). When students began firing, no one was trained to be a hero or a martyr. However, many spontaneously rose to the occasion. Their courage and compassion proved to be the first line of defense against the madness around them.

At the first round of shots, many teachers and students acted with amazing courage. When a gunman aimed at 12-year-old Emma Pittman in Jonesboro, Arkansas, a teacher, Ms. Shannon Wright, "acted instinctively . . . jumped into the line of fire," shielded the student, and was killed (Ayres, 1998, p. A23). After Jerry Safely was shot in the leg and in his left foot, he "lay over his girlfriend to protect her" ("Witnesses Recount Shooting," 1998, p. A28).

Use ellipsis marks (. . .) to indicate material you have left out of direct quotations. Note in the second sentence of the first paragraph the use of the comma with ellipsis, necessary here to set off the non-restrictive adjective clause that describes Ryker.

Place question marks inside closing double quotation marks if the question is a part of the quoted material. See the final sentence of the first paragraph.

Copycat Killers   9

Several heroes stopped shootings in brave and almost casual ways. After Kip Kinkel killed a student and shot 23 others, five critically, Jacob Ryker, "who was shot in the stomach and hands, . . . fought with Kinkel and got the gun, . . . then pulled him to the floor." His father explained that Jacob "did what he had to do" (Ritter, 1998, p. A3). In another case, Benjamin Strong, a minister's son and a football player, talked Michael Carneal into giving up after he killed three students and wounded eight others in West Paducah, Kentucky. "Put down the gun," Strong is reported to have said. "Don't shoot anybody. What are you doing?" (Bragg, "Forgiveness," 1997, p. A16).

Also acting spontaneously, other students showed amazing concern and compassion for their classmates. In a tiny closet in Columbine High School, two students lifted two asthmatic classmates toward the ceiling so that they could breathe (Barron, 1999, p. A1). After the shooting in Kentucky, many

The conclusion of this paper does not stretch the evidence; neither does it offer easy answers. Rather, it objectively admits that answers may be hard to find and hard to recognize if found. It concentrates on the human capacity for selfless heroism in times of stress—for that is what the documented events also reveal—without didactic sentimentality.

of the victims forgave their attacker. Members of the
prayer group into which he fired held up a sign that
read, "We forgive you, Mike." Benjamin Strong, who
talked Michael into putting down his gun, wanted to
meet the assailant. His intent was not revenge, but
healing. "I'd talk to him like a friend," he said.
"I'd see why he did it and I would pray with him"
(Bragg, "Forgiveness," 1997, p. A16).

Mass school shootings have been a nightmare for
many students, parents, and teachers. No doubt, the
tragedy of this needless violence will not be
restricted to the twentieth century. Psychologists
and educators have looked for answers, but they
have found few that really can help them anticipate
and prevent random, apparently unmotivated acts of
violence. Metal detectors, school evacuation plans,
and improved counseling can reduce the likelihood
of another tragic killing spree. However, if and
when violence erupts, the first line of defense
will remain heroic teachers and students who, in
times of crisis, act courageously and selflessly to
save others and to start the process of healing.

Begin on a new page for the list of sources called, in the APA style, *References.* Center the word on the page, double-space, and then list entries in alphabetical order. Each new entry begins at the left margin; indent additional lines in individual entries five spaces.

When listing a title, capitalize only the first letter of the first word, of a word coming after a colon, and of any proper noun. Do not place titles of articles in quotation marks.

References

Ayres, D. B., Jr. (1998, March 26). Bloodshed in a schoolyard. <u>New York Times</u>, p. A23. [Online] Retrieved March 28, 2000, from LEXIS-NEXIS database on the World Wide Web: http://web.lexis-nexis.com/universe

Barron, J., & Sink, M. (1999, April 21). Terror in Littleton. <u>New York Times</u>, p. A1. [Online] Retrieved March 23, 2000, from LEXIS-NEXIS database on the World Wide Web: http://web.lexis-nexis.com/universe

Besag, V. E. (1989). <u>Bullies and victims in schools: A guide to understanding and management</u>. Philadelphia: Open University Press.

Bragg, R. (1997, December 3). Forgiveness, after three die in shootings in Kentucky. <u>New York Times</u>, p. A16. Retrieved March 23, 2000, from LEXIS-NEXIS database on the World Wide Web: http://web.lexis-nexis.com/universe

Bragg, R. (1998, April 14). Jonesboro dazed by its darkest day. <u>New York Times</u>, Sec. 1, p. 1.

Retrieved March 23, 2000, from LEXIS-NEXIS
    database on the World Wide Web: http://
    web.lexis-nexis.com/universe

Cumming, D. (1996, September 26). Slain teacher:
    "He wanted to make a difference." <u>Atlanta
    Journal and Constitution</u>, p. A1.

Devine, J. (1996). <u>Maximum security: The culture of
    violence in inner-city schools</u>. Chicago:
    University of Chicago Press.

Egan, T. (1998, June 14). Where rampages begin. <u>New
    York Times</u>, Sec. 1, p. 1. Retrieved March 25,
    2000, from LEXIS-NEXIS database on the World
    Wide Web: http://web.lexis-nexis.com/universe

Farrington, J. (1998). When violence comes to
    school. <u>Current Health, 2</u> (24), 6.

Health and Administration Development Group. (1999).
    <u>Stopping school violence: An essential guide:
    Special report</u>. Gaithersburg, MD: Aspen.

Helmore, E. (1997, November 18). Inside story:
    Murder at Pearl High. <u>The Guardian</u> [London],
    p. 6.

Copycat Killers   13

Kolker, Claudia. (1999, December 7). 13-year-old
    shoots four schoolmates. <u>Los Angeles Times</u>,
    p. A16. Retrieved March 25, 2000, from LEXIS-
    NEXIS database on the World Wide Web:
    http://web.lexis-nexis.com/universe

Lore, D. (1999, May 23). Failed romances helped
    trigger school violence. <u>Atlanta Journal and
    Constitution</u>, p. A1.

McBrien, R. P. (1999, June 4). It's our response to
    evil that matters. <u>National Catholic Reporter</u>,
    p. 19.

<u>NBC Evening News</u>. (1999, December 13). WXIA.

Oglesby, C. (1996, October 11). Student in DeKalb
    claims self-defense. <u>Atlanta Journal and
    Constitution</u>, p. H1.

Ritter, J. (1998, May 22). "Nobody took him
    seriously": Oregon student "joked" he would
    "get people." <u>USA Today</u>, p. A3. [Online]
    Retrieved March 26, 2000, from LEXIS-NEXIS
    database on the World Wide Web:
    http://web.lexis-nexis.com/universe

Since the entries for the last three sources are unsigned articles, the title is given first, and the entry is alphabetized in the list according to the first letters of the title. Several entries show the APA style for indicating articles taken from online sources.

Copycat Killers   14

School violence continues to decline; Multiple

homicides in schools rise. (2000, April 3).

<u>Safe and Drug-Free Schools Program: Current

Headlines</u>. [Online] http://www.ed.gov/

offices/OESE/SDFS/news.html

Student guns down science teacher chaperoning

school dance. (1998, August 12). <u>New York

Times</u>, p. A1. [Online] Retrieved March 30,

2000, from LEXIS-NEXIS database on the World

Wide Web: http://web.lexis-nexis.com/universe

Witnesses recount shooting at Mississippi high

school. (1998, June 11). <u>New York Times</u>,

p. A28. [Online] Retrieved March 26, 2000,

from LEXIS-NEXIS database on the World Wide

Web: http://web.lexis-nexis.com/universe

Glossary of
Usage

45 Glossary of Exactness and Usage *gl/us*

A glossary cannot list all of the words that a writer needs to know or to check. Only a dictionary can do that. The following list treats selected problems that are not treated elsewhere in this handbook. Entries will help a speaker and a writer to reject some words and to select others that are exact and pleasing. The entry words listed here are often misused. Learn these words and their meanings. Watch carefully for others you will need to look up.

No dictionary can tell all you need to know about graceful and effective words or about the overuse of worn-out words. *Very,* for example, means "complete," "absolute," or "actual"; it gives importance to the word that it modifies. Dictionaries, however, do not say that *very* has been used so often that it has lost much of its punch and does not contribute great power to the word it modifies. Words like *cute, lovely,* and *wonderful* stand unlabeled; they are therefore regarded as formal in a dictionary. In a glossary or in the opinion of a skillful writer, they may be considered worn and inexact words of approval, even gushy and false if used too often. A writer trying to select the niceties of language should listen, reject, savor, and be aware of the word choices used by others—and then make selections with discrimination.

If this glossary does not contain a particular word or address a problem that concerns you, consult the general Index and then a dictionary. Idioms, redundant and wordy phrases, bad grammar, words used as the wrong part of speech, spellings, parts of verbs, *-self* words, and double negatives—some items often found in glossaries—are discussed in the text along with other problems of a similar kind.

Many of the entries in this glossary show words that are similar in sound or in spelling (*principal, principle*) but different in meaning. They are called *homonyms.* Some words often thought to be alike have meanings that are opposite (*imply, infer*). Some words that are similar but not exactly alike in sound or spelling (*accept, ex-*

cept) may cause as many or more problems than homonyms. One verb expresses the action of a person offering knowledge or opinion to another (*advise*); a noun written almost exactly like the verb except for the difference of one letter (*c, s*) names the thing that is offered (*advice*). *Already* refers to a time; *all ready* describes the status of people or things.

Some words that do not resemble each other in sound or in spelling have a relationship or kinship that may cause a writer to mistakenly use one for another. *Number* and *amount* both refer to quantity: one tells how many; the other tells how much. One word in a certain sense or usage is often preferable to another (*as* meaning *because,* for example, is weak).

Of course, it is impossible to name all of the pairs or sets of words or even to categorize the difficulties writers have with them. Reasoning may not determine which word to use. Habit and memory may help. You already know the differences between many of the words shown in pairs and sets in this glossary. A speaker or a writer needs to know which word to use or when to look up a word in a list, a glossary, or a dictionary. Determine which words you know well and which you will need to look up again and again.

Choose your words deliberately. Careless language often does not convey exact meaning. Bad usage may be inaccurate, out of date, ungrammatical, abstruse, or even culturally and morally offensive. A listener or a reader may become irritated, even angry, about the use or misuse of words. Language that offends is not likely to persuade a listener to spend money or to fall in love.

For serious and formal occasions, do not choose the informal, especially not the vulgar or the blasphemous. Achieve identity and personality by preferring words that please you and convey your moods, impressions, and meanings with casual yet calculated effectiveness.

Usage is personal. Even dictionaries disagree. One person may dislike a word and regard the use of it as in bad taste even though others may regard it as a perfectly acceptable word. Watch your own choices of words, but do not be quick to condemn others when usage is doubtful or the subject of disagreement among people and in dictionaries. The chief authority used and cited in this glossary is *The American Heritage Dictionary of the English Language,* Third Edition, 1997. Its Usage Panel considers the opinions of nearly one hundred writers, educators, political figures, scholars, and other distinguished users of the English language. The richness and the complexities of words are indicated by the varied opinions of these experts and the infrequent unanimity among them.

Accept, except   The verb *accept* means "to receive":

> The editor *accepted* the reporter's story.

The verb *except* means "to exclude."

> Students with high averages were *excepted* from the final examination.

The preposition *except* means "but."

> Every bird *except* the blue jay made a joyful noise.

> Read every page of every book on the list *except* the dictionary.

Accessorize   See *-ize.*

Advice, advise   *Advice* is a noun; *advise* is a verb.

Affect, effect   The verb *affect* means "to act upon," "to influence."

> Encouragement seems to *affect* athletes.

The noun *effect* means "a result," "a consequence."

> The prescribed drug had no *effect* on the athlete's sleeping pattern.

The verb *effect* means "to cause," "to bring about."

> The operation did *effect* [bring about] an improvement in the athlete's health.

Ain't   This contraction is used incorrectly for *am not, are not, have not, is not.* The *American Heritage Dictionary* Usage Panel asserts that it "has such a stigma that it is beyond any possibility of rehabilitation." In speech, sometimes *ain't* is used for a jocular or popular note or for emphasis. Many use *aren't I?* but in writing there is no acceptable substitute for the admittedly stilted *am I not?*"

All ready, already   *All ready* means "entirely prepared."

> The riders were *all ready* to mount.

Already means "by a specified time" or "so soon."

> The sun had *already* set.

All together, altogether   *All together* describes a group as acting or existing collectively.

>   The sprinters managed to start *all together*.

>   *Altogether* means "wholly, entirely."

>   The adviser did not *altogether* approve of the course.

Allusion, illusion   An *allusion* is an indirect reference. An *illusion* is an erroneous concept or belief.

Among, between   Use *among* with three or more persons or things.

>   Choosing *among* so many candidates is difficult.

>   Use *between* with only two persons or things.

>   Choosing *between* these two candidates will be difficult.

Amount, number   *Amount* refers to mass or quantity. *Number* refers to things that may be counted.

>   The *number* of turtles in the pond is large for such a small *amount* of water.

Anyways   Non-Standard for "in any case."

Awesome   Means "inspiring awe." *Awesome* used to describe something that is merely remarkable is slang.

Awhile, a while   *Awhile* is an adverb.

>   Stay *awhile*.

>   The expression *a while* consists of an article and a noun.

>   Stay here for *a while*. [object of preposition]

Beside, besides   *Beside* means "by the side of."

>   Sit *beside* the pool.

>   *Besides* means "in addition to," "also."

>   No one *besides* the minister spoke at the service.

Between   See Among.

Bring, take   *Bring* indicates movement toward the speaker.

>   *Bring* the ball to this side of the fence.

>   *Take* indicates movement away from the speaker.

>   *Take* the ball to the other side of the fence.

Bunch   Informal for "a considerable number or amount" or "a group of people with a common interest."

Can, may   For clarity, use *can* to indicate physical or mental ability.

> I *can* ski.

May indicates permission.

> The rule is that I *may* not ski on paved walkways.

Capital, capitol   *Capitol* designates a building that is a seat of government. Use *capital* for all other meanings.

Climactic, climatic   *Climactic* refers to a climax, a moment of greatest intensity in a series. *Climatic* refers to climate or weather.

Compare to, compare with   Use *compare to* when describing resemblances between two things.

> The poet *compared* the young girl *to* a summer day.

Use *compare with* when describing similarities and differences of two things that are alike in some ways.

> The collector *compared* the fake coin *with* the original.

Complement, compliment   As a verb, *complement* means "to complete, to bring to perfection."

> Her delicate jewelry *complemented* her simple but elegant gown.

As a noun, *complement* refers to something that completes or brings to perfection.

> Her delicate jewelry was a *complement* to her simple but elegant gown.

As a verb, *compliment* means "to praise."

> Departing guests *complimented* the gracious hostess.

Conscience, conscious   The noun *conscience* refers to the source of moral judgment that prefers right over wrong.

> *Conscience* dictated the return of the money.

Conscious means being physically or psychologically aware.

> The youth was *conscious* of the disapproval of his elders.

Contact   In 1969, only 34 percent of the Usage Panel accepted *contact* as a verb meaning "to get in touch with." By 1997, it had become acceptable to 65 percent of the Panel.

Continual, continuous   *Continual* refers to actions that recur at intervals.

> Every evening the bats returned *continually* to the cave.

Continuous means "uninterrupted in time."

> Several kinds of night creatures—frogs and insects—kept making a *continuous* noise.

Cool   The noun *cool,* meaning "poise" (as in "keep your cool"), and the verb phrase *cool it* (meaning "calm down") are slang. The adjective *cool,* meaning "acceptable," "excellent," or "first-rate," is probably the most common use of the word as slang.

Differ from, differ with   *Differ from* means "to be unlike."

> Travel by sea *differs* greatly *from* travel by air.

Differ with means "to disagree."

> A marine biologist and a stockbroker might *differ with* each other about basic purposes in life.

Disinterested, uninterested   *Disinterested* means "free from selfish interest or bias."

> Good referees in ball games must be *disinterested.*

Uninterested means "indifferent."

> Fans who are *uninterested* in a game seldom buy tickets.

Due to   Use *because of* instead of *due to* in a prepositional phrase modifying a verb.

> DO NOT USE *due to:*
>
> The game was canceled *due to* the hurricane. (modifies a verb)
>
> USE *because of:*
>
> The game was canceled *because of* the hurricane.
>
> USE *due to* or *because of:*
>
> The cancellation of the game was *due to* the hurricane. (modifies a noun)

Effect   See **Affect.**

Emigrate, immigrate   *To emigrate* means "to leave a home country and settle in another." The word refers to a point of departure. *To immigrate* means "to come into a country from another." The word refers to the destination.

Eminent, imminent   *Eminent* means "distinguished." *Imminent* means "about to happen."

Et cetera, etcetera, etc.   Use of *and so forth* instead of these terms will help you to avoid censure for misspelling, incorrect compounding of words, and self-conscious display of your knowledge of a Latinate term.

Ever, every   *Ever* means "at all times," "in any way," or "at any time," as in *forever, ever and anon,* or *ever so humble.* Or it is an intensive, as in *"Did you ever!"* *Every* means "all possible" or "all members of a group without exception," as in *everybody, every other,* and *every one.*

Except   See Accept.

Explicit, implicit   *Explicit* means "fully and clearly expressed."

A good parent or teacher should make every important rule *explicit*.

Implicit means "implied or understood."

The sexual meanings of the poem were only *implicit*.

Farther, further   Many writers use these two words interchangeably. But 74 percent of the Usage Panel of *The American Heritage Dictionary* prefers *farther* for physical distance.

The walking gets more difficult as you walk *farther* into a wilderness.

Further, referring to degree or time, is preferred by 64 percent of the Panel.

The vocabulary usually becomes more polysyllabic as a philosopher gets *further* along in his thinking.

Fewer, less   *Fewer* denotes number; *less,* amount or quantity.

Each year *fewer* people come to the reunion.

Most people eat *less* as they grow older.

Fine   The adverb *fine,* meaning "very well," is informal.

Fix   The word *fix* has a wide variety of meanings and of levels of usage. Naming "a predicament," it is formal. Meaning "to make preparations for," *fix* is used chiefly in the American South ("*fixing* to go to the game"). Naming an "injection of a narcotic into a vein," *fix* is slang.

Flunk   Meaning "to fail a course or an examination," *flunk* is informal. Used orally for *fail, flunk* may connote a more hopeless condition than *fail.*

Further   See Farther.

Great   Words like *great* may lose some of their strength from frequent use. Meaning "first-rate" or "very good," *great* is informal.

Guys   *Guy* is informal for a male. The plural *guys* is informal for either sex or both sexes.

Hopefully   Do not use *hopefully* as a vague sentence modifier. State clearly whether it is the writer, another person, or a group who hope.

The candidate has been *hopefully* proposing a cut in taxes.

If, whether   *If* means "on the condition that," "granting that," or "in the event that."

The character Job in the play says, "Even *if* God slays me, yet will I love Him."

Whether introduces alternatives.

> A friend remains loyal *whether* you win or lose.

Illusion   See **Allusion**.

Immigrate   See **Emigrate**.

Imminent   See **Eminent**.

Impact on   The use of *impact on* as a verb-adverb combination is widely regarded as pretentious and bureaucratic.

> During the strike uncollected garbage *impacted* heavily *on* even the souls of the people.

Implicit   See **Explicit**.

Imply, infer   *Imply* means "to hint."

> The director *implied* that the comedy had profound meanings.

Infer means "to conclude from evidence."

> When the mayor reversed her position on the tax bill, the panel *inferred* that she had a new financial adviser.

Individual   Use *individual* to refer to a single person contrasted with a social group.

GOOD USAGE

> In some countries an *individual* who believes in democracy must remain silent in order to be safe.

Without the contrast to a social group, *individual* and *individuals* are affectations.

AFFECTATION

> Three *individuals* in the boat could not swim.

Its, it's   *Its* is the possessive case for *it*. *It's* is a contraction of *it is* or *it has*. Carelessness often causes the misuse of one for the other.

-ize   The suffix *-ize* turns adjectives or nouns into verbs. Some words (like *radicalize*) with the suffix are acceptable. Others (like *accessorize, prioritize,* and *privatize*) are regarded as pretentious and bureaucratic.

Kind of, sort of   Informal when used as modifiers meaning "rather" or "somewhat."

INFORMAL

> *Kind of* pleased
>
> *Sort of* disgusted

FORMAL

> That *kind of* man (or book)

Less See Fewer.

Lead, led There are many possible causes of errors in writing words that sound similar or are written similarly: misspelling, carelessness in writing, or mispronunciation (*lead* rhymes with *bead; led* rhymes with *bed*). A spell-checker may fail to catch the use of the wrong word or spelling. Similar confusion may occur with *lose, loose; than, then; who's, whose; your, you're.*

Like In formal writing *like* is a preposition, not a conjunction. Preferred usage is *as* or *as if.*

> The tailback limped as if (not *like*) he had been hurt.

Literally Do not misuse *literally* (which means "actually" or "really") for *figuratively* (which means "metaphorically").

AVOID

> After the sale of the painting, the artist was *literally* walking on air.

Man A word that designates one sex instead of both is objectionable to many in words like *chairman, freshman, fireman,* and *unsportsmanlike.* Substituting *a person* (or *persons*) or *people* to designate any or all of the human race can mean a gain in accuracy and even in good manners. Words that can be substituted include *chair, chair of the department,* or *chairwoman* (when the sex is known). Instead of *freshman* or *freshmen, first-year student* is being used. For some words (*unsportsmanlike,* for example) no good substitutes have yet been found. Some words that omit *man* are improvements, like *firefighter* for *fireman.*

May See Can.

Media *Media,* as the plural for *medium,* refers to several news agencies that collect, publish, transmit, and broadcast the news. Many regard the use of *media* to refer to one entity (such as *television* in the following sentence) as a grammatical error in number.

> Television is the *media* that sometimes strives to invent news as well as to report it.

Minimize The verb *minimize* means "to reduce to the least possible amount." Adverbs like *greatly* and *considerably* should not be used to modify *minimize* because the verb itself carries the implication of a superlative: that is, of substantial reduction.

Most, almost   *Most* (which should mean "the greatest in number or amount") should not be used as a substitute for *almost,* to mean "nearly."

AVOID

One who is chronically tardy is late *most* all the time.

Neat   *Neat* used to mean "wonderful" or "terrific" is slang.

Scenery where mountains meet the sea is *neat*. (Use *wonderful* or perhaps *astonishing*.)

Nowhere near   Informal, clumsy, perhaps even dialect for "not nearly."

In those old days students claimed they had *nowhere near* enough money.

OK, O. K., okay   Informal.

Percent, percentage   Use *percent* when you give a specific number: 8 *percent*. Use *percentage* when no number is specified: a *percentage* of the stock.

Precede, proceed   These two words may be confused because their sounds are nearly the same except for the vowel in the first syllable.

Precede means "to come, exist, or occur before in time."

First-year students *precede* seniors on the waiting list for housing.

Proceed means "to go forward."

The instructor tried to ignore the loud noise of the planes and *to proceed* with the lecture.

Principal, principle   The adjective *principal* means "the main, the foremost, the most important." The noun *principal* names the leader, one in high position. The noun *principle* refers to rules and standards.

The *principal* reason for success in almost any field is hard work.

The *principal* of a small school sometimes teaches classes.

A leader of students should have high *principles*.

Quote, quotation   *Quote* as a verb is always acceptable, and *quotation* is acceptable as a noun. However, many object to the use of *quote* as a noun.

Respectfully, respectively   *Respectfully* means "showing proper respect."

Respectfully, each student thanked the president for the diploma.

Respectively means "singly in the order mentioned."

Each graduate passed *respectively* by the speaker and the registrar.

Sensual, sensuous *Sensual* refers to gratification of the physical, especially the sexual, appetites.

> The lithe young dancer's movements were undeniably *sensual*.

Sensuous refers appreciatively to what is experienced through any of the five senses.

> The *sensuous* beauty of the setting was accentuated by the colors and the aromas of the flowers.

So, so that Use *so that* (not *so*) to express intent or purpose.

> Live honorably *so that* you will sleep well and not have bad dreams.

Sometime, some time, sometimes The adverb *sometime* refers to an indefinite or unstated time in the future.

> The head of the school board said only that the committee would meet *sometime* in the future.

The two-word form *some time* consists of an adjective and a noun.

> The announcement stated only that the committee would meet at *some time* in the future.

The adjective *sometime* may mean "former."

> The *sometime* broker bought a motor scooter when she retired.

Sometimes means "at times" or "now and then."

> The grand jury *sometimes* does not meet for months.

Stationary, stationery *Stationary* is an adjective meaning "not moving" or "not capable of being moved." *Stationery* is a noun meaning "writing paper and other writing materials."

Super As a noun naming a superintendent or an adjective meaning "excellent," *super* is informal.

Take See **Bring.**

Thusly In educated usage, *thusly* sometimes occurs, but *thus, this way,* and *like this* also are and sound more natural.

Uninterested See **Disinterested.**

Unique Do not use *more, most,* or other modifiers that state a qualifiable extent or degree (such as *quite*) to modify *unique,* which means "the only one." Something either is unique or it is not. Some other absolute terms (not listed individually in this glossary) are *dead* and *equal.*

Utilize Prefer the shorter and simpler *use* instead of *utilize* in most cases. See *-ize*. *Utilize* meaning "to find a profitable or practical use for" is acceptable.

Ways In naming a distance in formal writing, use *way:* "a long *way* to travel."

Whether See If.

Whose, who's *Whose* is the possessive of *who; who's* is a contraction of *who is.*

-wise Do not use the suffix *-wise* to mean "with reference to" in words like *saleswise, budgetwise,* and *businesswise.*

Your, you're *Your* is the possessive of *you; you're* is the contraction of *you are.*

English as a Second Language (ESL)

---

46 English as a Second Language (ESL)

For those with English as a second language (ESL), this entire hand-book offers a review of such basics as grammar, usage, sentence construction, and mechanics. The following checklist (with cross-references to sections of this book) and the lists after it will help ESL writers to solve special problems.

46a   ESL Checklist

Omissions

- Do not omit the **subject** of a sentence.

    NOT: Checked my ticket before boarding the plane.
    SUBJECT ADDED: *I* checked my ticket before boarding the plane.

- Do not omit the **verb** of a sentence.

    NOT: The work in pewter both rare and beautiful.
    VERB ADDED: The work in pewter *is* both rare and beautiful.

         Consult: Subjects, pp. 96–97
                    Sentences, p. 106
                    Verbs, p. 86
                    Completeness, pp. 173–174
                    Fragments, pp. 110–112
                    Other omissions, pp. 173–174

Repetitions

- Do not repeat the subject (in the same **clause**) in the form of a **pronoun**.

    NOT: The pewter vase *it* is rare, and it is also beautiful.

SUBJECT NOT REPEATED: The pewter vase is rare, and it is also beautiful.

- Do not repeat an **object.**

    NOT: Freedom is what the flag stands for *it.*
    OBJECT NOT REPEATED: Freedom is what the flag stands for. [*What* is
    the **object of the preposition** *for;* delete *it.*]

> Consult: Subjects, pp. 96–97
> Clauses, pp. 104–106
> Pronouns, pp. 83–86
> Objects, pp. 99–101

Articles *(a, an,* and *the)*

- Use the **articles** *a* or *an* with singular **count** (countable) **nouns** (persons, places, or things that can be counted).

    The room contained *a* file cabinet, *an* old floor lamp, *a* desk, and *a* chair.

- Do not use *a* or *an* with **noncount (mass) nouns** (persons, places, or things) that are not usually counted.

    NOT: Rene asked for *a* money to buy *a* gas.
    BUT: Rene asked for money to buy gas.

- Use *the* with **count nouns** that name things, people, or places specifically.

    CORRECT: *The* desks in the room were antiques. [specific desks]
    NOT: *The* desks are not always antiques. [desks in general]

- Generally, do not use *the* with most singular **proper nouns.**

    NOT: *The* Alaska is still an unspoiled state.
    BUT: Alaska is still an unspoiled state.

> Consult: Articles, p. 89
> Nouns, p. 83

Verbs

- Learn **regular** and **irregular verb forms** (see lists, pp. 465–468).

- Learn the meanings of two-word (phrasal) verbs (see list, pp. 465–466). A two-word or **phrasal verb** is a verb plus a preposition or **adverb** together making up an **idiom**.

- Use the **base form of a verb** with *do, does, did, can, could, may, might, must, shall, should, will, would,* and *ought to.*

  NOT: *Do* magazine sweepstakes really *pays* off?
  BUT: *Do* magazine sweepstakes really *pay* off?
  NOT: You *must allows* three weeks for delivery.
  BUT: You *must allow* three weeks for delivery.

- Use the **past participle** with *has, have,* and *had.*

  NOT: *I have try* to explain the situation.
  BUT: *I have tried* to explain the situation.

- Learn when to use the **present participle** with forms of the verb *to be (am, are, is, was, were).*

  NOT: Summer *is pass* quickly.
  BUT: Summer *is passing* quickly.

  Consult: Verbs, pp. 86–88
              Verb forms, pp. 117–123
              Tenses and sequence of tenses, pp. 123–128
              Idioms, pp. 303–305

46b ESL Lists

These lists are not complete; they are merely intended to present some frequently encountered noncount nouns, irregular verbs, and two-word (phrasal) verbs.

Common Noncount Nouns

NOTE: Though all of the nouns listed next are normally noncount nouns (and have no article before them), some of them are occasionally used as count nouns.

advice	fish	luck
air	flour	makeup
anger	fun	money
bacon	furniture	news
baggage	garlic	oxygen
beauty	gas	pride
beef	gasoline	poverty
bread	gold	rice
butter	grass	salt
cement	gravy	sand
cereal	homework	silver
cheese	ice cream	sleet
clothing	intelligence	spinach
coffee	jam	sugar
dirt	jewelry	tuition
employment	junk	traffic
entertainment	lettuce	wealth
equipment	lipstick	wheat

Common noncount noun (*fish*) without *the* before it.

We try to avoid fish that are fried.

The same noun used with *the* before it.

The fish on that tray are grilled.

Irregular Verbs

This list supplements those lists of irregular verbs on pp. 118–119.

BASE	PAST TENSE	PAST PARTICIPLE
bend	bent	bent
bet	bet, betted	bet, betted
bite	bit	bitten, bit
bleed	bled	bled
breed	bred	bred
catch	caught	caught
cling	clung	clung
creep	crept	crept
cut	cut	cut
fall	fell	fallen
feed	fed	fed
feel	felt	felt
fight	fought	fought
find	found	found
flee	fled	fled
forget	forgot	forgotten
forgive	forgave	forgiven
have	had	had
hear	heard	heard
hide	hid	hidden
hit	hit	hit
hold	held	held
keep	kept	kept
make	made	made
meet	met	met
pay	paid	paid
read	read	read
ride	rode	ridden
say	said	said
seek	sought	sought
sell	sold	sold
send	sent	sent
shake	shook	shaken
show	showed	shown
sleep	slept	slept
slide	slid	slid
speak	spoke	spoken

BASE	PAST TENSE	PAST PARTICIPLE
spend	spent	spent
spring	sprang, sprung	sprung
stand	stood	stood
steal	stole	stolen
stick	stuck	stuck
stink	stank	stunk
strike	struck	struck, stricken
swear	swore	sworn
tear	tore	torn
tread	trod	trodden
weave	wove	woven
weep	wept	wept
win	won	won
wind	wound	wound

Common Two-Word (Phrasal) Verbs

ask out (invite on a date)
back up (go backward, support)
blow over (pass quietly)
blow up (explode)
break down (collapse)
break up (separate)
bring up (to rear *or* to initiate)
call off (cancel)
call on (visit, ask to participate)
call up (telephone)
catch up (cease to be behind)
clean up (cleanse)
come about (happen)
come across (remit, impress as)
come back (return)
come over (visit)
come up [with] (invent)
do over (do again)
drop in (visit)
drop off (slacken, take someone to)
drop out (stop attending)

fall behind (lag)
fill out (to complete, to become larger)
fill up (fill to capacity)
get along (progress)
get along [with] (relate harmoniously)
get away (escape)
get by (succeed—barely)
get into (become involved in)
get over (recover from)
get through (endure, finish)
get up (arise)
go out [with] (accompany)
go over (review)
grow up (mature)
hand in (submit)
hand out (distribute)
hang up (end talking on phone)
help out (assist)
hold up (to delay *or* to rob)
hurry up (hasten)

keep on (continue)
keep up (maintain)
leave out (omit)
look into (investigate)
look out (be on the alert)
look over (survey)
look up (search for)
make sure (verify)
make up (reconcile, invent)
make up [for] (compensate)
mix up (confuse)
pick out (choose)
pin down (identify specifically)
point out (show)
put away (save, store)
put off (postpone)
put out (extinguish)
put together (assemble)

put up [with] (tolerate)
run across (discover)
run into (encounter by chance)
run out [of] (exhaust)
show up (appear)
shut off (prevent passage
    through)
speak up (express opinions)
talk over (discuss)
think over (ponder)
try out (to test)
turn down (reject, decrease
    volume)
use up (exhaust supply of)
wake up (awaken)
wear out (use as long as
    possible)
wrap up (wrap a package, end)

Glossary of
Terms

47 Glossary of Terms *gl/trm*

Absolute concepts   Adjectives or adverbs (such as *dead* or *unique*) that describe absolute states have neither comparative nor superlative forms. See p. 163.

Absolute modifiers   See **Absolute concepts.**

Absolute phrase   See p. 218.

Abstract noun   See **Noun.**

Active voice   See **Voice.**

Adjectival   A term describing a word or word group that modifies a noun.

Adjective   A word that modifies a noun or a pronoun. See p. 159.

Adjective clause   See **Dependent clause.**

Adverb   A word that modifies a verb, an adjective, or another adverb. See p. 159.

Adverbial clause   See **Dependent clause.**

Agreement   The correspondence between words in number, gender, person, or case. A verb agrees in number and person with its subject. A pronoun must agree in number, person, and gender with its antecedent.

Alternating structure of a paragraph   Comparing or contrasting with movements back and forth between the subjects under discussion. See p. 74.

Analogy   A figurative comparison that explains one thing in terms of another. See p. 72.

Antecedent   A word to which a pronoun refers.

>   *antecedent*   *pronoun*
>   ↓   ↓
> When the ballet *dancers* appeared, *they* were dressed in pink.

Appositive   A word, phrase, or clause used as a noun and placed beside another word to explain it.

        appositive

The poet *John Milton* wrote *Paradise Lost* while he was blind.

Argumentation ad hominem   Reasoning that attacks a person rather than a real issue. See p. 7.

Article   *A* and *an* are indefinite articles; *the* is the definite article.

Auxiliary verb   A verb used to help another verb indicate tense, mood, or voice. Some principal auxiliaries are forms of the verbs *to be, to have,* and *to do.* See p. 87.

Balanced sentence   A sentence characterized by parallel elements, similar in structure, length, and thought. See p. 197.

Base form of verb   The first principal part of a verb, also called the **infinitive form** (without *to*) or the **simple form.**

Bibliography card   A full, documented record of bibliographical information on a researched work, often on a file card. See p. 360.

Block form   A format for letters that presents all main elements flush with the left margin. See p. 260.

Block structure of a paragraph   Comparing or contrasting one subject completely in a paragraph, followed by another subject completely in a separate paragraph. See p. 74.

Brainstorming   Opening the mind to sudden flurries of ideas. See p. 18.

Case   English has remnants of three cases: subjective, possessive, and objective. Nouns are inflected for case only in the possessive (*father, father's*). An alternative way to show possession is with the "of phrase" (*of the house*). Some pronouns, notably the personal pronouns and the relative pronoun *who,* are still fully inflected for three cases:

SUBJECTIVE OR NOMINATIVE (acting)
   I, he, she, we, they, who

POSSESSIVE (possessing)
   my (mine), your (yours), his, her (hers), its, our (ours), their (theirs), whose

OBJECTIVE (acted upon)
   me, him, her, us, them, whom

Clause   A group of words containing a subject and a predicate. See **Independent clause** and **Dependent clause.** See p. 105.

Clustering   Graphically drawing relationships among ideas, often with diagrams. See p. 20.

Collective noun   A word identifying a class or a group of persons or things. See p. 83.

Colloquialism   A word or expression used in familiar conversation but generally inappropriate in formal writing.

Comma splice (or comma fault)   An error that occurs when two independent clauses are incorrectly linked by a comma with no coordinating conjunction. See p. 112.

Common noun   See **Noun.**

Comparative and superlative degrees   See p. 162.

Complement   A word or group of words used to complete a predicate. Predicate adjectives, subjective complements, direct objects, and indirect objects are complements. See p. 99.

Complete predicate   The simple predicate, its modifiers, and any complements. See **Predicate.**

Complete subject   All the words that form a group and function together as the subject of a sentence. See **Subject.** See p. 97.

Complex, compound, compound-complex sentences   A *complex sentence* has one independent clause and at least one dependent clause. A *compound sentence* has at least two independent clauses. A *compound-complex sentence* has two or more independent clauses and one dependent clause or more. See p. 106.

Compound predicate   Two or more verbs that express action or conditions of a subject. See **Predicate.**

Compound subject   Two or more subjects of a sentence, joined by a conjunction and functioning together. See **Subject.** See p. 97.

Concrete noun   See **Noun.**

Conjugation   The inflection of the forms of a verb according to person, number, tense, voice, and mood.

Conjunctions   Words used to connect sentences or sentence parts. See also **Coordinating conjunctions, Correlative conjunctions, Subordinating conjunctions,** and p. 91.

Conjunctive adverb   An adverb used to relate two independent clauses that are separated by a semicolon: *besides, consequently, however, moreover, then, therefore,* and so on. See p. 90.

Connotation A meaning suggested by a word beyond its direct meaning. See p. 296.

Contraction The shortening of two words combined by replacing omitted letters with an apostrophe. See p. 279.

> *I've* for *I have. Isn't* for *is not.*

Coordinate adjectives Two or more adjectives that modify a noun independently and are separated by commas. See p. 207.

Coordinate clause See **Independent clause.** When there are two independent clauses in a compound or a compound-complex sentence, they may be called coordinate clauses.

Coordinating conjunctions Simple conjunctions that join sentences or parts of sentences of equal rank (*and, but, for, nor, or, so, yet*). See p. 91.

Correlative conjunctions Conjunctions used in pairs to join coordinate sentence elements. The most common are *either . . . or, neither . . . nor, not only . . . but also, both . . . and.*

Count nouns See **Noun.**

Cumulative adjective An adjective that modifies a cluster of subsequent adjectives and a noun and is not followed by a comma. See p. 207.

Dangling modifier A modifier that is not clearly attached to a word or element in the sentence.

DANGLING MODIFIER
Following a regimen of proper diet and exercise, Alan's weight can be controlled.

REVISED
Following a regimen of proper diet and exercise, Alan can control his weight.

Declension The inflection of nouns, pronouns, and adjectives in case, number, and gender. See p. 83.

Deduction See **Deductive method.**

Deductive method Applying generalizations and principles to new facts, situations, or circumstances.

Degrees of modifiers See p. 89.

Demonstrative adjective or pronoun A word used to point out (*this, that, these, those*).

Denotation The exact meaning of a word. See p. 294.

Dependent (subordinate) clause A group of words that contains both a subject and a predicate but that does not stand alone as a sentence. A dependent clause is frequently signaled by a subordinator (*because, since, that, what, who, which,* and so on). It always functions as an adjective, adverb, or noun.

adjective clause
The tenor *who sang the aria* had just arrived from Italy.

noun clause
The critics agreed *that the young tenor had a magnificent voice.*

adverb clause
When he sang, even the sophisticated audience was enraptured.

Diagramming Diagramming uses systems of lines and positioning of words to show the parts of a sentence and the relationships between them. Its purpose is to make understandable the way writing is put together. (See the example below.)

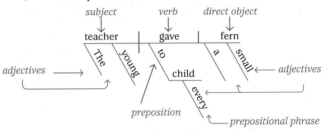

Dialect Regional, occupational, or ethnic words and usages. See p. 292.

Diction Choice of words.

Direct object A noun, pronoun, or other substantive that receives the action of the verb. See p. 100.

The angler finally caught the old *trout.*

Direct quotation Material quoted precisely and exactly as found. Requires quotation marks or, if lengthy, blocked indention. See p. 363.

Double comparative Illogical use of *-er* and *more* together. See p. 162.

Double negative Nonstandard use of two negative words within the same sentence.

DOUBLE NEGATIVE
I do *not* have *hardly* any problems with my car.

REVISED
> I have *hardly* any problems with my car.

Double superlative   Illogical use of *-est* and *most* together. See p. 162.

Ellipsis points   Three spaced periods used to indicate the omission of a word or words in a quotation.

Elliptical clause   A clause in which one or more words are omitted but understood.

understood
↙   ↘

> The director admired no one else as much as (*he admired* or *he did*) Faith DeFelice.

Expletives   *Here* and *there* used when the subject follows the verb. They cannot be subjects of a sentence. See p. 137.

Faulty predication   Errors occur in predication when a subject and its complement are put together in such a fashion that the sentence is illogical or unmeaningful. See p. 181.

FAULTY
> A reporter taking pictures meant that there would be publicity. [It is illogical to say that *taking pictures meant*.]

BETTER
> Since a reporter was taking pictures, we knew that there would be publicity.

Fragment   Part of a sentence written and punctuated as a complete sentence.

FRAGMENT
> *Jostling and bantering with one another.* The team headed for the locker room.

REVISED
> Jostling and bantering with one another, the team headed for the locker room.

Freewriting   Expressing in words any thoughts that come to mind. See p. 19.

Fused (or run-on) sentence   An error that occurs when two independent clauses have neither punctuation nor coordinating conjunctions between them.

FUSED
> The average adult has about twelve pints of blood this amount is roughly 9 percent of total body weight.

REVISED
> The average adult has about twelve pints of blood; this amount is roughly 9 percent of total body weight.

Future perfect tense See **Perfect tense.**

Future progressive tense See **Progressive tense.** See p. 124.

Future tense A verb form that expresses an action or condition expected to occur after the time of writing. See p. 124.

Gender The classification of nouns or pronouns into masculine, feminine, or neuter categories.

Gerund See **Verbal.**

Global revision Revising larger matters of a paper first. See p. 36.

Grouping See **Clustering.**

Helping verb See **Auxiliary verb.**

Homonyms Words that sound alike but have different meanings (*their, there*).

Idiom An expression peculiar to a given language. The meaning of an idiom must be memorized, for it cannot be determined simply from an understanding of the words themselves (*Tuesday week*). See p. 301.

Imperative mood See **Mood.**

Indefinite adjective An adjective that takes the same form as an indefinite pronoun (*any, each, every, none*).

Indefinite pronoun A pronoun not pointing out a particular person or thing. Some of the most common are *any, anybody, anyone, each, everybody, everyone, neither, one,* and *some.*

Indented form A format for letters that requires indention of main structured elements. See p. 260.

Independent (main) clause A group of words that contains a subject and a predicate and that can stand alone grammatically as a sentence.

Indicative mood See **Mood.**

Induction See **Inductive method.**

Indirect object   A word that indirectly receives the action of the verb. See p. 99.

Inductive method   Moving from factual knowledge to a conclusion or generalization.

Infinitive   See **Verbal.**

Inflection   A change in the form of a word to indicate its grammatical function. Nouns, adjectives, and pronouns are inflected by declension; verbs, by conjugation. Some inflections occur when *-s* or *-es* is added to nouns or verbs or when *'s* is added to nouns.

Informal or colloquial English   The more casual spoken language used in English-speaking countries. See p. 292.

Intensifier   A modifier (such as *very*) used to lend emphasis. Use sparingly.

Intensive pronoun   A pronoun ending in *-self* and used for emphasis.

The director *himself* will act the part of Hamlet.

Interjection   A word used to exclaim or to express (usually strong) emotion. It has no grammatical connection within its sentence. Some common interjections are *oh, ah,* and *ouch.* See p. 95.

Interrogative pronoun   See pp. 85 and 152.

Intransitive verb   See **Voice.**

Inversion   A change in normal word order, such as placing an adjective after the noun it modifies or placing the object of a verb at the beginning of a sentence.

Irregular verb   A verb that does not form its past tense and past participle by adding *-d* or *-ed* to its infinitive form—for example, *give, gave, given.*

Jargon   Technical terminology or the language of a special group.

Limiting modifier   A qualifying modifier, such as *only, about,* or *merely.* See p. 186.

Linking verb   A verb that does not express action but links the subject to another word, one that names or describes the verb. See pp. 87 and 160. Common linking verbs are *be, become,* and *seem.*

Logical fallacies   Errors in reasoning. See p. 2.

Loose sentence   A sentence that presents its main point early and further comment later. See p. 196.

Main clause   See **Independent clause.**

Mass noun   See **Noun.**

Mixed construction   A sentence with two or more parts that are not grammatically compatible.

MIXED CONSTRUCTION
> By cutting welfare benefits will penalize many poor families.

REVISED
> Cutting welfare benefits will penalize many poor families.

Modified block form   A format for letters that requires indention of main structured elements, excluding paragraphs. See p. 260.

Modifier   A word or group of words that limits or describes another word. See p. 89.

Mood   The mood (or mode) of a verb indicates whether an action is to be thought of as fact, command, wish, or condition contrary to fact. Modern English has three moods: the indicative, for ordinary statements and questions; the imperative, for commands and entreaty; and the subjunctive, for certain idiomatic expressions of wish, command, or condition contrary to fact.

INDICATIVE
> *Does* she *play* the guitar?
> She *does.*

IMPERATIVE
> *Stay* with me.
> *Let* him stay.

The imperative is formed like plural present indicative, without *-s.*

SUBJUNCTIVE
> If I *were you,* I would go.
> I wish he *were* going with you.
> I move that the meeting *be* adjourned.
> It is necessary that he *stay* absolutely quiet.
> If this *be* true, no man ever loved.

The most common subjunctive forms are *were* and *be.* All others are formed like the present-tense plural form without *-s.*

Nominal   A term for a word or a word group that is used as a noun—for example, the *good,* the *bad,* the *ugly.*

Nominative case   See **Case.**

Nonrestrictive (nonessential) modifier   A modifier that is not essential to understanding.

Non sequitur   A conclusion that cannot be drawn from what has just been stated. See p. 9.

Nonstandard English   Usages, spellings, and pronunciations not usually found in the speech or writing of educated people. See p. 292.

Noun   A word that names and that has gender, number, and case. There are proper nouns, which name particular people, places or things (*Thomas Jefferson, Paris,* the *Colosseum*); common nouns, which name one or more of a group (*alligator, high school, politician*); collective nouns (see pp. 000 and 000); abstract nouns, which name ideas, feelings, beliefs, and so on (*religion, justice, dislike, enthusiasm*); concrete nouns, which name things perceived through the senses (*lemon, hatchet, worm*); mass nouns (also called noncount nouns), which name things generally not counted (*silver, sugar*).

Noun clause   See **Dependent clause.**

Number   A term to describe forms that indicate whether a word is singular or plural.

Object   A noun, pronoun, or word group that receives the action of the verb (direct object), tells to or for whom the action is done (indirect object), or completes the meaning of a preposition (object of the preposition).

Object of preposition   See p. 153.

Objective case   See **Case.**

Objective complement   A word that accompanies a direct object and either modifies or renames the object. See p. 100.

Paragraph of analysis   A paragraph that stresses differences and dissimilarities, in spite of apparent similarities. See p. 75.

Paragraph of classification   A paragraph that stresses similarities or common denominators, in spite of seeming differences. See p. 75.

Paragraph of description   A paragraph that describes a scene or person, moving from detail to detail in a logical order, often appealing to the five senses. See p. 70.

Paragraph of narration   A paragraph that presents events over time and sometimes across space, usually beginning with the first event and concluding with the last. See p. 69.

Parallelism   Parallelism occurs when corresponding parts of a sentence are similar in structure, length, and thought.

FAULTY

The staff was required to wear black shoes, red ties, and *shirts that were white*.

PARALLEL

The staff was required to wear black shoes, red ties, and white shirts.

Paraphrase   An expression of ideas found in a source but not in the same words and often about the same length as the original source. See p. 363.

Participle   See **Verbal.**

Parts of speech   See pp. 82–95.

Passive voice   See **Voice.**

Past participle   The third principal part of a verb. Past participles generally end in *d, ed, en, n,* or *t* (*learned, known, dwelt*). See p. 102.

Past perfect tense   See **Perfect tense.**

Past progressive tense   See **Progressive tense.** See p. 125.

Past tense   A verb form that expresses a completed action or condition before the time of writing. See p. 125.

Perfect tense   A verb form that indicates one time or action completed before another. See p. 125.

Periodic sentence   A sentence that withholds an element of the main thought until the end. See p. 197.

Person   Three groups of forms of pronouns (with corresponding verb inflections) used to distinguish between the speaker (first person), the person spoken to (second person), and the person spoken about (third person).

Personal pronoun   A pronoun like *I, you, he, she, it, we, they, mine, yours, his, hers, its, ours, theirs.*

Phrasal verb   See **Verb.**

Phrase   A group of closely related words without both a subject and a predicate. There are subject phrases (*the new drill sergeant*), verb phrases (*should have been*), verbal phrases (*climbing high mountains*), prepositional phrases (*of the novel*), appositive phrases (my brother, *the black sheep of the family*), and so forth. See pp. 101–102.

Plagiarism   Using the words or ideas of others without giving credit; avoided by giving full references to sources. See p. 365.

Post hoc, ergo propter hoc Asserting that one thing or event causes another because it precedes another. See p. 9.

Predicate The verb in a clause (simple predicate) or the verb and its modifiers, complements, and objects (complete predicate). See pp. 96–98.

Predicate adjective An adjective following a linking verb and describing the subject. See pp. 89 and 99.

> The rose is *artificial*.

Predicative nominative See **Subjective complement**.

Predication See **Faulty predication**.

Preposition A connective that joins a noun or a pronoun to the rest of a sentence. See p. 93.

Prepositional phrase A word group introduced by a preposition (*in the rain, over the bridge*).

Present participle A participle formed by adding the suffix *-ing* to the base (simple) form of a verb (*searching, reading*). See p. 102.

Present perfect tense See **Perfect tense**. See p. 124.

Present progressive tense See **Progressive tense**. See p. 124.

Present tense A verb form that expresses an action or condition that is currently occurring, regularly occurring, or consistently true. See p. 123.

Primary sources Works or subjects about which other materials are written. See p. 356.

Principal parts The verb forms present (*smile, go*), past (*smiles, went*), and past participle (*smiled, gone*). See p. 117.

Progressive tense A verb form that shows that an action or condition is ongoing. See p. 124.

Proper noun See **Noun**.

Red herring A device that shifts a subject from one topic to another to ensure that the first is forgotten or ignored. See p. 7.

Reflexive pronoun A pronoun ending in *-self* and indicating that the subject acts upon itself.

Relative pronoun See p. 85.

Restrictive (essential) modifier A modifier essential for a clear understanding of the element modified. See **Nonrestrictive** (nonessential) **modifier**.

Run-on sentence See **Fused sentence.**

Scratch outline The simplest kind of outline, consisting of a list of points in order but without subdivisions. See p. 22.

Secondary sources Writings about primary sources. See **Primary sources.** See p. 356.

Sentence fragment See **Fragment.**

Sentence modifier A word or group of words that modifies the rest of the sentence (*for example, frankly, in fact, on the other hand,* and so forth).

Sentence outline A formal, detailed structure that organizes material in complete sentences. See p. 24.

Simple predicate The main verb and any auxiliary verbs of a sentence. See **Predicate.** See p. 98.

Simple sentence A sentence consisting of only one independent clause and no dependent clauses. See p. 106.

Simple subject The essential elements in a sentence's subject, usually consisting of a single word. See **Subject.** See p. 96.

Singular count nouns See **Noun.**

Slang Nonstandard vocabulary of cultural or subcultural groups. See p. 301.

Split infinitive An infinitive with an element interposed between *to* and the verb form (to *highly* appreciate). Avoid. See p. 190.

Standard English The generally accepted language of educated people in English-speaking countries; it is used in most public documents. See p. 292.

Style The ways through which writers express their thoughts in language; the ways they connect words. See p. 309.

Subject A word or group of words about which the sentence or clause makes a statement. See p. 96.

Subjective case See **Case.**

Subjective complement A noun following a linking verb and naming the subject.

> The flower is a *rose.*

Subjunctive mood See **Mood.**

Subordinate clause See **Dependent clause.**

Subordinating conjunctions Conjunctions that connect subordinating clauses to the rest of the sentence. Some common subordinating conjunctions are *after, although, as, as if, as long as, as soon as, because, before, if, in order that, since, so that, though, unless, until, when, where, whereas,* and *while.* See p. 92.

Substantive A noun or a sentence element that serves the function of a noun.

Summary An expression of the essence of a source but not in the same words and usually in fewer words. See p. 363.

Superlative degree See p. 162.

Syntax The grammatical ways in which words are put together to form phrases, clauses, and sentences.

Thesis statement A clear, concise sentence that presents a paper's central idea or purpose. See p. 28.

Tone The quality in writing that conveys the author's attitude toward his or her subject.

Topic outline A formal, detailed structure that helps to organize materials. See p. 22.

Topic sentence See **Thesis statement.**

Transitive verb See **Voice.**

Upside-down subordination Placing the main idea of a sentence in a subordinate clause. See p. 170.

URL Uniform resource locator, a vital part of an online address. It must be included in bibliographical entries for Internet sources.

Verb A word or group of words expressing action, being, or state of being. See p. 86.

> Automobiles *burn* gas.
>
> What *is* life?

Verb phrase See **Phrase.**

Verbal A word derived from a verb and used as a noun, an adjective, or an adverb. A verbal may be a gerund, a participle, or an infinitive. See p. 102.

Verbal phrases Verbals (gerunds, participles, infinitives) and the words associated with them. See **Verbal.**

Voice Transitive verbs have two forms to show whether their subjects act on an object (active voice) or are acted on (passive voice). See p. 128.

Index

Abbreviations Used in Marking Papers

GENERAL EDITING MARKS